# Why
# I Killed
# the Mahatma

# Why
# I Killed
# the Mahatma

## UNCOVERING GODSE'S DEFENCE

KOENRAAD ELST

RUPA

Published by
Rupa Publications India Pvt. Ltd 2018
7/16, Ansari Road, Daryaganj
New Delhi 110002

*Sales Centres:*
Allahabad Bengaluru Chennai
Hyderabad Jaipur Kathmandu
Kolkata Mumbai

Copyright © Koenraad Elst 2018

ISBN: 978-81-291-xxxx-x

First impression 2018

10 9 8 7 6 5 4 3 2 1

The moral right of the author has been asserted.

Printed at Repro Knowledgecast Limited, India

*Dedicated to the memory of Ram Swarup (1920–1998)*
*and Sita Ram Goel (1921–2003),*
*two Gandhian activists who lived through it all and were able to*
*give a balanced judgement of Mahatma Gandhi and his assassin*

# Contents

# Foreword

Historical writing and political purposes are usually inseparable, but a measure of institutional plurality can allow some genuine space for alternative perspectives. Unfortunately, post-independence Indian historical writing came to be dominated by a monolithic political project of progressivism that eventually lost sight of verifiable basic truths. This genre of Indian history and the social sciences more generally reached a nadir, when even its own leftist protagonists ceased to believe in their own apparent goal of promoting social and economic justice. It descended into a crass, self-serving political activism and determination to censor dissenting views challenging their own institutional privileges and intellectual exclusivity. One of the ideological certainties embraced by this coterie of historians has been the imputation of mythical status to an alleged threat of Hindu extremism and its unforgivable complicity in assassinating Mahatma Gandhi.

Historian Dr Koenraad Elst has entered this crucial debate on the murder of the Mahatma with a skilful commentary on the speech of his assassin, Nathuram Godse, to the court that sentenced him to death, the verdict he preferred to imprisonment. Dr Elst takes seriously Nathuram Godse's extensive critique of India's independence struggle, particularly Mahatma Gandhi's role in it and its aftermath, but he points out factual errors and exaggerations. He begins with a felicitous excursion into the antecedent context of the Chitpavan community to which Nathuram Godse belonged and its important role in the history of Maharashtra as well as modern India. The elucidation of Godse's political testament becomes the methodology adopted by Dr Elst to engage in a wide ranging and thoughtful discussion of the politics and ideology of India in the immediate decades before Independence and the period after its attainment in 1947.

Godse's lengthy speech to the court highlights the profoundly political nature of his murder of Gandhi. Nathuram Godse surveys the history of India's independence struggle and the role of Mahatma Gandhi and judges it an unmitigated disaster in order to justify Gandhi's assassination. But he murdered him not merely for what he regarded as Gandhi's prior betrayal of India's Hindus, but his likely interference in favour of the Nizam of Hyderabad whose followers were already violently repressing the Hindu majority he ruled over. In the context of discussing Godse's political testament, many issues studiously ignored or wilfully misrepresented by the dominant genre of lssweftist Indian history writing are subject to withering scrutiny. The impressive achievement of Dr Elst's elegant monograph is to highlight the actual ideological and political cleavages that prompted Mahatma Gandhi's tragic murder by Godse. A refusal to understand its political rationale lends unsustainable credence to the idea that his assassin was motivated by religious fanaticism and little else besides. On the contrary, Nathuram Godse was a secular nationalist, sharing many of the convictions and prejudices of the dominant independence movement, led by the Congress party. He was steadfastly opposed to religious obscurantism and caste privilege, and sought social and political equality for all Indians in the mould advocated by his mentor, Vinayak Damodar Savarkar (also called Veer Savarkar).

Godse's condemnation for the murder of Mahatma Gandhi cannot detract from the extraordinary cogency of his critique of Gandhi's political strategy throughout the independence struggle and a fundamentally misconceived policy of appeasing Muslims, regardless of long-term consequences. His latter policy merely incited their truculence, and far from eliciting cooperation on a common agenda and national purpose, intensified their separatist tendencies. His perverse support for the Khilafat Movement, opposed by Jinnah himself, was compounded by wilful errors at the Round Table Conference of 1930–32. He took upon himself the task of representing the Congress alone during the second session without adequate preparation, and eagerly espoused the Communal Award of separate electorates. And by conceding the creation of the province of Sindh in 1931 by severing it from the Bombay Presidency, as a result of Jinnah's threats, guaranteed an eventual separatist outcome. Godse also denounced the Congress strategy of first participating in the provincial governments of 1937 without the Muslim League and then withdrawing hastily from them, thereby losing influence over political developments at a critical juncture. He also censures the bad faith of Gandhi's unjust critique of the reformist Arya Samaj and Swami Shraddhananda's social activism and Gandhi's shocking failure to condemn his murder by a Muslim.

Nathuram Godse even espoused the very conclusions of the progressive strand of historical writing in independent India that blamed the British for accentuating communalism (i.e. religious division) to perpetuate imperial rule. What he did oppose was the kind of communal privileges he felt Mahatma Gandhi accorded to Muslims, though in the end he accepted them as unavoidable for the pragmatic reason of eliciting Muslim support for a united, independent India.

Of course, Gandhi's populism transformed both Congress and Muslim politics into a more volatile mass movement. In the case of Muslim politics, over which the constitutionalist Mohammed Ali Jinnah had presided until 1916 before retiring for a time to his legal practice, Gandhi's appeasement helped nurture unequivocal separatism. What Godse implacably opposed was India's partition, which underlined the failure of Gandhi's attempt to appease Muslims. Most of all, Godse was outraged by Gandhi's continued solicitude towards them after Partition and despite the horrors being experienced by Hindus inside newly-independent Pakistan. In particular, he was appalled by Gandhi's insistence on releasing Pakistan's share of accumulated foreign exchange reserves, which Jawaharlal Nehru also counselled Mahatma Gandhi against, (while India was at war with it in Kashmir), because the funds would immediately aid their war effort.

Revealingly, Godse appears to have grasped the imperative to negotiate wisely with the British in order to achieve the intact legacy of a united India. He was critical of the posturing of the Congress that ended in the disastrously misconceived Quit India Movement of 1942 that was quickly succeeded by Gandhi's total capitulation. The latter could have meant the abandonment of all democratic pretensions and handing over the governance of independent India to the Muslim League to prevent Partition. Quite clearly, Gandhi's assassin was not the raving Hindu lunatic popularly depicted in India, but a thoughtful and intelligent man who was prepared to commit murder. In some respects, Dr Bhimrao Ambedkar was an even fiercer critic of Gandhian appeasement of Muslims, sentiments echoed by no less political giants of India and the Congress like Sri Aurobindo Ghose and Annie Besant.

Dr Elst also provides a brief, but persuasive account of the political lapses of Congress and its iconic personalities, as well as the fate of the Hindu Mahasabha and its prominent leaders, Veer Savarkar and Dr Syama Prasad Mookerjee. He points out the utter folly of Congress politicians in their dealings with British in the 1940s. The highly respected Sri Aurobindo Ghose, a former Congress leader himself, had urged support for Britain's war effort and excoriated Subhas Bose for allying with the Japanese, but to no avail. In addition, Dr Elst carefully highlights Godse's disapproval of the glaring inconsistencies in Gandhi's pacifism, both intellectual

and political, counter posing them to the lofty principle of absolute
non-violence it supposedly represented. But Dr Elst is fully aware of
the tragic impact of the Mahatma's assassination on India and the
profoundly debilitating impact it had on Indian nationalist politics
subsequently. In his conclusion, he balances Nathuram Godse's
critique of Mahatma Gandhi by revisiting its substantial rejection
by leading Hindutva scholars, Ram Swarup and Sita Ram Goel. In
a lengthy concluding section, he adds his own careful assessment
of Gandhi's successes as well as perversity in promoting hostile
Islamic and Christian interests. His comments on contemporary
Indian political life and the significance of Gandhi's continuing
legacy for it are astute.

It is also relevant to reiterate that an important additional
contribution of Dr Elst's excellent monograph is to underline
the insuperable contradictions posed by the Indian discourse
on secularism and communalism. In his convincing account,
Dr Elst judges that it has turned logic on its head by accusing
secular nationalists, represented, for example, by the alleged
Hindu nationalists of the RSS, of the very political transgression
of communalism that its own support for sectarian privilege,
however politically well-meaning, clearly entails. Ironically, Indian
politicians of all hues continue to maintain, in a triumph of hope
over experience, that true Islam would guarantee Hindu-Muslim
amity. And the paradox of independent India is that it evolved
into an armed modern entity as secular nationalists like Nathuram
Godse ardently wished.

Dr Gautam Sen
(Former Lecturer in the Politics of the World Economy,
London School of Economics & Political Science)

# Preface

Mohandas Karamchand Gandhi, better known as the Mahatma, was shot dead by the Hindu nationalist journalist Nathuram Godse on 30 January 1948, half a year after the independence and partition of India. During his trial, which ended in a death sentence, Godse was permitted to explain his motives in a speech. The present book is largely a critical comment on that courtroom speech. One of our findings is that while Godse's act was by definition extremist, his criticism of Gandhi was in fact shared by many.

The first version of the present book was *De moord op de Mahatma* in Dutch (The Murder of the Mahatma'), published by the Davidsfonds in Leuven, Belgium, in January 1998, in time for the assassination's fiftieth anniversary. News of the publication led to my being invited by the leading Dutch radio anchor Marjolein Uitzinger of AVRO broadcasting foundation and by the Dutch Hindu broadcaster *OHM-Vani* for lengthy interviews. By contrast, after initial calls for interviews on the news programmes of Flemish (i.e. Dutch-speaking Belgian) state radio and TV, I was disinvited, apparently because the book did not contain the expected hagiographical indignation over Godse's radical incomprehension of Gandhi's presumed greatness. Its message was not deemed fit for a commemoration of a holy man's martyrdom. Of the two leading Flemish dailies, *De Morgen* gave it a review mixing praise with indignation, while *De Standaard* burned it down completely.

At the publisher's request, I had included in the Dutch edition a long introduction of Indian history, the caste system and the Hindu-Muslim conflict. I left these out in the English editions, judging that separate publications on those topics are sufficiently available. The first English edition, *Gandhi and Godse: A Review and a Critique*, was published in 2001 by Voice of India, a Delhi-based Hindu publishing house founded and managed by the late great historian, Sita Ram Goel. I had my doubts about having the book published through an ideologically marked publisher, but it seemed there was little alternative. I expected mainstream publishers to be wary of publishing it as it cited most of Godse's speech verbatim, and India's ban on the publication of his speech had never formally been lifted. Like many laws in India, that ban had become dead letter and Godse's own political party, the Hindu Mahasabha, had effectively brought out the speech as a booklet; but a serious publisher with a reputation to uphold might choose to be more prudent. However, when Mr Goel heard of my Dutch book detailing Godse's motives for murdering Gandhi, he himself offered to publish an English translation. He had been a Gandhian activist in his youth and an eyewitness to some of the events discussed in the speech. He always retained a soft corner for the Mahatma, even after narrowly escaping with his life, his wife and his first child during the Muslim League's 'Direct Action Day' in Kolkata, the prelude to the great Partition massacres for which many Hindus and Sikhs hold Gandhi co-responsible. His skepticism vis-à-vis the Hindu nationalists' tendency to blame Gandhi for the Partition is discussed here in chapter 6–8.

A French translation of the Indian edition, *Pourquoi j'ai tué Gandhi: Examen et Critique de la Défense de Nathuram Godse* (*Why I Killed Gandhi: Investigation and Critique of Nathuram Godse's Defense*), was prepared at the request of the Paris-based publisher Michel Desgranges in 2007. His prestigious publishing house *Les Belles Lettres*, otherwise specialized in the Greco-Roman classics, had started a series of books on India directed by François Gautier, Indian correspondent for several French dailies. It was a step forward to be published alongside top-ranking Indology scholars like Prof. Michel Angot.

Meanwhile, the English-Indian edition was getting some recognition. It was, after all, a rare entrance into the real thoughts of a Hindu nationalist, as opposed to one of those 'expert' analyses by a biased academic Indologist. Even those Westerners who are in the pocket of the Indian secularists can recognize a reliable source when they are presented with one. That is why Prof. Martha Nussbaum used my book as a source in her own book *The Clash Within* (Harvard 2007, p. 165 ff., p. 362 ff.). Not that she wrote anything that Nehruvians in India would disapprove of, but at least she got the Godse part right.

A much updated Dutch edition was published by Aspekt Publishers in Soesterberg, the Netherlands, in 2009. It was included in its series of biographies under the simple title *Mahatma Gandhi*. This amounted to a first-class burial, obscuring the specificity of the book and making it look like just another biography. But at least I am happy it became available in print again for the Dutch-medium public.

Now the book, updated once more, may well have found its definitive shape in this English edition. I thank Professor Gautam Sen for writing an insightful foreword.

1

# The Murder of Mahatma Gandhi and Its Consequences

*'It is very necessary throughout to view Gandhi as he is and not what he poses to be.'*[1]

## CHRONICLE OF THE MAHATMA MURDER

Between 5.00 and 5.30 p.m. on 30 January 1948, on the way to his daily public prayer session in the garden of Birla House, Delhi, Mohandas Karamchand Gandhi, leader of the movement that had presided over India's independence from Britain in August 1947, was killed with three revolver shots by Nathuram Vinayak Godse, editor of the Pune-based Marathi daily *Hindu Rashtra*. The old man (born 1869) fell down with a barely audible groan, *'Hey Ram'* ('Oh God') according to the official legend, then breathed his last.

This way, Godse (born 1910) exacted 'punishment' for Gandhi's alleged pro-Muslim policies. These were particularly his acceptance in June 1947 of the plan to partition India into a secular state, retaining the name India and a Muslim state called Pakistan; and more immediately his fast, earlier in January 1948, on behalf of the safety of the Delhi Muslims threatened by angry Hindu refugees pouring in from Pakistan, and in support of Pakistan's demand that India pay them ₹550 million as their share from the treasury of British India. Under protest, the Indian Government had given in to the latter demand because of Gandhi's pressure, and in spite of the presence of Pakistani invasion troops on Indian territory in Kashmir. Surely this was the first time in history that a country deliberately financed its battlefield opponent, and not everyone was pleased with this display of Gandhian values.

Godse offered no resistance when the police arrested him, and effectively saved him from being lynched by the crowd.[2] The next morning, the very last issue of the *Hindu Rashtra* carried the news of Gandhiji's death on the cover in jubilant language.[3]

An earlier attempt on Gandhi's life, on 20 January 1948, had failed. The perpetrator of the clumsy bomb attack, Madanlal Pahwa, a refugee from Pakistan living in Mumbai, had been arrested on the spot. The police soon discovered that the two attempts on Gandhiji's life were connected, thanks to partial confessions extracted from Pahwa under torture, and to the help of Pune arms merchant Digamber Badge, who during a routine questioning revealed that he had provided Pahwa some weaponry.[4] Badge was arrested on 31 January and soon turned approver, so that he did not sit in the dock during the Mahatma murder trial and even received state housing and a pension afterwards.

In the next few days, the police arrested as accomplices the manager of *Hindu Rashtra,* Narayan Dattatreya Apte; Nathuram's brother Gopal Godse; entrepreneur Vishnu Karkare, refugee benefactor and sometime collaborator of *Hindu Rashtra*; Badge's home servant Shankar Kistaiyya; and Dr Sadashiv Parchure from Gwalior, who had provided the murder weapon. It transpired that Pahwa's bomb explosion had been meant as a signal for a shoot-out by the others, who had been present but hesitated at the last moment. Vinayak Damodar Savarkar, ideologue of the Hindu Mahasabha ('Hindu great-assembly', HMS), and one of the 25,000 Hindu nationalist activists who had been arrested immediately after the murder under Preventive Detention laws, was also included among the co-accused. Even under torture, all the others had denied Savarkar's complicity.

## THE VERDICT

The Mahatma murder trial took place in Delhi's Red Fort.[5] Godse and Apte were sentenced to death, Savarkar was acquitted, the others were given prison sentences on conspiracy charges. Godse appealed against the verdict, not because he claimed innocence of the murder, but because he denied that there had been a conspiracy. In effect, the thrust of his (and his accomplices') appeal was that all the others had to be acquitted, because none of them had been a party to the murder. Eventually, the appeals trial did not substantially alter the verdict, except for Kistaiyya and Parchure, who got the benefit of the doubt and were acquitted.

According to the Godse family, Law Minister Dr Bhimrao Ambedkar contacted Nathuram's lawyer to convey the message that if Nathuram would like his sentence commuted to life imprisonment, he would be able to arrange it. After all, it was easy enough to invoke Gandhiji's non-violence to this effect, e.g.: 'Killing this misguided activist could hardly be a fitting tribute to Gandhiji's legacy of non-violence.' But Nathuram's reply was: 'Please, see to it that mercy is not imposed on me. I want to show that through me, Gandhiji's non-violence is being hanged.' Taken aback by this reply, Ambedkar, who had never thought highly of Gandhiji's eccentric ideas, actually praised Godse.[6]

Godse and Apte were hanged in the early morning of 15 November 1949 in Central Gaol, Ambala. Their ashes were secretly submerged in the nearby Ghaggar River (the ancient Saraswati river of Vedic fame), though it had been Godse's last wish that his ashes be thrown into the Indus River, in what had now become Pakistan, as soon as the Pakistan territory was liberated from Islamic rule. Every anniversary of the hanging, small gatherings in Pune and Mumbai commemorate Godse's and Apte's 'sacrifice' and renew the pledge to undo India's partition.

## POLITICAL CONSEQUENCES

The immediate political consequences of the murder were chiefly the following four:

Firstly, the communal tension in India stopped at once (not in Pakistan; in its eastern sector, i.e., today's Bangladesh, pogroms of the minorities continued until 1950). When earlier that month the Mahatma had started a fast unto death for communal harmony, the riots in Delhi had already stopped; Hindu and Sikh refugee organizations had promised to Gandhi that they would vacate the Muslim houses and mosques which they had occupied. But this victory for Gandhian non-violence and 'change of heart' was wearing off, especially because new refugees kept coming; because there was still no news from Pakistan of any similar abating of the violence against the minorities there; and because many people, including Godse, were indignant at the Government's paying ₹550 million to Pakistan under Gandhi's pressure. But just when communal violence was about to resume, Gandhi's death sent a shock wave through India which stopped the anti-Muslim agitation completely and ushered in a period of relative communal peace which was to last well into the 1960s.

Secondly, the Hindu Mahasabha, the pro-Hindu political party with which Godse, Apte and their newspaper had been associated, was knocked out as a political force. Even its leader Dr Syama Prasad Mookerjee, a member of independent India's first and broad-based government (which included some non-members of the Indian National Congress in spite of the latter's comfortable majority), left the party. In the subsequent decades, it never got more than three seats in the Lok Sabha. Today, it is a small organization and only a shadow of the party it once was.

Thirdly, the Hindu nationalist organization Rashtriya Swayamsevak Sangh (RSS, National Volunteer Corps, or simply 'the Sangh') of which Godse had been a member, was banned and forced to comply with Government demands, especially the drafting of a written Constitution to remove the impression of its being a secret society. Only after complying was it unbanned and its leadership released from prison. The subsequent RSS habit of paying insistent lip service to the dominant ideologies and institutions might be partly due to this humiliating episode.

Fourthly, the total lack of support from politicians in other parties during this ordeal convinced the RSS rank and file of the need to start a party of their own. This way, Gandhi's death was a factor in the foundation of the Jana Sangh (1951–77), later refounded as the Bharatiya Janata Party (BJP), that ruled India in 1998–2004, and is the ruling party now since May 2014.

Note that we are not including among the murder's consequences any change in the party-line of the Congress. The power equation of the next few years, viz. Nehru's breakthrough to unchallenged hegemony, had essentially been put into place by Gandhi himself. Before Independence, against the preference of the Congress Working Committee, the Mahatma had forced the highly esteemed Sardar Vallabhbhai Patel to withdraw his candidature for the Congress presidency, effectively imposing Nehru as party leader on an unwilling party, and therefore also as Prime Minister on the country. There is no indication whatsoever that in the subsequent power struggle between the leftist Nehru and conservatives like Patel, Purushottamdas Tandon and C. Rajagopalachari in 1948–50, a surviving Gandhi would have sided with the latter. To that extent, Gandhi's absence should, in theory, be deemed a setback for Nehru, but he made up for it with an extra measure of his Machiavellian cleverness. Gandhi's heir drew a moral advantage from the murder, which Patel as Home Minister had not been able to prevent, and he carried the day.

## A TABOOED DOCUMENT

What remains of Nathuram Godse is the statement he gave in his own defence during the trial, on 8 November 1948. After the statement was read in court, its publication was prohibited. However, after the release of Godse's accomplices from prison in the 1960s, translations in Indian languages started appearing, and in 1977, Nathuram's brother Gopal published the English original under the cautious title *May It Please Your Honour*. A new edition, with a long epilogue by Gopal on the background and the events in prison, was published in 1993 under the more revealing title *Why I Assassinated Mahatma Gandhi*.[7]

To my knowledge, before the present book no serious discussion of Godse's speech has ever been published. For example, in spite of its title and project, B.R. Nanda's book *Gandhi and His Critics* does not even mention Godse, let alone his self-justification. There is no such thing as a rebuttal of Godse's argumentation against Gandhi, but there is no sympathizing commentary either. The Hindu Mahasabha has merely published the speech itself, and some eye-witnesses have laid down in writing their memories of the atmosphere in court when Godse spoke.

Justice Gopal Das Khosla, one of Godse's judges, and whose sympathies were certainly not with 'Hindu Communalism',[8] has left this impression in his book *Murder of the Mahatma*: 'The audience was visibly and audibly moved. There was a deep silence when he ceased speaking. Many women were in tears and men were coughing and searching for their handkerchiefs. (...) I have, however, no doubt that had the audience on that day been constituted into a jury and entrusted with the task of deciding Godse's appeal, they would have brought in a verdict of 'not guilty' by an overwhelming majority.'

In 1998, a Mumbai playwright, Pradeep Dalvi, tried to recreate some of the atmosphere in his play *Me Nathuram Godse Boltoy* ('This Is Nathuram Godse Speaking'). After seven performances, Prime Minister Atal Bihari Vajpayee managed to convince the Maharashtra state government, a Hindu nationalist coalition of Shiv Sena and BJP, to withdraw clearance for the play. This was somewhat unexpected, considering that Shiv Sena leader Bal Thackeray was on record as saying that future generations will venerate Godse rather than Gandhi. It was left to Mumbai's liberals, led by filmmaker Shyam Benegal, to protest against this act of censorship.[9]

Nathuram Godse's defence statement is a historical document, and in this book we will quote it at length. The numeration of its paragraphs as given here is present in the original as published by his brother. Godse develops his critique of Gandhi in a chronological order as the events of the Mahatma's political career took place, and the numbering in his statement follows accordingly. Yet, references to some topics remain scattered, so at some places in this book, I have brought together these scattered references. Paragraphs in which he repeats himself or which are not relevant for his political self-justification have not been reproduced, but the greater part of his text is reproduced verbatim before being commented upon.

## FACTS OF THE MURDER PLOT

The first part of Godse's statement merely states his position in the trial. He claims sole responsibility for the murder, and rejects the thesis of the prosecution that there was a conspiracy:

'I, Nathuram Vinayak Godse, the first accused above-named, respectfully beg to state as under:

'1. Before I make my submission as regards the various charges

I respectfully submit that the charges as framed are not according to law, in as much as there is a misjoinder of charges and there ought to have been two separate trials, one relating to the incident of the 20th of January 1948 and the other relating to the incident of the 30th of January 1948. The two having been mixed up together the whole trial is vitiated. (...)'

'4. It appears from the charge sheet that the prosecution takes the events that have happened on 20 January 1948 and thereafter on 30 January 1948 as one and the same or a chain of events in continuation of one and the same object culminating in the murder of Gandhiji. I, therefore, wish to make it clear at the outset that the events up to 20 January 1948 are quite independent and they have no connection whatsoever with what happened thereafter and on 30 January 1948.'[10]

What follows is a list of specific allegations made by approver Badge which Godse denies one by one—no one ever helped him or even knew of his murder plans, no one of the co-accused supplied the murder weapon. Instead, he had bought the revolver from an unknown merchant in Delhi refugee circles (paragraphs 1–25).

The court was quite right in ignoring this plea. Certainly there had been a conspiracy, in which all the accused except Savarkar were involved. There were enough witnesses who had seen the conspirators together in late January 1948, in hotels, airplanes, railway stations, etc. The conspiracy, though denied to the last minute of the trial by all the conspirators, was also confirmed to me by the two accomplices who survived into the 1990s—Madanlal Pahwa and Gopal Godse.[11] As Gopal Godse told me: 'Of course I was involved, but I had a right to deny it. Nathuram was bound to be hanged, but for the rest of us it made a big difference, so we all—Nathuram included—pleaded against the conspiracy thesis.'

One man could not be saved by this defence plea—the manager of the paper *Hindu Rashtra*, Narayan Apte, son of famed historian and Sanskrit scholar Vaman Shivram Apte, whose *The Student's Sankrit-English Dictionary* is still widely in use. A Brahmin like Godse, he was much more a man of the world. At the time of the events under discussion, he had a wife with a handicapped little son as well as a mistress who was expecting his daughter. He was the only real accomplice in the actual murder, planning the second attempt along with Godse and encouraging him till the end. Nathuram Godse preferred to act (almost) alone in the attack on 30 January 1948 because in his judgement, the first attempt had failed due to the excess number of participants. In that light, the court was right in distinguishing between Godse and Apte on the one hand and the rest of the conspirators on the other, imposing the death penalty on the former and prison sentences on the latter.

The rest of Godse's statement was devoted entirely to a discussion of politics, both Gandhiji's and his own. It is built up as a crescendo of indignation at what he saw as the Mahatma's accumulating errors, culminating in the unabashed justification of the murder. After having tried to keep his friends outside the reach of judicial punishment, he stands up to claim the full guilt or merit of the murder as the logical consequence of his own long-standing political convictions in confrontation with Gandhi's policies.

It has not been noticed either by his admirers or his detractors that quite a few of his political convictions were the same or very similar to those held by Gandhi. The fact that he murdered the Mahatma has eclipsed every other fact in his fairly long and detailed statement. We hope that this study will enable the readers to see Godse with their own eyes rather than through the eyes of those who have thus far monopolized the discourse on the *Mahatma murder*.

## NOTES

1. Lord Willingdon, Viceroy of India, 1933; quoted in B.R. Nanda: *Gandhi and His Critics*, p. vii.

2. The policeman who made the arrest, Dasondha Singh, a Sikh, was murdered on 15 May 1995 in his village in Hoshiarpur, East Punjab. The retired policeman had been involved in a quarrel with people close to the state government (Congress), which may explain the speed with which the investigation was closed without result (*Indian Express*, 27 May 1997). Probably there is no connection with the Mahatma murder, though it remains true that among Sikhs, a community which was hit particularly hard by the Partition, Godse is more popular than Gandhi.

3. The story of the murder plot is told in detail in Tapan Ghosh's *The Gandhi Murder Trial* (1973), ch. 1–5; Manohar Malgonkar: *The Men Who Killed Gandhi* (1978, I have used the 1981 reprint); and an inside account by Nathuram's brother Gopal Godse: *Gandhiji's Murder and After* (1989), ch.1–3.

4. Saira Menezes; 'I Regret I Wasn't The Man To Kill Gandhi', *Outlook*, 2 February 1998, https://www.outlookindia.com/magazine/story/i-regret-i-wasnt-the-man-to-kill-gandhi/204997

5. Accounts of the trial include G.D. Khosla's *The Murder of the Mahatma and Other Cases* (1963), ch. 10; P.L. Inamdar's *The Story of the Red Fort Trial 1948–49* (1979); T. Ghosh's *Gandhi Murder Trial*, ch. 7–27.

6. Interview with Gopal Godse, January 1992.

7. Gopal Godse had also published another account, richer in details but with the focus more on personal than on political aspects, in 1966, written immediately after his release from prison in 1964; in 1989, an English translation from the Marathi original was published: *Gandhiji's Murder and After*.

8. One indication of G.D. Khosla's convictions—his book on the matter, *Murder of the Mahatma*, is dedicated to the militantly secularist writer Khushwant Singh. Moreover, on p. 261 he explicitly supports the demands for which the Mahatma went on his final fast (esp. payment by India of ₹550 million to Pakistan), and which had triggered the initiative to kill him. On the Partition and the ensuing refugee

problem, Khosla wrote *Stern Reckoning. A Survey of the Events Leading up to and Following the Partition of India.*

9. Vide Masseh Rahman: 'Bombay's culture cops', *Time*, 3 August 1998.

10. Nathuram Godse: *Why I Assassinated Gandhi*, pp. 15–16.

11. Interview with Gopal Godse, January 1992; and with Madanlal Pahwa, February 1996.

# 2

# Nathuram Godse's Background

## NATHURAM GODSE'S CASTE

The Mahatma's assassin, Nathuram Vinayak Godse, was a bachelor and teetotaller, completely devoted to his political work. The city where he lived was in itself a continuous encouragement to a servant of the Hindu cause: Pune, capital of the Peshwa Empire (1713–1818), the last great Hindu power before British rule. Godse was an ardent follower of Vinayak Damodar Savarkar, also known as swatantryaveer ('hero of independence') or just veer, 'hero', who, though formally retired as president of the Hindu Mahasabha, was still its undisputed ideological leader.

Both Savarkar and Godse belonged to the Chitpavan Brahmin caste of coastal Maharashtra, a very prominent community in India's history since the eighteenth century. The members of this caste are still physically distinct by their taller and lighter features (some even have blue eyes), pointing to their immigrant origins. They are said to be Maga Brahmins whose original homeland was Shakadweep, 'the Shaka (Scythian) continent', i.e., Central Asia.[1] Apparently, as Shrikant Talageri in *Aryan Invasion Theory and Indian Nationalism* (p. 244) observes, they came as refugees from

Seistan in western Afghanistan at the time of the Muslim conquest in the ninth century (as would a few centuries later the Saraswat Brahmins from Kashmir, now largely settled in Goa). According to their own traditions laid down in the Sahyadri Khanda, they were washed ashore as corpses but Vishnu's incarnation Parashurama 'brought the corpses back to life' by a reversal of the cremation process: the pyre (chita) merely purified (pavanam) them, hence their name 'Chitpavan'. For a long time, they were looked down upon and used for menial services by the native Deshasth Brahmins.[2] But at the turn of the eighteenth century, a Chitpavan clan shot to prominence in the wake of the Maratha commander Shivaji's successful liberation of parts of Maharashtra from Moghul rule.

Shivaji's progeny proved incapable of ruling and extending the Maratha empire, and in 1713 effective control passed into the hands of their prime ministers, the Chitpavan Peshwas.[3] For half a century, Peshwa-led armies scored victory upon victory, until they overplayed their hand and suffered a shattering defeat in the third battle of Panipat in 1761 against the Afghan invader Ahmad Shah Abdali. In spite of this setback, they remained the main power centre in India until their decisive defeat by the British East India Company troops in 1817.

At the end of the nineteenth century, Chitpavan Brahmins like V.K. Chiplunkar, G.K. Gokhale and B.G. Tilak took a leadership role in the fledgling freedom movement against British colonial rule.[4] The British rulers considered them the most dangerous caste in India; in jest, they abbreviated the caste's alternative name *Konkanasth Brahmins* as *KoBra*. At any rate, the Chitpavan Brahmins had a strong sense of vocation as India's leaders on the road to freedom and national honour. Though politically committed to the abolition of caste, Godse and Savarkar undoubtedly had this caste-bound sense of vocation.

REVENGE ON GODSE'S CASTE

One immediate consequence of the murder which is usually left unmentioned in the numerous hagiographies of the Mahatma is the wave of revenge which hit the Hindu Mahasabha, the RSS and most of all, the Chitpavan Brahmin caste. It seems that most hagiographers were embarrassed with the way the apostle of non-violence was mourned by his fans as well as by others who merely used the opportunity for, as in *Red Fort Trial* (p. 4) P.L. Inamdar puts it, 'the manhunt of Maharashtrian Brahmins irrespective of their party allegiance by non-Brahmins in Poona and other districts.' Offices and houses were burnt down, numerous people were molested and at least eight people were killed, according to an official tradition.

However the article 'Gandhi is killed by a Hindu', published by *The New York Times* on 31 January 1948, puts the number of mortal victims in Bombay (now called Mumbai) alone, and on the first day alone, already at fifteen. Locals in Pune (where of course the *Hindu Rastra* office was set on fire, along with the offices of other pro-Hindu papers) told me they estimated the death toll in Pune alone at fifty. One of the rare studies of the event, by Maureen Patterson, concludes that the greatest violence took place not in the cities of Mumbai, Pune and Nagpur, centres of Hindu nationalism, but in 'the extreme southwest of the Deccan plateau—the Desh—of the Marathi linguistic region', including Satara, Belgaum and Kolhapur.[5] Then, as now, press reporting on communal rioting was under strict control, and Maureen Patterson reports that even decades after the facts, she was not given access to relevant police files. So, we may not know the exact magnitude of this 'Gandhian violence' until all the records are opened, but the death toll may well run into several hundreds.

In a second phase, the violence became purely casteist—the middle castes, particularly the Marathas aspiring to dominate at the expense of the Brahmins, joined the riots bandwagon to settle scores with their main rivals, e.g., in Pune: 'Godse's act, which first set off anti-RSS attacks, before long became the opportunity non-Brahmans had been waiting for to retaliate against Chitpavans for long years of real or imagined domination. Crowds in lorries reportedly owned by leading Maratha politicians and hundreds on foot surged through Brahman wards bent on revenge.'[6]

In the Satara district, Chitpavans were 'disproportionately' active in highly visible positions, and thereby 'symbolized the power that they had in the past two centuries taken over from the Maratha king in Satara as his Peshwas', which had led to a long-standing Maratha resentment. In February 1948, one thousand of their houses were officially reported as having been burnt down, and an unspecified number were killed, e.g.: 'one family named Godse was said to have lost three male members.' In this case, the ground had been prepared by decades of anti-Brahmin agitation by the Satyashodhak Samaj (founded by the nineteenth century anti-Brahmin ideologue Mahatma Jyotirao Phule) with anti-Brahmin hate theatre and social boycotts.[7]

The destruction was even larger in Kolhapur, where attacks on HMS and RSS offices, and on a film studio owned by a pro-HMS Maratha, were followed by a massive wave of terror against all Brahmins.[8] Here it was the Maratha princely court itself which had for long given the lead in anti-Brahmin policies, such as job reservations for non-Brahmins and attracting anti-Brahmin teachers (both Christian missionaries and Veda-fundamentalistic Arya Samaj reformists) to run the schools. Maratha resentment was often expressed in a constructive manner, such as support to the actual uplift of low-born people to positions held mostly by Brahmins, e.g., the studies and career start of India's first Law Minister, Dalit leader Dr Bhimrao Ambedkar, had been sponsored by the ruler Shahu Maharaj of Kolhapur and Sayajirao Gaekwad of Baroda, descendents of Maratha generals. Shahu Maharaj had actively collaborated with the British against the freedom movement, which was locally identified with Chitpavan Brahmins like B.G. Tilak. Note the combination of anti-Brahminism with aggressive Hinduism in the Marathas as heirs of Shivaji, a combination which many feel in recent decades has got embodied in the Shiv Sena.

The biggest violence took place in the seven Patwardhan (Chitpavan) princely states such as Sangli, where the remarkably advanced factories owned by Chitpavans were largely destroyed. Here, Jains and Lingayats joined the Marathas in the attacks. The events hastened the integration of the Patwardhan states (viz. by March 1948) into the Bombay province, an integration opposed by the Brahmins fearing Maratha predominance in the integrated province.

In a mythological aside, Maureen Patterson muses that the Marathas, who claim Kshatriya (warrior aristocracy) status, had finally found a way and a position to avenge the mythical actions of the Brahman Parashurama who, as it is believed, exterminated the Kshatriyas from the face of the earth at one point. It is believed that the same Parashurama created the Chitpavan Brahmins from corpses that lay on the Konkan coast.[9]

However, lest Gandhians and Congress apologists use this casteist development to disown their own responsibility, it merits emphasis that the first phase of the violence seemed to be in the name of Gandhism, targeting Hindu nationalists of various organizations, regardless of caste. Thus, in Mumbai: 'Mobs broke into Mahasabha and RSS offices, and ransacked houses and shops belonging to known members of these organizations. Trouble continued the next day when a mob estimated between 500 and 1000 gathered in front of [the house of] the fiery Hindu nationalist leader Vinayak Damodar Savarkar, and began stoning it. Reports, probably rumours, had circulated that people close to Savarkar had been distributing sweets to celebrate Gandhi's death. Congress supporters were incensed and swarmed around Veer Savarkar's house, but police intervention saved him from bodily harm. But police were not in time to prevent his brother, who lived nearby, from being hurt.'[10]

The best comparison in living memory for this massacre of Hindu nationalists and Brahmins is provided by the massacre of Sikhs by Congress secularists in Delhi and elsewhere after the murder of their leader Indira Gandhi by her Sikh bodyguard in 1984. (The anti-Jewish pogrom of the *Kristallnacht*, 9–10 November 1938, comes to mind. It was triggered by the murder of a German diplomat in Paris by a Jewish youngster.) But unlike in the case of the anti-Sikh pogrom, where a few local Congress leaders were brought to trial after a long delay, and where references to the events keep on being made in studies of 'communalism', the Mahatma riots had no consequences for the perpetrators and were flushed down the memory hole, probably because the accused in the latter case did not have a high profile.

## GODSE, THE SWAYAMSEVAK

The ideological helplessness of the contemporary Hindu nationalists comes out immediately when you question them about Mahatma Gandhi. The assessment of Gandhi's significance for Hindu society and the fact of his murder by a Hindu are embarrassing topics for them, which the opponents of the Hindu movement are still exploiting to the hilt.

Invariably, the so-called secularists seemed to regard the RSS (with its *parivar* or 'family' of affiliated organizations including the BJP) as the 'alleged murderers of the Mahatma'. As Craig Baxter, in *The Jana Sangh* (p. 50), has remarked, this allegation is in defiance of the judicial verdict in the Mahatma murder trial: 'The RSS and the Jana Sangh do, however, frequently face accusations of being the 'murderers of Gandhi'. These most commonly come from the Congress 'left' or from the Communists, are used as political slogans, and, of course, show a disregard for the legal decision in the case.' But no matter how much the RSS connection with Godse's act may have been disproven, in *The Jana Sangh* (p. 229), Baxter notices that Gandhi's murder has been 'a millstone around the neck' of the political Hindu movement and especially the RSS.

Faced with this allegation, sticky though disproven, two attitudes are possible: continuing in a defensive position by issuing denials whenever the allegation is uttered, or taking it in one's stride and even defiantly accepting it. It is believed that the latter was generally the rhetorical tactic of Bal Thackeray, leader of the national-populist Shiv Sena. Thus, when the demolition of the Babri Masjid on 6 December 1992 was ascribed to Shiv Sena volunteers, Thackeray declared, as *The Times of India* reported, 'If Shiv Sainiks did it, I am proud of them.' On the Gandhi murder too, he had taken a defiant stand, even though he never accepted that the assassination could be attributed to the Shiv Sena in anyway. In 1992, he shocked the opinion-makers by declaring that future generations would erect statues for Godse rather than for the Mahatma.

The RSS family's line has been just the opposite: they have exhausted themselves in denials and condemnations of the murder. Because of their enemies' persistence, this has meant that in this respect, as in many others, the RSS family has been continually on the defensive. In fact, seeing the RSS on the defensive has obviously fuelled their opponents' gusto in using this allegation. The RSS leaders keep on repeating that the RSS had been officially cleared of all charges of complicity, but to no avail: the media in India and abroad just keep on associating them with the murder of the Mahatma.[11]

To prove its innocence, the RSS family has invested a lot of words in denouncing the murder and praising the Mahatma. Immediately after the murder, the RSS supremo Madhav Sadashiv Golwalkar called it a 'heinous crime' and directed all branches to suspend normal routine for the thirteen days of Hindu mourning

'out of respect and sense of sorrow at the tragic demise of Mahatmaji.'
Years later, he still gave speeches in praise of the Mahatma, just
like any average Congressman. In his case, however, no outsider
was willing to credit him with sincerity, perhaps wrongly.[12]

## THE GODSE BROTHERS' TESTIMONY ON THE RSS

Here is Nathuram Godse's own version on his involvement with
the RSS:

'29. I have worked for several years in RSS and subsequently
joined the HMS and volunteered myself as a soldier under its
pan-Hindu flag.'[13]

'114. About the year 1932 late Dr. Hedgewar of Nagpur
founded the Rashtriya Swayamsevak Sangha in Maharashtra also.[14]
His oration greatly impressed me and I joined the Sangha as a
volunteer thereof. I am one of those volunteers of Maharashtra
who joined the Sangha in its initial stage. I also worked for a
few years on the intellectual side in the Province of Maharashtra.
Having worked for the uplift of the Hindus, I felt it necessary to
take part in the political activities of the country for the protection
of the just rights of the Hindus. I therefore left the Sangha and
joined the Hindu Mahasabha.'[15]

However, Nathuram Godse's straightforward declaration has
lately been challenged by none other than his brother and accomplice
Gopal. On the occasion of the annual Nathuram Godse memorial
meeting (Mumbai, 17 November 1993), Gopal was interviewed
and said, against the umpteenth statement by Hindu nationalist
leader L.K. Advani disowning Nathuram, that Nathuram had been
a *baudhik karyavah* ('intellectual officer', i.e., the above-mentioned
'work on the intellectual side'), an RSS worker of some rank at least
at the local level. The four Godse brothers had been groomed by
the RSS at the initiative of the eldest, Nathuram.[16] Though their
locus of activity shifted somewhat, there never was a clean break

with the RSS.

It is true that their guru, Veer Savarkar, had spoken with mild contempt of the RSS, a well-known fact which gave credibility to Godse's court statement that he had left the RSS at about the time of Savarkar's accession to the presidency of the HMS in December 1937. But then, Savarkar had no personal connection with the RSS, while the Godse brothers had spent time in RSS meetings in their young days and developed a close link with it, not so easy to disown. Therefore, Nathuram contrived to create the impression that the RSS had little to do with him, simply to avoid creating more trouble for the RSS in the difficult post-assassination months. Gopal explains that Nathuram did not leave the RSS, he only stated so because Golwalkar and the RSS were already in a lot of trouble after Gandhi's murder.[17]

There is really no controversy here. Nathuram Godse never rejected the RSS, but he was not functioning within the RSS structure in the years before the murder. He had chosen to do political work whereas the RSS scrupulously stayed out of party politics. Ideologically, he still was an RSS man. That is why he sang the nationalist RSS song *Namaste sada vatsale matribhume* ('I bow to thee, loving Motherland, always'),[18] a fixed part of every RSS shaakhaa (branch) meeting, when he walked to the gallows.

It remains true, moreover, that the RSS had professed a very negative opinion of the Mahatma's failed policy of 'Hindu-Muslim unity', an opinion which was also Nathuram Godse's motive for the murder. Much of Godse's speech consisted of comments which Hindu activists of any affiliation, including the RSS, had been making ever since the Mahatma's involvement in the pan-Islamist Khilafat Movement of 1920–21 (discussed below). There is just no denying that while the murder was the handiwork of a small group of conspirators, their motive had been an indignation over Gandhi's policies which they shared with the entire Hindu Mahasabha, with the RSS and with many common Hindus and Sikhs besides.

However, being of the same political opinion does not constitute complicity in the crime. When a great man is murdered, you always see vultures descend on the great opportunities for political exploitation which the concomitant quantity of guilt and blame offers. When Yitzhak Rabin was murdered in 1995, many in the Israeli Labour Party blamed the opposition Likud bloc, alleging that with its virulent anti-Rabin propaganda, it had 'created the right climate' for the murder. Likewise, after Mahatma Gandhi had criticized Swami Shraddhananda's work of reconverting Indian Muslims to Hinduism, a Muslim killed the Swami; and so, Nathuram Godse alleged that Gandhi had 'created the right climate' for the murder, or words to that effect: he 'provoked a Muslim youth to murder the Swami.'[19] But we need not emulate Godse in his conflation of criticism and murder, do we?

The RSS may rightly disown the responsibility for Godse's act. It never believed in assassination as a method of conducting politics. Before and after 1948, the RSS has been involved in many a street fight, but never in targeted assassinations of public figures. Even during Godse's trial, no evidence was ever produced that the organization had ordered or condoned Godse's initiative to murder the Mahatma. If not for moral reasons, then at least out of self-interest, the RSS was most certainly disinclined to associate itself with a crime of this magnitude. After all, the negative consequences that actually followed were perfectly foreseeable. And yet, the RSS ought to publicly (as most of its sympathizers do privately) own up at least Godse's argumentation, for that was the view of Gandhi's policies commonly held by the RSS activists in the 1940s.

## INSPIRED BY SAVARKAR

In paragraphs 26–47, Nathuram Godse details the story of his involvement in the Hindu Sanghatan movement ('self-organization', of which the HMS and the RSS were instances) and his political relation with Veer Savarkar:

'29. I have worked for several years in RSS and subsequently joined the Hindu Mahasabha and volunteered myself to fight as a soldier under its pan-Hindu flag. About this time Veer Savarkar was elected to the Presidentship of the Hindu Mahasabha. The Hindu movement got verily electrified and vivified as never before, under his magnetic lead and whirlwind propaganda. Millions of Hindu Sanghatanists looked up to him as the chosen hero, as the ablest and most faithful advocate of the Hindu cause. I too was one of them. I worked devotedly to carry on the Mahasabha activities and hence came to be personally acquainted with Savarkarji.'[20] And that, to Godse, is all there is to say about their personal relationship.

Godse explains how Savarkar encouraged and financially supported Apte and him when on 28 March 1944 they started their Marathi daily *Agrani* ('forerunner, vanguard'). This paper was closed down in 1946 by the authorities for flouting the ban on clear and factual reporting on communal violence (i.e., detailing the genesis of the riots and the community-wise breakdown of the victim numbers), but immediately restarted under the name, *Hindu Rashtra*. Though they sometimes met at the HMS office in Bombay, Savarkar never involved himself in Godse's enterprise, not even to contribute a regular column as Godse had requested him to do. As Partition came near, Godse lost his faith in the HMS's ability to stem the tide and keep India united:

'34. Some three years ago, Veer Savarkar's health got seriously impaired and since then he was generally confined to bed. (...) Thus deprived of his virile leadership and magnetic influence, the activities and influence of the Hindu Mahasabha too got crippled and when Dr. Mookerji became its President, the Mahasabha was actually reduced to the position of a hand-maid to the Congress. It became quite incapable of counteracting the dangerous anti-Hindu activities of Gandhiite cabal on the one hand and the Muslim League on the other. (...) I determined to organise a youthful band of Hindu Sanghatanists and adopt a fighting programme both against the Congress and the League without consulting any of those prominent but old leaders of the Mahasabha.'[21]

The 'youthful band' was the Hindu Raksha Dal ('Hindu protection squad') with a membership never exceeding 150. Godse was now his own man directing his own political activities, independent of the RSS and HMS. Whatever their ideological kinship, they cannot be held responsible for Godse's act.

## DISAPPOINTED WITH SAVARKAR

Let us now look in more detail into the organizational estrangement between Godse and his mentor Savarkar. Of the events 'which painfully opened my eyes about this time to the fact that Veer Savarkar and other old leaders of the Mahasabha could no longer be relied upon' (para 35–44), Godse mentions the following examples. In 1946, Savarkar went out of his way to personally reprimand Godse when Apte and he had heckled Gandhiji during a prayer-meeting in a Hindu temple in Bhangi Colony (Delhi), where Gandhiji had read passages from the Quran in spite of protests by the Hindu worshippers, and where he had spoken in defence of Bengal Chief Minister Huseyn Shaheed Suhrawardy, the man possibly politically (and probably also directly) responsible for anti-Hindu pogroms in Calcutta and Noakhali. Godse quotes Savarkar:

'37. (...) "Just as I condemn the Congressites for breaking up your party meetings and election booths by disorderly conduct, I ought to condemn any such undemocratic conduct on the part of Hindu Sanghatanists also."'[22]

Of greater political importance was the fact that Savarkar and the other HMS leaders recognized the post-Partition State of India, hoisted its flag, and accepted Nehru's invitation that their party president, S.P. Mookerjee, join the provisional government:

'41. (...) To my mind to recognise a State of Divided India was

tantamount to being a party to the cursed vivisection of India. (...)
Veer Savarkar went further and actually insisted that the tri-colour
flag with the wheel should be recognised as a National Flag.

'42. (...) In addition to that, when Dr. Mookerji asked his
permission through a trunk call to Veer Savarkar as to whether Dr.
Mookerji should accept a portfolio in the Indian Union Ministry,
Veer Savarkar emphatically replied that the new Government must
be recognised as a National Government whatever may be the party
leading it, and must be supported by all patriots (...).'[23]

By inviting the HMS president into his Cabinet, Nehru
effectively neutralized the HMS. In the opposition, the party could
have been a dangerous adversary, especially as the champion of the
Indian unity which Congress had betrayed; but as a partner in
the government, and one with little influence at that, it became
harmless. In terms of political strategy, Godse's critique of the HMS
leadership's cooperationist line was probably correct. On the other
hand, one should concede to Nehru a certain genuine generosity
and a fitting sense that the first native Government should be a
truly national one, with representatives of all political tendencies.
Then again, it is also true that Dr Mookerjee and Dr Ambedkar
had been invited by him on advice from Mahatma Gandhi and
Sardar Patel; Nehru himself was rather reluctant at that time and
felt increasingly uncomfortable with them subsequently, as events
went to prove.

Savarkar, the veteran fighter for independence, was apparently
too happy with the long-awaited sovereignty as embodied in the
first native Union Government to think in terms of party politics.
But Godse did not believe that a truly sovereign and representative
government was compatible with the intrusive presence of Gandhiji:

'43. (...) I myself could not be opposed to a common front
of patriots, but while the Congress Government continued to be
so sheepishly under the thumb of Gandhiji and while Gandhiji
could thrust his anti-Hindu fads on that Congressite Government

by resorting to such a cheap trick as threatening a fast, it was clear to me that any common front under such circumstances was bound to be another form of setting up Gandhiji's dictatorship and consequently a betrayal of Hindudom.'[24]

If even Savarkar and Mookerjee were willing to surrender to Gandhiji's dictates, Godse judged that the time had come for a new and independent political activism:

'44. Every one of these steps taken by Veer Savarkar was so deeply resented by me that I myself along with Mr. Apte and some of the young Hindu Sanghatanist friends decided once and for all to chalk and work out our active programme quite independently of the Mahasabha or its old veteran leaders. We resolved not to confide any of our new plans to any of them including Savarkar.'[25]

Here, Godse denies once more that Savarkar had played a role in the assassination. Approver Digamber Badge kept on making this very allegation, possibly because he or the investigating police officers expected some reward from Pandit Nehru in exchange for catching such a big fish. HMS leader and Godse's lawyer L.B. Bhopatkar revealed several years later, in Manohar Malgonkar's *The Men Who Killed Gandhi* (a volume published by the Savarkar Memorial Committee on 16 February 1989), that Dr Ambedkar, the Law Minister in Nehru's Cabinet at that time, met him secretly to inform him that Nehru was *personally* interested in involving Savarkar, though there was no evidence to prove Savarkar's complicity. His mere imprisonment was successful enough in eliminating him from politics. Manohar Malgonkar, in *The Men Who Killed Gandhi* (p. 29) writes 'The strain of the trial, and the year spent in prison while it lasted, wrecked Savarkar's health and finished him as a force in India's politics.'

At any rate, the prosecutor could not produce the slightest evidence connecting Savarkar with the murder. In August 1974, Badge admitted to an interviewer that his testimony against Savarkar had been false.[26] Ever since, journalists reluctant to give up the polemical advantage of connecting the main Hindutva ideologue with the murder, glibly introduce him as 'a *co-accused* in the Mahatma murder trial.'[27] In Nehruvian 'secularism', superficiality of thought is compensated for by thoroughness in dishonesty.

## A RUMOUR ABOUT GODSE AND SAVARKAR

At this point, we cannot altogether ignore a rumour which frequently appears in the secondary literature on Hindutva. According to Larry Collins and Dominique Lapierre, the writers of the overrated book *Freedom at Midnight*, the most widely-read introduction to the history of India's attainment of independence, including the Mahatma murder story, Godse had had a homosexual relation with Savarkar.[28]

As usually happens with rumours, this one too has spread. Thus, in M.J. Akbar's Nehru biography (p. 428), the claim becomes a curt statement of fact: 'Nathuram Godse, thirty-seven, homosexual, fanatic, ascetic, ...' Akbar's book has been republished as a Penguin paperback, available in the whole world. Similarly, the French edition of *Freedom at Midnight* claims that Savarkar was a homosexual and frequent opium user, even though few people knew about it. And of Godse, that before he chose to remain a celibate, 'he had had, so it is believed, only one sexual experience, with his political mentor Veer Savarkar, as initiator.'[29]

In his psychological comment on the relation between Gandhi and Godse, well-known psychologist Ashis Nandy registers Collins' and Lapierre's claim and expresses serious doubts about it, but also mentions those very facts that seem to make it plausible to Freudians.[30] Firstly, as a child, Godse had been treated like a girl by his parents, in the hope of magically warding off the fate of their three earlier sons, who had all died in infancy. *Nathuram* literally means 'nose-ring Ram' (his given name was *Ramachandra*, or *Ram* for short), because he had been made to wear this feminine ornament. Secondly, Savarkar, who spent a decade in the Andaman penal colony, must have been familiar with aberrant sexual practices common in prisons; the Pathan camp guards had a grisly reputation in this regard. These conjectures don't prove anything, but they provide the infrastructure of plausibility on which rumour-mongers build their inferences.

Fact is that serious reporters on the Gandhi murder trial mention nothing of the kind, and that the claimed source of the rumour, Nathuram Godse's brother Gopal, strongly denies (to Nandy as well as to myself) ever having told any such thing to Collins and Lapierre. According to him, the authors had meanwhile given an undertaking to his lawyer that the passage would be deleted from future editions of the book. The newer Indian prints have indeed left out the offending passages.[31] The burden of proof definitely lies with those who persist in repeating the rumour, and until they discharge it, we must hold them guilty of slander.

Having disposed of this alleged intimate relationship, we are left with the more relevant and undisputed fact that Godse was a devoted political follower of Savarkar. Godse joined the HMS just around the time when Savarkar, an acclaimed hero of the independence struggle, became its president (December 1937). For Godse, this was the latest step in a career as an activist for the Hindu cause, which included years of active membership of the RSS (which can be inferred to cover the period 1932–37). But to outsiders, the truly surprising and ironical fact must certainly be that Godse had started his involvement in politics as a Gandhian activist.

## GODSE THE GANDHIAN

Numerous Hindu revivalist leaders and authors started their public life in Gandhian activism. Godse began his political career as a volunteer in Mahatma Gandhi's Civil Disobedience campaign of 1930–31. During this involvement, he discovered the organized

Hindu movement.

On some important points, the RSS line and the Savarkar line in the Hindu Mahasabha coincided with the Gandhian line. Thus, without any formal affiliation to Congress, Nathuram Godse took a leadership role in local initiatives to cure Hindu society of casteism and untouchability. As a youngster, he had earned the wrath of his parents by saving the life of a Mahar (untouchable) child, thus 'polluting' himself with its touch, and then walking into the family home without taking a bath first. As soon as he made his own living, he ignored the traditionalist objections and involved himself in organizing inter-caste meals and other symbolic offences to the untouchability taboo.

In its attempts at kindling mass agitation, the HMS also used Gandhian methods. In 1938, Godse led a group of Hindu Mahasabha activists in a campaign of Gandhian-style unarmed resistance against the anti-Hindu discrimination in the Muslim-dominated princely state of Hyderabad. He was arrested and spent a year in prison.

Ashis Nandy has pointed out the parallels between Gandhi's and Godse's personalities: they were both deeply religious, ascetic, given to sexual abstinence, and strongly attached to the Bhagavad Gita. We may add that both believed they had a supernatural sense: as a child already, Godse had acted as the oracle of the family goddess, while Gandhi always invoked his 'inner voice' to overrule rational considerations. Moreover, their political commitment was largely the same as well, as Nandy, in *At the Edge of Psychology* (p. 82), observes:

> Both were committed and courageous nationalists; both felt that the problem of India was basically the problem of the Hindus because they constituted the majority of Indians; and both were allegiant to the idea of an undivided free India. Both felt austerity was a necessary part of political activity.

Gandhi's asceticism is well-known, but Godse too lived like a hermit. He slept on a wooden plank, using occasionally a blanket and even in the severest winter wore only a shirt. Contrary to the idea fostered by the popular Hollywood film on him, *Nine Hours to Rama*, Godse neither smoked nor drank. In fact, he took Gandhi's rejection of sexuality even further: he never married and remained a strict celibate. Like Gandhi, Godse considered himself a *sanatani* or traditional Hindu and, in deference to his own wishes, he was cremated according to *sanatani* rites.

By contrast, the atheist Savarkar ordered for his own cremation to be conducted with only the barest minimum of ritual.

Yet, and in this respect too he resembled Gandhi, he said he believed in a casteless Hindu society and in a democratic polity. He was even in favour of Gandhi's attempts to mobilize the Indian Muslims for the nationalist cause by making some concessions to the Muslim leadership. Perhaps it was not an accident that Godse began his political career as a participant in the civil disobedience movement started by Gandhi and ended his political life with a speech from the witness stand which, in spite of being an attack on Gandhi, none the less revealed a grudging respect for what Gandhi had done for the country.

Note that a number of authors have grossly misstated Godse's difference of opinion with that of Gandhi's. Richard Waterstone, in *De Wijsheid van India* (p. 151), claims Godse killed Gandhi because he was against Gandhi's policy that tried to reconcile Hindus with Muslims. Joachim Betz writes: 'The murderer, a Brahmin, explained after his arrest that he had killed Gandhi because he had conceded equal rights to the Muslim minority in India.'[32]

If Joachim Betz had written in his own name that this was

Godse's reason, it would have been a wrong interpretation, a mistake. But putting this explanation into Godse's mouth is simply a lie. Perhaps not Betz's own lie, but then at least a lie by one of his Indian sources. For determined opponents of the Partition like Godse, giving 'equal rights' to the Muslims in non-partitioned India would have been a very reasonable price for keeping India united. His objection was, on the contrary, that Gandhi rarely treated Hindus and Muslims as equals, giving preferential treatment to the Muslims instead.

Another motive falsely attributed to Godse is that he opposed Gandhi's campaign against untouchability, when in fact he took an active part in it. This much is true, that a murder attempt on Gandhi had been tried during his visit to Pune in 1935, when caste reform was indeed the focus of his attention. On 25 June 1935, a Hindu suspected of opposing equality for Harijans had thrown a bomb in a car thinking mistakenly that the Mahatma was in it,[33] but Godse is not known to have been involved. A related claim is that Godse, as 'a member of the RSS, an "orthodox" fascist Hindu organization', had been angered by Gandhi's relative repudiation of the authority of the shastras, the ancient Hindu ethical codes: 'With this, he [i.e., Gandhi] wiped the traditional wielders of authority from the map, and signed his own death warrant.' Gandhi became a mortal threat to the orthodox Hindus.[34] The Hindu nationalist movement was far from orthodox, and has always been criticized by the truly orthodox (e.g., Swami Karpatri and the Puri Shankaracharya-s) for its neglect of and hostility to the doctrine of caste, i.e., for the same reasons as the Mahatma.

## PUNISHING HIS OWN KIND

Logically following from the conviction, common to both Gandhi and Godse, that 'the problem of India was basically the problem of the Hindus', there is another important parallel: both were hard on their own Hindu society, not on Muslims.

Gandhi was uncompromising in demanding from Hindus that they remedy the 'evils of Hindu society', starting with untouchability. He never pointed a finger at the evils of Muslim society, on the ground that one should set one's own house in order, not that of others. This position is reasonable but in contradiction with Gandhi's vision of Hindu-Muslim unity and of himself as more than a mere Hindu leader. The Mahatma coerced Hindus (and the Congress, a party almost completely manned by Hindus) with his numerous fasts, but never used this pressure on Muslims.

Even Gandhi's admirer B.R. Nanda, in *Gandhi and His Critics* (p. 6), admits about Gandhi's 'most potent weapon', the coercive fast, which he never used against his opponents, but only against people who loved and admired him. Nanda reasserts his claim by stating that Gandhi did not use this weapon to force 'the Muslim League to give up its demand for Pakistan.' Indeed, Gandhi's own promise: 'India will only be vivisected over my dead body', would have meant in practice that he staked his life for a Muslim retreat on the Pakistan demand; Godse was not the first nor the last to remark that on this crucial occasion, Gandhi refused to use the one weapon at his disposal.

Like Gandhi, Godse refused to let Hindus lay the blame for their sufferings elsewhere but on themselves. In the case of Partition, he looked for Hindu culprits: the Congress leadership and Gandhi. Looking at the Partition story from a distance, it is obvious that Pakistan was not Gandhi's but Jinnah's creation. Not Gandhi was the 'father of Pakistan', as Godse alleged, but Jinnah (and behind Jinnah were Muslim ideologues like Rahmat Ali and Sir Muhammad Iqbal).

At worst, Gandhi could be called a passive accomplice, one who had not done his utmost to prevent Partition; the actual initiative to Partition obviously emanated from sections of the Muslim community.[35] But Godse took Muslim separatism for granted as a natural given for which no blame was to be apportioned, and only passed judgement on the Hindu way of dealing with this separatism. In this, Gandhi had failed, and so he was 'guilty of Partition'. This is truly similar to Gandhi's position that the victim is co-guilty of the aggression which he suffers, e.g. when the Mahatma wrote: 'Need the Hindu blame the Mussalman for his cowardice? Where there are cowards, there will always be bullies.'[36]

Therefore, Godse did not mete out his punishment to the Muslim leadership, but to the most revered and most responsible Hindu leader, Mahatma Gandhi. If Godse had killed Jinnah (which he and Apte had vaguely considered when in the spring of 1947, the Pakistan Constituent Assembly was meeting in Delhi), it would still have been murder, but perhaps it would have been regarded as more consistent with his own logic: avenging the Partition of the Motherland on the man who had achieved this Partition by ruthless means. Instead, he killed a leader who had opposed Partition, even if not to the utmost, and who still professed the belief that the Partition could and should be undone in the near future. Like the Mahatma, Godse was harsher on his own kin than on the opposing camp.

## GODSE THE SECULARIST

To locate Godse on the ideological map, it is important to know his position vis-à-vis secular principles. In the next section of his statement, Godse's object is to distance himself from any semblance of religious fanaticism:

'48. The background to the event of the 30th January, 1948, was wholly and exclusively political and I would like to explain it at some length. The fact that Gandhiji honoured the religious books of Hindus, Muslims, and others or that he used to recite during his prayers verses from the Gita, the Quran and the Bible never provoked any ill will in me towards him. To my mind it is not at all objectionable to study comparative religion. Indeed it is a merit.'[37]

Here, Godse wisely leaves undiscussed the difference between a sober comparative *study* of religions and the mindless claim of a fundamental *unity* of all religions, as propagated in embryonic form by Gandhi and in full-fledged form by Gandhi's disciples. We just saw that Godse once objected publicly to Gandhi's reading from the Quran in a Hindu temple, but he seems to have realized his mistake when chided for it by Savarkar. At any rate, he swore by the equality in law for the practitioners of all religions:

'49. The territory bounded by the North Western Frontier in the North and Cape Comorin in the South and the areas between Karachi and Assam, that is the whole of pre-partition India, has always been to me my motherland. In this vast area live people of various faiths and I hold that these creeds should have full and equal freedom for following their ideals and beliefs. In this area the Hindus are the most numerous. They have no place which they can call their own beyond or outside this country. Hindusthan is thus both motherland and the holy land for the Hindus from times immemorial. To the Hindus largely this country owes its fame and glory, its culture and art, knowledge, science and philosophy. Next to the Hindus, the Muslims are numerically predominant. They made systematic inroads into this country since the 10th century and gradually succeeded in establishing Muslim rule over the greater part of India.

'50. Before the advent of the British, both Hindus and Muslims as a result of centuries of experience had come to realise that the Muslims could not remain as masters in India; nor could they be driven away. Both had clearly understood that both had come to stay. Owing to the rise of the Mahrattas, the revolt of the Rajputs and the uprise of the Sikhs, the Muslim hold on the country had become very feeble and although some of them continued to aspire for supremacy in India, practical people could see clearly that such hopes were futile. On the other hand, the British had proved more powerful in battle and in intrigue than either the Hindus or Mussalmans, and by their adoption of improved methods of administration and the assurance of the security of the life and property without any discrimination both the Hindus and the Muslims accepted them as inevitable.

'50 (continued). Differences between the Hindus and the Muslims did exist even before the British came. Nevertheless it is a fact that the British made the most unscrupulous use of these differences and created more differences in order to maintain their power and authority. The Indian National Congress which was started with the object of winning power for the people in the governance of the country had from the beginning kept before it the ideal of complete nationalism which implies that all Indians should enjoy equal rights and complete equality on the basis of democracy. This ideal of removing the foreign rule and replacing it by the democratic power and authority of the people appealed to me most from the very start of my public career.'[38]

It is remarkable that Godse, who profiles himself as a secular nationalist, puts a decisive part of the blame for the Pakistan movement on the British. He makes no attempt to link the contemporary phenomenon of Islamic separatism with the fundamental doctrines of Islam. More ideologically developed Hindu thinkers hold that the British role in the development of Muslim separatism was auxiliary at most, that separatism is an intrinsic feature of Islam (at least when it is the weaker party, unable to grab the whole territory), and that there was a continuity and unity of purpose between Pakistan and earlier Islamic states on Indian soil. Pakistani ideologues too claim that Pakistan came into existence the day Muhammad-bin-Qasim stepped into Sindh in AD 712, and that modern Pakistan is the successor-state of the Moghul Empire. By contrast, militant secularists agree with Godse that British rule was decisive in poisoning previously friendly Hindu-Muslim relations.

The one difference between Godse and the so-called secularists in India is that Godse swore by genuinely secular and democratic principles, so that 'all Indians should enjoy equal rights and complete equality on the basis of democracy' and no special privileges on the basis of communal identity, such as weightage in parliamentary representation for the Muslims. Congressite and leftist secularists, by contrast, supported communal representation and weightage back then, and still support separate Personal Law systems for different communities defined by religion today. If words still have a meaning, Godse's vision of independent India's polity was more secular than that of the self-styled secularists.

## NOTES

1. Maga Brahmins are worshippers of Surya, the Sun God, who is iconographically depicted with boots, like a Shaka (Scythian) horseman. *Maga* is probably the same root as in the *Magians*, the Mazdean priesthood of Iran, which once included much of Central Asia.

2. In her dissertation on the Chitpavans (ESP/20, University of Bombay, Kalina Campus Library, 1928), Mrs Iravati Karve reports that 'as late as AD 1200, they were poor farmers leading a life of seclusion and poverty (...) We are told that they were ignorant and despised, and were usually employed as cooks and peons (...) At first, the Deshasthas would not dine with these intruders.' (pp. 1–2, quoted by Talageri: *Indian Nationalism*, p. 244). She also mentions an alternative story of the caste's creation, viz. that Parashurama simply taught 60 fisherman families the Brahminical rituals (p. 22), apparently reflecting their original lowly status in the eyes of the Deshasth Brahmins.

3. This process devolving power from a dynasty to its ministers has parallels elsewhere, e.g., in the eight century, the Frankish Merovingians were sidelined by their 'court mayor', Charles the Hammer (who defeated the Moors in Poitiers AD 732), whose Carolingian descendants included Charlemagne.

4. Vide Stanley A. Wolpert: *Tilak and Gokhale*, with a consideration of

their caste background in ch. 1.

5. Maureen L.P. Patterson: 'The shifting fortunes of Chitpavan Brahmins: focus on 1948', in D.W. Attwood et al., eds.: *City, Countryside and Society in Maharashtra*, p. 37. Her account is confirmed by members of the directly affected Telang family in Sangali and Haripur and the Sidhaye family of Jaysinghpur, as by eye-witness Ram Sidhaye, whom I interviewed in Atlanta, Georgia in 2010. He and his mother and siblings were sent away by his father and uncle, who suffered yet another form of government-supported harassment, viz. being jailed without charges.

6. Maureen L.P. Patterson: 'The shifting fortunes of Chitpavan Brahmins: focus on 1948', in D.W. Attwood et al., eds.: *City, Countryside and Society in Maharashtra*, p. 39.

7. ibid, p. 40.

8. Maureen L.P. Patterson: 'The shifting fortunes of Chitpavan Brahmins: focus on 1948', in D.W. Attwood et al., eds.: *City, Countryside and Society in Maharashtra*, pp. 43–47. In passing, we learn here (p. 45) that Bal Gangadhar Tilak, Congress leader until his death in 1920 and a Chitpavan Brahmin, had 'pre-empted the Maratha king Shivaji as a major symbol in the cause of nationalist, anti-British activity'; which in turn becomes more understandable when we hear that in 1818, Shivaji's successor in Kolhapur had been 'siding with the British in the final struggle with the Peshwa.'

9. Maureen L.P. Patterson: 'The shifting fortunes of Chitpavan Brahmins: focus on 1948', in D.W. Attwood et al., eds.: *City, Countryside and Society in Maharashtra*, pp. 50–51.

10. ibid, p. 37.

11. 'The double murder of Mahatma Gandhi', Scroll.in, accessed on 4 December 2017

12. A.G. Noorani: 'The RSS and Gandhi: A Necessary Backstory', *The Wire*, 24 July 2016, https://thewire.in/53045/the-rss-and-gandhi-2/

13. Nathuram Godse: *Why I Assassinated Gandhi*, p. 27.

14. By 'Maharashtra' is not meant the present-day province of that name, but the Marathi-speaking part of the Bombay Presidency, which did not include Nagpur, the city where the RSS was founded in 1925.

15. Nathuram Godse: *Why I Assassinated Gandhi*, p. 102.
16. Gopal Godse interviewed by Arvind Rajagopal: 'Resurrecting Godse. The *Hindutva* Continuum', *Frontline*, 28 January 1994.
17. Arvind Rajagopal: 'Resurrecting Godse. The *Hindutva* Continuum', *Frontline*, 28 January 1994.
18. Full text with translation is given in Nathuram Godse: *Why I Assassinated Gandhi*, p. 139.
19. Nathuram Godse: *Why I Assassinated Gandhi*, pp. 53–54 (para 70.d.i of his speech), discussed below.
20. Nathuram Godse: *Why I Assassinated Gandhi*, p. 27.
21. ibid, p. 29.
22. ibid, pp. 30–31.
23. ibid, pp. 32–33.
24. ibid, p. 33.
25. ibid, p. 34.
26. Manohar Malgonkar: *The Men Who Killed Gandhi*, p. 93.
27. I recall the phrase being used in a column by M.J. Akbar, but in his Nehru biography (*Nehru*, p. 178), Akbar tries another insinuating phrase, which is not even glib: he wrongly claims that Savarkar was HMS president 'until he retired in guilt after the assassination of Mahatma Gandhi in 1948.' Savarkar actually stepped down in 1943, and was not burdened with any guilt in 1948.
28. Collins and Lapierre: *Freedom at Midnight*, ch. 16.
29. Collins and Lapierre: *Cette nuit la liberté*, 1983, p. 553: 'Vieux fumeur d'opium, il était aussi homosexuel, mais peu de gens le savaient.' And p. 561: '... il n'avait eu, croit-on, qu'une seule expérience sexuelle avec pour initiateur son mentor politique, Vir Savarkar.'
30. Ashis Nandy: 'The Politics of the Assassination of Gandhi', *At the Edge of Psychology*, pp. 85–86. Typically, Nandy submerges Godse's clear-cut political motive in a psycho-soup of 'male prototype', 'heightened sensitivity to man-woman relationships', 'the assassin's ego ideal', etc.
31. Thus, the edition of *Freedom at Midnight* which I have used, by Tarang Paperbacks, 1988.
32. Joachim Betz: 'Indien: Geschichtliche Entwicklung', *Informationen zur politischen Bildung*, p. 9. Though some sub-chapters are devoted

to Hindu revivalism, the bibliography does not contain a single title by a Hindu revivalist.

33. Louis Fischer, *The Life of Mahatma Gandhi*, p. 406.

34. Winand Callewaert: 'Mahatma Gandhi, een hindoe?', *Inforiënt* (Leuven), November 1986, p. 1.

35. In this context, it is remarkable that some Pakistani and even Indian authors (notably H.M. Seervai's *Partition of India: Legend and Reality*), agree with Godse in laying a much larger part of the blame for Partition with the Congress leadership. However, that the Congress's tactical mistakes accelerated the swing in Muslim opinion towards the Pakistan idea, was a development entirely dependent on the presupposed existence of a Pakistan project, which was obviously a Muslim initiative for which Gandhi and Congress cannot be blamed.

36. M.K. Gandhi in *Young India*, 29 May 1924.

37. Nathuram Godse: *Why I Assassinated Gandhi*, p. 36.

38. ibid, pp. 36–7.

3

# Critique of Gandhi's Policies

## GENESIS OF MUSLIM SEPARATISM

Nathuram Godse comes to the point when he introduces his analysis of Gandhiji's politics:

'51. In my writings and speeches, I have always advocated that the religious and communal consideration should be entirely eschewed in the public affairs of the country, at elections, inside and outside the legislatures and in the making and unmaking of Cabinets. I have throughout stood for a secular State with joint electorates and to my mind this is the only sensible thing to do. (...)'[1]

It should be clear by now that the conflict between Gandhi and Godse was not one between secularism and communalism (i.e., a system of community-based rights, of allotting privileges to or imposing disabilities on citizens on the basis of their communal identity, especially their religious community membership), except if we identify Godse with secularism and Gandhi with communalism. Both were religious men, but Godse wanted a secular polity while Gandhi condoned political arrangements along communal lines. It was also in Gandhi's more than in Godse's case that religion continuously spilled over into his political rhetoric.

Yet, the Congress had started with simple and straightforward democratic aims before being tricked into communal compromise by the Muslim League:

'51 (continued). Under the influence of the Congress, this ideal was steadily making headway amongst the Hindus. But the Muslims as a community first stood aloof and later on under the corroding influence of the Divide and Rule Policy of foreign masters were encouraged to cherish the ambition of dominating the Hindus. The first indication of this outlook was the demand for separate electorates instigated by the then Viceroy Lord Minto in 1906. The British Government accepted this demand under the excuse of minority protection. While the Congress party offered a verbal opposition, it progressively supported separatism by ultimately adopting the notorious formula of "neither accepting nor rejecting" in 1934.'

'52. Thus had originated and intensified the demand for the disintegration of this country. What was the thin end of the wedge in the beginning became Pakistan in the end. The mistake however was begun with the laudable object of bringing out a united front amongst all classes in India in order to drive out the foreigner and it was hoped that separatism would eventually disappear.'[2]

Here, Godse shows quite a measure of understanding and respect for Gandhi's initial promise of achieving Hindu-Muslim unity in the interest of national freedom. It is certainly not an unfair reading of Gandhi's mind to state that he offered 'hope that separatism would eventually disappear.' This separatism had become an official part of India's political landscape with the creation of the Muslim League in 1906 as a party advocating loyalty to the British Empire, along with special privileges and reservations for the Muslim community. But the Mahatma consistently mishandled the issue and helped solidify Muslim communal politics. By 1934, when the communal division of political power and government jobs was being consolidated in law, his Congress movement was reduced to looking the other way, or what Gandhi called 'neither accepting nor rejecting'.

The phrase of 'neither accepting nor rejecting' summed up Gandhiji's position vis-à-vis the 'Communal Award', the plan to thoroughly communalize the legislatures under the Government of India Act 1935. The secular position would have been to oppose the plan outright and to insist on non-communal assemblies elected by a single electorate comprising all voting citizens, regardless of religion, who were free to vote for any candidate, regardless of the latter's religion. But to Godse's disappointment, Gandhiji took an unclear position which amounted to an unspoken acceptance of the communalization of the democratic process, a stepping-stone on the way to Partition. In particular, separate electorates meant that Muslim candidates needed to cater only to Muslim opinion, which encouraged them to take ever more sectarian positions. Regardless of any judgement of the political choices involved, Gandhi's refusal to take sides on such a crucial issue showed a painful lack of leadership and strategic insight: fence-sitting is rarely rewarded in politics. Moreover, far from being neutral, it effectively amounted to acquiescing in the definitive communalization of the polity.

Note once more how the secularist Godse repeats the Congressite sop story that Muslim separatism had been instigated by the British, and that the Muslims had been enticed into it by an outside agency. In reality, in starting the communalization of the polity, Lord Minto had merely approved a proposal by Agha Khan, the wealthy leader of the Ismaili Shiite Muslims. Later on, the colonial rulers gave in to the demands of Muslim League leader Mohammed Ali Jinnah, who was by no means their stooge. The British merely tried to harness the pre-existing and strong-willed stallion of Muslim separatism to their project of perpetual control over India.

## ENCOURAGEMENT OF MUSLIM SEPARATISM

Nathuram Godse keeps on emphasizing the democratic and reasonable character of his own political position:

'53. In spite of my advocacy of joint electorates, in principle I reconciled myself with the temporary introduction of separate electorates since the Muslims were keen on them. I however insisted that representation should be granted in strict proportion to the number of every community and no more. I have uniformly maintained this stand.'[3]

Though notorious as the Hindu fanatic par excellence, Godse was, in fact, willing to consider compromises if these were required by the goal of an independent and united India. Extremism and communal polarization, according to Godse, were introduced into Indian politics by the Muslim League, and nourished by the British and by the Congress:

'54. Under the inspiration of our British masters on the one hand and the encouragement by the Congress under Gandhiji's leadership on the other, the Muslim League went on increasing its demands on Communal basis. The Muslim community continuously backed the Muslim League; each successive election proved that the Muslim League was able to bank on the fanaticism and ignorance of the Muslim masses and the League was thus encouraged in its policy of separatism on an ever increasing scale year after year.'[4]

It is exaggerated to say that 'the Muslim community continuously backed the Muslim League.' First of all, there were not that many elections results of which could be compared. Secondly, the crucial elections of 1937, which had to give substance to the project of democratic provincial self-government under the new Government of India Act (1935), saw a humiliating defeat of the Muslim League at the hands of the Muslim electorate: only 9 per cent of the Muslim voters favoured the League, and it secured less than half of the reserved (Muslim) seats in its UP heartland, a third in

Bengal, and a negligible portion in the other provinces, including Muslim-majority Sindh.[5] It is only in the elections held at the turn of 1946 that the Muslim vote swung dramatically towards the Muslim League, which cornered 86.6 per cent, i.e., a resounding mandate for the creation of Pakistan.[6]

On the other hand, no credible political force effectively opposing Jinnah emerged from the 91 per cent of the Muslim electorate who had refused to support the League in 1937. While the HMS was sidelined as a political force by the Congress, no comparable anti-League operation was initiated by any section of the Muslim elite. Muslim-led multi-religious parties (e.g., Sikandar Hayat Khan's Unionists in Punjab, Fazlul Haq's Krishak Praja Party in Bengal) did not at all oppose the privileges which the Muslim League had demanded and achieved for the Muslims. In *Struggle for Freedom* R.C. Majumdar mentions that after a moment of Muslim disunity at the Round Table Conference of 1930–32, Muslims, of all shades of opinion, insisted that their claims must be met.

In his book, Majumdar further expounded that while opposing the League, they endorsed, at least passively, some of the League's communal policies, and it was their active support which 'put new life into the League' after its 1937 defeat. Similarly, the conservative Ulema opposed the Pakistan project (because they aimed at controlling the whole rather than a part of India) but supported most other communal demands of the League, thus strengthening further the communal outlook which underlay the Pakistan demand. Welcomed by the Congress as 'nationalist Muslims', they helped Gandhi and Nehru in suppressing all articulate Hindu voices in the Congress. This way, Muslim support for the League policies was considerably larger than the League's own vote percentage.

But the most important point to note about this part of Godse's statement is that Godse, the proverbial Hindu 'communalist', is accusing Gandhiji of nothing but introducing the 'communal' element into politics. This was to remain a constant in Hindutva political parlance, accusing the self-styled secularists in India of being 'communal' all while the self-styled secularists made the very same allegation against the Hindutva activists.

Historically, the characterization of the Hindutva forces as 'communal' is as absurd as calling the anti-Communists 'Communists', for 'communalism' is quite literally the enemy which the HMS was created to combat. The Hindutva spokesmen called their British and Muslim League enemies 'communal' and advocated unadulterated 'non-communal' democracy, while these enemies themselves called their own favoured policies 'communal': communal representation, communal weightage, Communal Award. Today, with shrill sloganeering pushing proper terminology out of common usage, the term 'communal' is inimically applied to people who never apply the term to themselves; but in those days, the HMS was entirely in agreement with its opponents' self-perception when it called them 'communal'.

The division of the electorate and the distribution of jobs on a 'communal' basis were explicit demands of the Muslim League, were explicitly proposed and imposed by the British authorities, were explicitly accepted by the Indian National Congress, and were explicitly rejected by the HMS. From its foundation till at least 1947, the distinctive identity of the HMS in Indian politics consisted in its pro-democracy and anti-communal stand.

## GANDHI'S NON-VIOLENCE

What follows is a selection from the central part of Godse's statement: the political justification of the murder. It is a scathing critique of the Mahatma's policies vis-à-vis the Muslim leadership. The first point concerns the doctrine of absolute non-violence:

'56. Since the year 1920, that is to say after the demise of Lokmanya Tilak, Gandhiji's influence in the Congress first increased and then became supreme. His activities for public awakening were phenomenal in their intensity and were reinforced by the slogan of truth and non-violence which he ostentatiously paraded before the country. No sensible or enlightened person could object to these slogans; in fact there is nothing new or original in them. They are implicit in every constitutional public movement. To imagine that the bulk of mankind is or can ever become capable of scrupulous adherence to these lofty principles in its normal life from day to day is a mere dream. In fact honour, duty and love of one's own kith and kin and country might often compel us to disregard non-violence. I could never conceive that an armed resistance to the aggressor is unjust. I will consider it a religious and moral duty to resist and if possible to overpower such an enemy by the use of force. (...)'[7]

'59. [Upon returning to India from South Africa,] Gandhiji began his work by starting an Ashram in Ahmedabad on the banks of the Sabarmati River, and made truth and non-violence his slogans. He had often acted contrary to his professed principles and if it was for appeasing the Muslims, he hardly had any scruple in doing so. truth and non-violence are excellent as an ideal and admirable as guides in action. They are, however, to be practised in actual day-to-day life and not in the air. I am showing later on that Gandhiji himself was guilty of glaring breaches of his much-vaunted ideals.'[8]

These are three different criticisms. The first is that absolute non-violence is a lofty ideal fit for saints but unfit for the average human being—still an endorsement of non-violence as a moral principle. The second is that non-violence is sometimes morally wrong, viz. when considerations of self-defence and honour force us to face a determined enemy in battle, i.e., when they force the violent option upon us as the only remaining way to ensure survival and justice. The third is that Gandhi himself broke his own principle of non-violence on a number of occasions, e.g., when he took non-combatant service in the British war effort against the Boers and the Zulus, or when he recruited Indian young men for the

British army in World War I in the vain hope of earning gratitude and political concessions.

A fourth criticism runs through this statement, in the sarcastic conclusions of different episodes, but is not explicitated—the paradox that non-violence applied in a blind and injudicious manner leads to violence in extra large amounts.[9] In the India of the 1930s and 40s, the HMS position was essentially that of Cicero when he said: '*Si vis pacem, para bellum*', 'If you want peace, be prepared for war.' In a climate of frequent and increasing Muslim aggression, Savarkar and his followers thought that the organization of Hindu self-defence units would be the best guarantee of communal peace; or what American foreign-policy makers in the Cold War used to call 'peace through strength'.

On the international scene, this principle was being illustrated by the Munich Agreement: concluding a peace treaty with Hitler was not wrong per se, but it could only have worked if France and Britain had backed up their signatures with an increased military force capable of keeping Hitler to his word. Instead, the democratic powers, in their aversion to the militaristic hubris of the dictators, had been cutting down on defence spending. This way, an anti-militaristic policy created a strategic vacuum which made Hitler's Blitzkrieg possible. The lesson for India was obvious—weakness invites aggression and leads to more violence than strength and armed preparedness would have done.

## HINDUTVA AND GANDHIAN NON-COWARDICE

In his statement, Nathuram Godse failed to mention that on a number of occasions, Gandhi did concede the common sense view that a preparedness to fight the aggressor generally prevents violence; and that even if the violence cannot be avoided, it is at least better to defend yourself than to surrender to aggression. Whereas Gandhi had advocated a strictly non-violent strategy in most cases, including an unarmed defence against the impending Japanese invasion in 1942, the Hindu parties have always advocated a strong defence capability. Yet, even here the Hindutva movement is more Gandhian (or at least capable of selecting some Gandhi lines in support) than one would expect.

The famous quotation of Mahatma Gandhi on Hindu cowards and Muslim bullies deserves to be read in full:

'There is no doubt in my mind that in the majority of quarrels the Hindus come out second best. But my own experience confirms the opinion that the Mussalman as a rule is a bully, and the Hindu as a rule is a coward. I have noticed this in railway trains, on public roads, and in the quarrels which I had the privilege of settling. Need the Hindu blame the Mussalman for his cowardice? Where there are cowards, there will always be bullies.

'They say that in Saharanpur the Mussalmans looted houses, broke open safes and, in one case, a Hindu woman's modesty was outraged. Whose fault was this? Mussalmans can offer no defence for the execrable conduct, it is true. But I, as a Hindu, am more ashamed of Hindu cowardice than I am angry at the Mussalman bullying. Why did not the owners of the houses looted die in the attempt to defend their possessions? Where were the relatives of the outraged sister at the time of the outrage? Have they no account to render of themselves? My non-violence does not admit of running away from danger and leaving dear ones unprotected. Between violence and cowardly flight, I can only prefer violence to cowardice.'[10]

To be sure, this is still Gandhi, which means that it is an unbalanced and extreme view. Gandhi declares that the owners of the looted houses ought to have chosen to 'die in the attempt to defend their possessions.' But why should the lawful owner die, and in punishment of what crime? If anyone has to die at all, would it not be fairer, more just, to let the aggressor die rather than his victim? Justice does not figure in Gandhi's calculus of non-violence.

People should innocently die by way of moral gesture rather than inflict a just punishment on the aggressor: here we see a misplaced kind of personal asceticism eclipsing any socially responsible concern for public justice.

Or does Gandhi merely mean that people should expose themselves to the risk of dying by fighting the aggressor rather than flee? In any case, Gandhi's statement can be interpreted both ways. In his earlier writings, he says again and again that though non-violent resistance was the better and braver way, aggression should be resisted by violence if one is not capable of following the superior way. For him, running away from battle (palâyanam) was the way of the coward, as Krishna tells Arjuna in the very first chapter of the Bhagavad Gita. While Gandhi did make extreme statements about the virtue of getting killed, here he talks common sense: 'I prefer violence to cowardice.' Gandhi is ashamed that Hindus failed to put up an effective self-defence, and wants them to do better next time.

Here, for once, Gandhi seems to link up with a whole tradition of mature thinkers who have taken a proportionalist view of the acceptability of violence: in cases where force can reasonably be expected to make the difference (not when the situation is hopeless), it is lawful to use force to ward off aggression. In its own view of itself, the RSS (and likewise other Hindu organizations from Godse's Hindu Raksha Dal to the Shiv Sena) has precisely taken up the challenge formulated here by Gandhi: 'Need the Hindu blame the Mussalman for his own cowardice?' Gandhi calls on Hindus not to be cowards in the face of Muslim bullies. In response, the RSS claims it builds martial qualities and equips its workers with the strength to face bullies. So, in a way, there is nothing un-Gandhian about RSS martial arts practice.[11]

During Partition, some Sangh workers were active in taking revenge on Muslims inside India (as eyewitnesses have told me), doing some bullying of their own. For instance, Vasant Mungre, president of Shanti Darshan Belgo-Indian Association, lived in Gwalior in 1947 when RSS people came and demanded (in vain) that his father deliver to them the Muslim family which he had hidden in his house; he himself ceased attending RSS shakhas after this incident. That similar martial RSS feats took place in the far more dangerous circumstances of the territory allotted to Pakistan, has been disputed by the movement's habitual critics.[12] However, recently the RSS has collected and published a series of testimonies of RSS sacrifice and bravery, of how they saved Hindus in Pakistan and escorted them to the safety of remainder-India.[13]

Even in a stern and hostile letter to RSS leader M.S. Golwalkar, Home Minister Vallabhbhai Patel had acknowledged: 'In the areas where there was the need for help and organisation, the young men of the RSS protected women and children and strove much for their sake.'[14] This is a rather mild way of describing the pathetic dependence of the unprepared Congress people in the Pakistani territories on whatever help the RSS and local ad hoc Hindu militias could offer to cover their escape to the border. In the face of Islamic terror, the Gandhian method was abandoned forthwith by its nominal adherents, who entrusted their lives to the more usual methods of fight and flight.

## GANDHI VERSUS KRISHNA

Godse contrasts Gandhiji's non-violence with the forceful methods used by historic Hindu heroes in defence of their family honour or their motherland. This also implies a defence of the Freedom Fighters who had opted for violence, the so-called revolutionary terrorists (including the young Savarkar and the young Hedgewar), against Gandhi's claims of the moral superiority of non-violence. At the time of the hanging of Bhagat Singh for a bomb attack in 1931, and on other occasions, Gandhi had condemned them as 'misguided patriots'. He had made a similar statement about the historic military leaders Rana Pratap, Shivaji and Guru Govind Singh.

But the strongest argument to embarrass the followers of Gandhi is provided by the two religious heroes whose names were frequently invoked by Gandhiji himself, Rama and Krishna:

'56 (continued). Shri Ramchandra killed Ravan in a tumultuous fight and relieved Sita. Shri Krishna killed Kansa to end his wickedness. In the Mahabharat, Arjun had to fight and slay quite a number of his friends and relations including the revered Bhishma, because the latter was on the side of the aggressor. It is my firm belief that dubbing Rama, Krishna and Arjuna as guilty of violence is to betray a total ignorance of the springs of human action. It was the heroic fight put up by the Chhatrapati Shivaji Maharaj that first checked and eventually destroyed Muslim tyranny in India. It was absolutely correct tactics for Shivaji to kill Afzal Khan as the latter would otherwise have surely killed him. In condemning Shivaji, Rana Pratap and Guru Govind as misguided patriots, Gandhiji has merely exposed his self-conceit.

'57. Each of the heroes in his time resisted aggression on our country, protected the people against the atrocities and outrages by alien fanatics and won back the motherland from the invader. On the other hand, during more than thirty years of the undisputed leadership of the Mahatma, there were more desecrations of temples, more forcible and fraudulent conversions, more outrages on women and finally the loss of one third of the country. It is therefore astounding that his followers cannot see what is clear even to the blind, viz. that the Mahatma was a mere pygmy before Shivaji, Rana Pratap and Guru Govind. His condemnation of these illustrious heroes was to say the least, most presumptuous.

'58. The clique which has got into power with the patronage of British imperialism by a cowardly surrender to the Partition of India at the point of Muslim violence is now trying to exploit Gandhiji's death in hundred hectic ways for its own selfish aims.

But history will give to them their proper place in the niche of fame. Gandhiji was, paradoxical as it may appear, a violent pacifist who brought untold calamities on the country in the name of truth and non-violence, while Rana Pratap, Shivaji and the Guru will remain enshrined in the hearts of their countrymen for ever and for the freedom they brought to them.'[15]

It is the height of absurdity that all his life, Gandhi saw the Bhagavad Gita as a manual of non-violence, when the book actually opens with Krishna's exhortation to Arjuna to do battle, refuting all the arguments offered by Arjuna to justify desertion from the battlefield. Interpreted metaphorically, this could still be construed as Gandhian, in the sense that Gandhi favoured involvement in political struggles rather than retirement into a quiet private life. But the Gita is not altogether metaphorical. It speaks quite explicitly about killing and getting killed, and convinces Arjuna not to mind some killing and dying with the plea, among others, that death is not so important, given that the indwelling immortal soul simply moves on from a discarded body to a newly conceived one.[16] The Gita teaches that for certain people and in certain circumstances, killing is the right thing to do.

## GANDHI VERSUS THE HMS

Godse contrasts the HMS policy, which seized the opportunity of World War II to have Hindu young men trained in the art of warfare, favourably with Gandhiji's non-violence:

'66. (...) The Muslims did not obstruct the war [World War II] efforts and the Congress sometimes remained neutral and sometimes opposed. On the other hand, the Hindu Sabha realised that this was an opportunity for our young men to have a military training, which is absolutely essential for our nation, and from which we were rather kept far away intentionally by the British. But due to this war, the doors of Army, Navy and Airforce were opened to us, and Mahasabha urged our countrymen to militarise Hindus. The result was that nearly 1/2 millions of Hindus learnt the art of war and mastered the mechanised aspect of modern warfare. The Congress Governments are enjoying the fruits of the Mahasabha's foresight because the troops they are using in Kashmir and had employed in Hyderabad would not have been there ready-made but for the effort of men with such outlook. (...)'[17]

Reference is to the military operations preventing the secession of Hyderabad and the conquest of most of Kashmir by Pakistani irregulars in 1948. India could succeed in these operations because it had a modern army, as the HMS had always wanted (along with most parties in most countries), in spite of the Mahatma's musings about an India without an army. There is nothing outlandish or extremist about the argument that absolute non-violence is unrealistic and, when it leads to the defencelessness of the innocent, even immoral.

In the case of Gandhi, this defect was compounded by his deliberate or implicit deviations from his own policy, e.g. when he campaigned for Indian recruitment into the British Army during World War I, or when he failed to exert pressure on Indian industrialists during World War II to refrain from selling to the British war machine. One of Gandhi's foremost financial sponsors apparently made a fortune out of the war effort; a leading Gandhian in Calcutta supplied imported tinned beef to the Allied forces in Assam. Gandhi was sometimes illogical and inconsistent even in the exercise of the principle which he propagated most.

Consider the positions of Savarkar and Gandhi regarding participation in World War II. While some HMS leaders, like N.C. Chatterjee, passionately supported the Allied cause for ideological reasons, viz. as a struggle of democracy against totalitarianism, Savarkar judged the situation purely in terms of India's interests, without much heartfelt preference for one camp or the other. The same is true of Gandhi, who rejected the image of the war as a struggle between good and evil.

Gandhi 'wanted to make it clear that a victory for the Axis would have been far worse' because it had espoused violence as a principle, while the Allies 'at least paid lip-service to peace and freedom, and truth and non-violence'; but he also pointed out that 'their action belied their profession', so that their victory was one of 'superior arms and superior man-power' rather than 'a victory of truth over falsehood.'[18] To President Roosevelt's claim that the Allies were fighting for freedom and the Axis for enslavement of the nations, Gandhi, in his speech at Bardoli on 8 January 1942, which was printed in *Harijanbandhu* the same day and later in *Collected Works* (vol. 79, p. 205), commented: 'But to me both the parties seem to be tarred with the same brush.'

Against those who glorify the Allies' war against the Axis as a holy and necessary war, Gandhi maintained his quintessentially pacifistic position that war itself was a crime: 'War criminals are not confined to the Axis powers alone. Roosevelt and Churchill are no less war criminals than Hitler and Mussolini.'[19] The bombings of Dresden, Hiroshima and Nagasaki confirmed this assessment. He explicitly preferred the uncomfortable position of siding with neither camp: 'Holding the view I do, it is superfluous for me now to answer your argument that "this war has split the world into two camps." Between Scylla and Charybdis, if I sail in either direction, I suffer shipwreck. Therefore I have to be in the midst of the storm.'[20]

That may be an honourable position, and perhaps it was not very different from Savarkar's, but the translation of this vision into practice was very different between these two Hindu leaders. Savarkar chose to 'militarize the Hindus', to seize the opportunity of giving military experience to Hindu young men. Having suffered years of torture in a British penal colony, Savarkar probably did not share Gandhi's sentimental anguish at the thought of London being bombed by the Luftwaffe, and as we shall see, Godse made no secret of his admiration for Subhas Chandra Bose, the Congress leftist who fought on the Japanese side. However, a simple look at strategic equations and basic geography made it clear to Savarkar that the only way to implement his plan was by siding with the British. He did not hesitate a minute and never wavered in his decision: his men would fight on the British side against Germany and Japan.

The Congress and Gandhi, by contrast, took all possible positions regarding participation in the war, in succession or even simultaneously. Congress nationalists refused cooperation with the British because the Viceroy hadn't had the courtesy to ask them for it, instead committing India to the war effort all on his own. Communist-influenced Congress leftists followed the Soviet line, viz., until June 1941, that this was an imperialist war between two imperialist powers, so that freedom-loving nations should abstain from taking sides; after the German invasion of the Soviet Union, they reversed their stand and joined the war effort.

In 1942, when Japan seemed all set to conquer India, Gandhi led a swing to the 'Quit India' position. Japan would have no interest in invading India if India ceased to be a British colony and a base for British and American operations; so it was in India's interest if the British were thrown out fast. But while pro-Congress youngsters were sabotaging the British-Indian infrastructure, pro-Congress industrialists were working to capacity for the British war production. Then, by 1944, when imprisonment had beaten the Congress leaders into submission (and irrelevance), they agreed to cooperate with the British for victory in the war, a victory which was by then already certain.

Gandhi, the anglicized lawyer, was sentimentally inclined to support Britain, but was held back by his pacifism. Under his impact, the Congress machinery was not employed to recruit young men for the British-Indian army, not even after the organization had agreed to support the Allied war effort. In World War I, he had recruited Indian young men for the pointless and wasteful battles in Flanders' fields, truly an imperialist war with no moral stake; but now his own followers were deriding Savarkar as a 'recruiting officer', though most observers would say that World War II was not a senseless war and that there was a considerable moral stake involved.

One factor in Gandhi's changed position may be that his services to the British war effort in World War I had not paid off politically, that India had not been rewarded for it with more political autonomy. But the overriding factor seems to be simply his pacifism: how could he be against violence and against war if he was going to condone the biggest war with the biggest bloodshed in history? If a war with more than fifty million mortal victims was defensible, how could any smaller conflict be condemned as wrong?

At this point, Gandhi subordinated his political concern for India to his moral concern for non-violence. Savarkar did the opposite—in general he believed in an 'economy of violence', in which a measured use of violence may sometimes avert a much bigger or more protracted conflagration; and in the particular world situation of 1939–45 he saw that a non-violent scenario was simply not on offer, so he decided to make the best of the war for India.

## GANDHI AND WORLD WAR II

While we are on the subject of World War II, we may insert a little intermezzo here about Gandhi's most remarkable interventions in that crisis. Regarding the persecution of the Jews in Germany, Gandhi showed his extremely pacifistic face, the face of militant meekness, of 'when slapped, turn the other cheek'. Hindutva publications regularly criticize this aspect of Gandhism, e.g., 'the fatuosity, naïveté and callousness of the Mahatma's advice to the Jews in Germany in 1938, that they should offer mass civil disobedience to the Nazis (...) even after the dimensions of that horror were revealed, he continued to insist that if the Jews had followed his advice, they would have won a moral victory, even though they would have died the same.'[21]

Telling people to score a moral victory at the price of their lives, is not the advice which many would receive gladly. Gandhi 'discredited his own position' by saying in 1946 that 'the Jews should have offered themselves to the butcher's knife (...) It would have aroused them and the people of Germany (...) As it is they succumbed anyway in their millions.'[22] It is true that refraining from Gandhian posturing had not saved the Jews, but surely other ways of saving them could have been explored. In this connection, we may recall that as a Muslim sympathizer, Gandhi steadfastly opposed the Zionist project in Palestine, which, to many Jews, was the logical road to salvation.[23]

Of course, we don't know what the effect would have been if the Jews in the Reich had offered resistance along satyagraha ('holding fast to truth', non-violent resistance) lines. Would it have melted the iron hearts of the SS men? A few prominent Jews had written to Gandhi to refute his assumption of a similarity between the position of Indians in South Africa (where non-violent action for civil rights scored its greatest success) and that of Jews in Germany. Unsurprisingly, they could not bring Gandhi to admit that his position had been less than 100 per cent correct.[24]

At this point, a distinction must be made between Gandhiji's belief that World War II had to be avoided even at an extremely high price, and his specific advice to Jews to offer themselves as meek sacrifices. The former position is not as outlandish as the latter, indeed it is necessarily implied in any genuine pacifism. Gandhi would not have been Gandhi if he had not believed in a non-violent way out of the European security crisis of the late 1930s. He would not have been true to his belief in 'change of heart' if he had not written his much-ridiculed letter to Adolf Hitler admonishing him to explore non-violent ways of achieving Germany's legitimate aims.[25]

Without recourse to extremist Gandhian gimmicks, we should make at least the mental exercise of exploring the possibilities for maintaining peace which diplomats had in the 1930s. If a hawk like Richard Nixon could make peace with a practised mass-murderer like Mao Zedong, why not Churchill with Hitler *before* the latter turned mass-murderer? Among other little-discussed possibilities, we should face the likelihood that the mass killing of the Jews could have been avoided by a negotiated safe-conduit if Britain and Germany had remained on speaking terms. The now-common argument that the Allies had to fight and win the war in order to save the Jews (on the entirely false assumption that saving the Jews had been one of their war aims) is simply not valid, for the war *was* fought and won, yet far too many of the Jews were not saved.

Worse, it was only under pressure of war circumstances that the Nazi leadership resolved to kill the Jews. Until 1941, it had been willing to 'solve the Jewish problem' by banishing them from the German Reich, whether to Madagascar or some other distant country. So, in spite of what some people may tell you today, there was nothing morally wrong in exploring ways to avoid war with Hitler, or to contain rather than escalate that war once it had broken out.

To be sure, in 1939 nobody could foretell what exactly the war would bring. Until 1941, it was even quite likely that Germany would retain control of the European mainland, and in that sense end the war in victory. It was not known who would enter the war, what weapons would be developed and by whom, nor what new horizons in inhumanity would be opened up. However, especially for the generation which had lived through World War I, it was entirely certain that the war would bring untold suffering and that its outcome could spring a few unpleasant surprises. Not to speak of what defeat might bring, even victory could bear bitter fruits.

Even the hawk Winston Churchill had been sobered by the 'victorious' outcome of the Great War. American isolationists still like to quote his analysis of the unforeseen fatal consequences of the American entry into World War I (entry which broke the stalemate and pushed Germany on the defensive): 'If you hadn't entered the war, the Allies would have made peace with Germany in the Spring of 1917. Had we made peace then there would have been no collapse in Russia followed by Communism, no breakdown in Italy followed by Fascism, and Germany would not have signed the Versailles Treaty, which has enthroned Nazism in Germany (...) and if England had made peace early in 1917, it would have saved over one million British, French, American and other lives.'[26]

A different outcome of World War I, which could have resulted from a number of factors including a different American view of the war, would have eliminated the proximate causes of the rise of Nazism, among other evils. No wonder that Gandhi, in his press statement published in Bombay Chronicle (21 December 1941) and reproduced in *Collected Works* (vol. 75, p. 180), took a dim view of USA's entry into World War II: 'I cannot welcome this entry of America. American tradition singles her out as an arbitrator and mediator between the warring nations. (...) It is tragic to contemplate that with America as party to the war there is no great Power left which can mediate and bring peace, for which I have no doubt the peoples of all lands are thirsting.' And again, in his interview in *Harijan* on 25 May 1942, which was reproduced in *Collected Works* (vol. 76, p. 115), he calls it unfortunate that 'America, instead of working, as she should have worked, for world peace, identified herself with war.'

This may not be the prevalent view today, but in the circumstances, it must have seemed reasonable. By contrast, Gandhi's advice to individual Jews, telling them to walk meekly into the slaughterhouse, is a different story. It was the same advice he gave to Hindus trapped in what was to become Pakistan, as we shall see.[27] If Gandhians want to keep on writing about their hero, a useful project would be to thoroughly analyze their hero's preoccupation with death, especially, as Godse would have remarked, with other people's death. The carelessness with which he counselled self-sacrifice deserves a deeper diagnosis.

## WHY HINDU-MUSLIM UNITY HAD TO FAIL

We should now return to the decades preceding World War II to evaluate Gandhi's policies in those slightly less dramatic times. Godse explains the circumstantial reason for Gandhi's failure in bringing about Hindu-Muslim unity in India:

'61. When Gandhiji finally returned to India at the end of 1914, he brought with him a very high reputation for courageous leadership of Indians in South Africa. (...) He was honoured and obeyed by Hindus, Muslims and Parsis alike and was universally acclaimed as the leader of all Indians in South Africa. His simplicity of life, his unselfish devotion to the cause which he had made his own, his self-sacrifice and earnestness in fighting against the racial arrogance of the Afrikaners had raised the prestige of Indians. In India, he had endeared himself to all.

'62. When he returned here to serve his countrymen in their struggle for freedom, he had legitimately hoped that as in Africa he would command the unchallenged confidence and respect of all communities. But in this hope he soon found himself disappointed. (...) In South Africa, Indians had claimed nothing but elementary rights of citizenship which were denied to them. (...) Hindus, Muslims and Parsis therefore stood united like one man against the common enemy. (...) The Indian problem at home was quite different. We were fighting for home rule, self-Government and even for independence. We were intent on overthrowing an Imperial Power, which was determined to continue its sway over us by all possible means, including the policy of 'Divide and Rule' which had intensified the cleavage between Hindus and Muslims. (...)'[28]

The stakes in South Africa were much lower than in India,

where Indians intended to rule the country, not merely to obtain some civil rights. The Indian minority in South Africa also stood together against a ruling white group larger than their own, and a black majority which, though by no means oppressing the Indians, was foreign to them and socially (if not politically) in an altogether different position. In India, no such conditions of clinging together against overwhelmingly stronger outsiders prevailed, so that the Indians had room for internal polarization along communal lines.

Also, in India, the Muslim leadership had a historic memory of empire, and felt entitled to its restoration. Muslim numbers in India were also larger than ever before, both in relative and in absolute terms, so there was no reason why Islam should fail to regain its lost position of dominance. The only dispute within the Muslim elite was whether they should aim for a gradual reconquest of the whole of India, or to settle for a partition and be secure in the control of a large part of the country. No Muslim leader is known to have explicitly accepted the prospect of a purely democratic polity in a united India without any special privileges for the Muslims.

## GANDHI'S ROLE IN THE FAILURE

Gandhiji became the unquestioned Congress leader with the demise of B.G. Tilak in August 1920. From the outset, he made Hindu-Muslim unity the central plank in his political platform, for the following reason:

'64. He saw that the foreign rulers by the policy of 'Divide and Rule' were corrupting the patriotism of the Muslims and that there was little chance of his leading a united host to the battle for Freedom unless he was able to cement fellow-feeling and common devotion to the Motherland. He, therefore, made Hindu-Muslim unity the foundation of his politics. As a counterblast to the British tactics, he started making the friendliest approaches to the Muslim community and reinforced them by making generous and extravagant promises to the Muslims. This, of course, was not wrong in itself so long as it was done consistently with India's struggle for democratic national freedom; but Gandhiji completely forgot this, the most essential aspect of his campaign for unity, with what results we all know by now.'[29]

The Congress, along with the constitutionalist Moderates, regularly extracted from the British some concessions amounting to mildly increased autonomy; that much of success has to be granted to Gandhi and his movement. But every bit of newly acquired power for the Indians was shared at once with Congress's Muslim communalist rivals. According to Hindu critics, the latter did not fight for the Indian cause, but shared (even disproportionately, partly thanks to British help in return for their loyalty) in the spoils whenever the Congress achieved anything for India. With every gain for India, Muslim communalism also gained. Before the determined British and Muslim League intrigues, wholly motivated by their respective self-interests, Gandhi as the new Congress leader proved to be a poor tactician, stumbling from compromise to defeat.

## GANDHI AND THE KHILAFAT

Gandhi's trail of fruitless concessions to Muslim demands started with the Khilafat Movement, the movement in support of the preservation of the Ottoman Caliphate and its restoration to sovereignty over the sacred places of Islam. This movement, opposed by Muslim modernists like Jinnah, was led by the brothers Muhammed and Shaukat Ali, to whom Gandhi offered the Congress as a platform and organizational instrument:

'65. Our British rulers were able, out of Indian resources, continuously to make concessions to Muslims and to keep the various communities divided. By 1919, Gandhiji had become desperate in his endeavours to get the Muslims to trust him and went from one absurd promise to another. He promised 'a blank cheque' to the Muslims. He backed the Khilafat Movement in this country and was able to enlist the full support of the National Congress in that policy. (...) the Ali Brothers became de facto Muslim leaders; Gandhiji welcomed this as the coming promise of leadership of the Muslims. He made most of the Ali Brothers, raised them to the skies by flattery and unending concessions; but what he wanted never happened.'

Indeed, the Khilafat Movement was a tragi-comical failure. Its demands lost their object when Turkish republicans under Mustafa Kemal Ataturk deposed the Caliph and abolished the very institution of the Caliphate (1923–24), in spite of the prestige which it used to confer on Turkey in the eyes of the Muslim world. But even before that, the agitation had been derailed when Gandhi's inner voice expressed its disapproval of the violent turn which the movement was taking. After the murder of some policemen in Chauri Chaura (UP) on 5 February 1922, Gandhi called off the agitation, to the surprise and dismay of his Muslim allies. Muslim anger at Gandhi's typically Hindu pusillanimity led to the biggest wave of Hindu-Muslim riots since the establishment of British paramountcy in India:

'65 (continued). The Muslims ran the Khilafat Committee as a distinct political religious organisation and throughout maintained it as a separate entity from the Congress; and very soon the Moplah Rebellion showed that the Muslims had not the slightest idea of national unity on which Gandhiji had set his heart and had staked so much. There followed, as usual in such cases, a huge slaughter of the Hindus, numerous forcible conversions, rape and arson. The British Government, entirely unmoved by the rebellion, suppressed it in a few months and left to Gandhiji the joy of his Hindu-Muslim unity. The Khilafat agitation had failed and let down Gandhiji. British Imperialism emerged stronger, the Muslims became more fanatical and the consequences were visited on the Hindus. (...)'[30]

There is no indication that Gandhi or other Congress leaders ever cared to study the Islamic concept of Khilafat, i.e., the theocratic empire ideally encompassing all Muslims and ultimately the whole world. Gandhi used to haughtily dismiss any questions about the intrinsically problematic aspects of Islam, an attitude which is, by no means, idiosyncratically Gandhian. As a friend of the Hindus, I hope I may be permitted the following observation of their mentality.

As a dim remnant of their ancient glory, when Indian science and civilization were most advanced and admired by neighbouring nations, many Hindus still cherish a superiority attitude, often buried underneath their more recent and more visible inferiority complex vis-à-vis the West. Among the harmless instances, I may cite the NRI ladies who dismiss Western sweets as tasteless stuff compared to Indian ones. Much more harmful is the haughty assumption by Hindu ideologues and polemicists that they know everything about everything.

This unspoken assumption explains why Gandhi, his follower Vinoba Bhave and numerous others pretentiously claimed to know Islam better than the Muslims themselves, e.g., to insist that Islam, too, teaches non-violence; or why *The Times of India* could confidently assert that the Taliban's destruction of the Buddha statues in Bamiyan, an act of outspoken Islamic iconoclasm, was 'un-Islamic'; or why the RSS mouthpiece *Organiser* sometimes carries articles arguing that 'true' Islam actually prohibits cow-slaughter. The anti-scriptural attitude among anglicized urban Hindus reinforces this tendency; they think that studying the boring old letter of the Book is unnecessary once you have seized its 'spirit', an imputed 'spirit' which turns out to be really only a projection of current ideological fashions.

Had Gandhi bothered to study Islamic doctrine, he would have known that the concept of Khilafat is intrinsically anti-nationalist. That may or may not be a good thing (e.g., under the Ottoman Caliphate, Turkish-Kurdish relations were much better than under the secular republic founded by Atatürk), but it was undeniably at cross-purposes with the freedom movement, which sought to unite Indian Hindus with Indian Muslims against colonialism, rather than uniting Indian Muslims with foreign Muslims against all infidels. It was a perfectly logical outcome that the Indian Muslim masses, consisting of native converts suddenly sensitized by their foreign-descended elites to the pan-Islamic cause, ended up attacking Hindus: the Khilafat is intrinsically an Islamic bulwark against the infidels.

Rabindranath Tagore commented thus on the post-Khilafat Hindu-Muslim riots: 'A very important factor which is making it almost impossible for Hindu-Muslim unity to become an accomplished fact is that the Muslims cannot confine their patriotism to any one country. I had frankly asked whether, in the event of any Mohammedan power invading India, they would stand side by side with their Hindu neighbours to defend their common land. I was not satisfied with the reply I got from them. (...) even such a man as Mr. Mohammed Ali has declared that under no circumstances is it permissible for any Mohammedan, whatever be his country, to stand against any Mohammedan.'[31]

After the debacle, Gandhi and the other Congress leaders refused to do any serious introspection about their intellectual failure regarding the Caliphate doctrine. They simply continued peddling cheap assertions about Islam as the religion of brotherhood, as if nothing had happened. Remark that Godse, while not repeating such assertions in his statement, doesn't analyze or refute them either. He describes barbaric behaviour by Muslims but neglects to trace it to its source. He felt resentment against Muslims for the sufferings they had inflicted on Hindus, but he was not articulately critical of Islamic doctrine. Setting the trend for later Hindu nationalist spokesmen (e.g., each of the RSS leaders from M.S. Golwalkar to K.S. Sudarshan), he lashed out at Muslims but refrained from indicting Islam as having inculcated in believers a hatred of infidels that motivated them to acts like the post-Khilafat pogroms.

# GANDHI AND JINNAH

'65 (continued). Mr. Jinnah who had staged a comeback was having the best of both worlds. Whatever concessions the Government and the Congress made, Mr. Jinnah accepted and asked for more. Separation of Sindh from Bombay [Presidency] and the creation of the N.W. Frontier [Province] were followed by the Round Table Conference in which the minority question loomed large. Mr. Jinnah stood out against the federation until Gandhiji himself requested Mr. McDonald, the Labour Premier, to give the Communal Award. Further seeds were thereby sown for the disintegration of this country. (...) The Congress continued to support the Communal Award under the very hypocritical words of "neither supporting nor opposing", which really meant its tacit acceptance. During the War, Mr. Jinnah (...) promised to support the war as soon as the Muslim rights were conceded; in April 1940, within six months of the War, Mr. Jinnah came out with the demand for Pakistan on the basis of his two-nation theory. (...)'[32]

The expression 'Jinnah had staged a comeback' might unintentionally obscure the fact that Jinnah had not been a communal extremist before he had been eclipsed as a Muslim leader by the Ali Brothers, the leaders of the Khilafat campaign. Jinnah had been a constitutionalist who believed in negotiated progress towards more autonomy, but his style of working had been knocked out by the mass politics which Gandhi and his Khilafat allies initiated. To be sure, Jinnah had piloted the 1916 Lucknow Pact which was, of course, a communal arrangement (the acceptance of communal electorates by the Congress in exchange for League cooperation in the freedom struggle), but it was integrated into a larger nationalist perspective; if Jinnah could already be called a communalist, he was at least by no means a separatist.

But the Jinnah who 'came back' was a different man from the constitutionalist sidelined by Gandhi's option for mass politics;

different also from the modernist Muslim leader and genuine 'nationalist Muslim' who had been pushed in the background by the pan-Islamist religious fervour of the Khilafatists. And the key agent in this transformation of Jinnah into the leading enemy of the nation had been none other than Gandhi himself.

Gandhi's seizing control of the Congress is described as follows by a historian: 'The Calcutta Congress gave Gandhi his first major victory, for though his non-cooperation program was strongly opposed by Bengal's leading politicians, C.R. Das and B.C. Pal who joined forces with Jinnah and Annie Besant against him, the Mahatma, with the Ali brothers and Motilal Nehru in his corner, emerged with a clear majority mandate to lead the march against the government. Khilafat trainloads of delegates, hired by Bombay's merchant prince Mian Mohamed Chotani, one of Gandhi's leading supporters, had been shipped cross-country to pack the Congress pandal and vote for their hero's resolution, transforming Congress into a populist political party. It marked a revolutionary shift in Congress's base of support to a lower-class mass, funded by wealthy Hindu Marwari and Muslim merchant-industrialists.'[33]

The humiliation which Gandhi inflicted on them knocked Pal out of politics for good and made an utterly disgusted Jinnah retire into his law practice for several years. When Jinnah came back, he had learned his lesson and started capitalizing on the religious sentiments which had over-grown Indian politics, thanks to Gandhi and the Ali Brothers. This way, Jinnah the separatist was largely Gandhi's creation.

Godse foregoes the occasion to point out Gandhi's role in this transformation of Jinnah's politics. For the rest, his account is generally accurate, though it is not true that 'Gandhiji himself requested' the Communal Award. Like with the Pakistan demand later, Gandhi only acquiesced in what he thought had become inevitable. A more detailed list of Gandhi's concessions to Muslim pressure is given in para 70, discussed in this book.

## THE QUIT INDIA MOVEMENT

Godse gives the following general impression of the deterioration of Gandhi's nationalism to all-out Muslim appeasement in the two decades following his accession to Congress leadership:

'65 (continued). The services began to be distributed on communal basis and the Muslims obtained high jobs from our British Masters not on merit, but by remaining aloof from the struggle for freedom and because of their being the followers of Islam. Government patronage to Muslims in the name of minority protection penetrated throughout the body-politic of the Indian State and the Mahatma's meaningless slogans were no match against this wholesale corruption of the Muslim mind. But Gandhiji did not relent. He still lived in the hope of being the common leader both of the Hindus and Muslims and the more he was defeated, the more he indulged in encouraging the Muslims by extravagant methods. The position continued to deteriorate and by 1925, it became patent to all that the Government had won all along the line; but like the proverbial gambler, Gandhiji increased his stake. He agreed to the separation of Sindh [from the Bombay Presidency] and to the creation of a separate province in the N.W. Frontier. He also went on conceding one undemocratic demand after another to the Muslim League in the vain hope of enlisting its support in the national struggle. (...)'[34]

The creation of Sindh and the NWFP as separate provinces meant that the small Hindu minorities there were left at the mercy of the Muslims. This had been a Muslim demand, and while Gandhi agreed to it, no one can tell what the Hindus got in return for it. Gandhi never claimed to represent the Hindus as such anyway: while the Muslims could press demands as Muslims, both through the Muslim League and through the intra-Congress Muslim lobby, the Hindus were only heard as nationalists. The only expressly Hindu lobby group, the HMS, was treated with indifference or hostility by the Congress leadership, much in contrast with the deferential treatment which the Muslim lobby and the Muslim League received.

The grand finale of this trail of concessions was Partition amid bloodshed. However, when World War II broke out in September 1939, this outcome was still not inevitable, with the Congress having far more democratic legitimacy than the Muslim League, and holding important trump cards, including a number of provincial governments. But the Congress and Gandhi played their cards very poorly, abdicating their government positions (in protest against the Viceroy's involving India in the war effort without consulting native leaders) and antagonizing the British needlessly, so that the Muslim League could fill the vacuum. The jump from a merely weak position to a total abdication of the struggle against Muslim separatism was made in the Quit India Movement of August 1942.

This was an agitation intended to force the British to leave India at once. While politically justified in a very general sense, it was the height of folly under the circumstances. Having the British quit India was a completely unrealistic demand considering that Britain was at war, had an unprecedentedly large army at the ready, considered India its vital base for action against Japan, and would treat any sabotage of its war effort as subversion. Possibly a well-organized guerrilla army could have succeeded in this operation, at least after a protracted struggle, but Gandhiji's unprepared and unarmed amateurs stood no chance at all. Wholly improvized and bereft of strategy, the Quit India Movement earned the Congress nothing except the deep mistrust and hostility of the British, who cooperated all the more eagerly with the Muslim League:

'66. The British Government liked the Pakistan idea as it kept the Hindus and Muslims estranged during the war and thereby avoided embarrassing the Government. (...) The Congress in 1942 started the 'Quit India' Movement in the name of Freedom; violent outrages were perpetrated by Congressmen in every Province. In the Province of North Bihar, there was hardly a railway station which was not burnt or destroyed by the Congress non-co-operators; but in spite of all the opposition of the Congress, the Germans were beaten in April, 1945 and the Japanese in August, 1945. (...) The "Quit India" campaign of 1942 had completely failed. The Britishers had triumphed and the Congress leaders decided to come to terms with them.

'Indeed in the subsequent years the Congress policy can be quite correctly described as "Peace at any Price" and "Congress in Office at all costs". The Congress compromised with the British who placed it in office and in return, the Congress surrendered to the violence of Mr. Jinnah, carved out one-third of India to him, an explicitly racial and theological State, and destroyed two million human beings in the process. Pandit Nehru now professes again and again that the Congress stands for a secular State and violently denounces those who remind him that only last year he agreed to a communal and theological State; his vociferous adherence to a "Secular State" is nothing but a case of "my lady protests too much".'[35]

The figure of 'two million' casualties during the Partition disturbances was frequently given during the aftermath of that catastrophic episode, though no one could know for sure. P. Johnson in *Modern Times* maintains that, today estimates are usually given as below one million, typically six lakhs, but it is still hard to tell. Figures of casualties in communal violence are often kept on the low side by the authorities in an attempt not to fan the flames of communal vengeance any further.

Other claims made here by Godse definitely suffer from quantitative exaggeration, e.g., that 'there was hardly a railway station' in North Bihar which had not fallen victim to the violence of Gandhian Congress activists. But it is true that the Quit India Movement had rapidly slipped out of Gandhi's control, and that his 'non-violent' agitation did turn violent on a good many occasions. Gandhi himself had given orders for acts of sabotage, i.e., violence against buildings and machinery, but not against people. But since buildings are also manned and guarded, violence against people was the inevitable result. After his imprisonment, Gandhi did penance for his undeniable role in the wave of violence—a rare occasion when he realized that he could not control the violent consequences of his own movement.

There can be no doubt that the Quit India Movement, which was predicated on the mistaken perspective of imminent British defeat against Japan, was a total failure in terms of Congress objectives. British power was not dislocated, the Congress leadership was reduced to passive by-standing in prison, the war effort continued with the active involvement (both economic and military) of Indian society, and the political field was left to the Muslim League, which strengthened its position and coolly prepared for the enforcement of its Partition demand. The Communist Party of India (CPI) had also been legalized and had prospered as never before under British patronage, political as well as financial. It joined wholeheartedly the Muslim League demand for Pakistan, and provided the ideological blitz which the Muslim League was incapable of mounting on its own. Leading Muslim-born Communists left the Congress to join the Muslim League in the hope of capturing it from within so that Pakistan could be used as a base near the Soviet Union, as Communists in China had done by their Long March under Mao. How the Muslim rulers of Pakistan defeated the Communist game and how Nehru rescued the Muslim Communists from that country is an interesting but different story.

## NOTES

1. Nathuram Godse: *Why I Assassinated Gandhi*, p. 38.
2. ibid, p. 38.
3. ibid, p. 38.
4. ibid, p. 39.

5. About the 1937 elections, see R.C. Majumdar: *Struggle for Freedom*, p. 561.

6. Full election results for December 1945 in R.C. Majumdar's *Struggle for Freedom*, p. 724 ff.

7. Nathuram Godse: *Why I Assassinated Gandhi*, p. 39.

8. ibid, p. 41.

9. Vide e.g., para. 58, where Godse says: 'Gandhiji was, paradoxical as it may appear, a violent pacifist who brought untold calamities on the country.'

10. 'Hindu-Muslim Tension: Its Cause and Cure', Young India, 29 May 1924; reproduced in M.K. Gandhi: *The Hindu-Muslim Unity*, pp. 35–36. Emphasis added.

11. Shome Basu, Photo Feature: An RSS Training Camp at Work, *The Wire*, 4 October 2017, https://thewire.in/184044/photos-rss-training-camp/

12. The martial performance of the RSS during the Partition catastrophe is questioned by RSS renegade V.M. Sirsikar: 'My Years in the RSS', in E. Zelliot & M. Berntsen, eds.: *The Experience of Hinduism*, p. 202, and utterly rejected by Des Raj Goyal: *Rashtriya Swayamsewak Sangh*, admittedly an extremely hostile source.

13. Manik Chandra Vajpeyi and Shridhar Paradkar: *Jyoti Jala Nij Pran Ki*, Suruchi Prakashan, Delhi 2000.

14. Letter dd. 11-9-1948, reproduced in Des Raj Goyal: *Rashtriya Swayamsewak Sangh*, p. 137. The letter continues: 'But the objectionable part arose when they, burning with revenge, began attacking Mussalmans.'

15. Nathuram Godse: *Why I Assassinated Gandhi*, p. 39–41. Emphasis added.

16. Bhagavad-Gita 2:11–30.

17. Nathuram Godse: *Why I Assassinated Gandhi*, p. 47.

18. Report on a speech by Gandhi in Bombay Chronicle, 11 June 1945, reproduced in *Collected Works*, vol. 80, p. 294.

19. Interview given to Ralph Coniston, 'before April 25, 1945', reproduced in *Collected Works*, vol. 79, p. 423.

20. Addressing his followers (and answering a query by one of them) at

Sevagram, 30 July 1944, reproduced in *Collected Works*, vol. 77, p. 434.

21. V.P. Bhatia: 'When the AICC disowned Gandhian non-violence', *Organiser*, 15 June 1997, quoting with approval from Michael Edwards: *The Myth of the Mahatma*, p. 258. Gandhi tendered his advice to the Jews in the first *Harijan* issue after the *Kristallnacht* pogrom, 9–10 November 1938.

22. Quoted with comment by Dennis Dalton: *Mahatma Gandhi, Nonviolent Power in Action*, p. 37.

23. Vide P.R. Kumaraswamy: 'Mahatma Gandhi and the Jewish national home: an assessment', Asian and African Studies, 1992, pp. 1–13.

24. Letters by Martin Buber and J.L. Magnes and the correspondence between Gandhi and Hayim Greenberg are discussed by D. Dalton: *Mahatma Gandhi*, pp. 134–137.

25. Letter to Hitler, 23 July 1939, *Collected Works* vol. 70, p. 20–21. A second letter was written on Christmas Eve 1940. Both are discussed in detail in K. Elst: *Return of the Swastika*, ch. 2. During Germany's successful Blitz offensive, Gandhi wrote in a letter to Lord Linlithgow, 26 May 1940 (reproduced in *Collected Works*, vol. 72, p. 100): 'But assuming that things are as black as they appear to be for the Allied cause, is it not time to sue for peace for the sake of humanity? I do not believe Herr Hitler to be as bad as he is portrayed. He might even have been a friendly power as he may still be. It is due to suffering humanity that this mad slaughter should stop.' (emphasis added)

26. Winston Churchill speaking to *New York Enquirer* editor William Griffin, 1936, quoted in *Chronicles*, December 1995, p. 42. For the same reason, Major General J.F.C. Fuller had called 6 April 1917, day of the USA's entry into the war, 'the most fateful day in European history since Varus lost his legions'; quoted ibidem. Varus was the Roman general who lost his whole army in the battle of the Teutoburg forest against the Germans, thus defining the limit of Roman power in Europe.

27. Vide para 93, discussed in ch. 5.

28. Nathuram Godse: *Why I Assassinated Gandhi*, pp. 42–43. Even in South Africa, the Muslim residents had raised accusing fingers at him

several times, threatened to replace him with Ameer Ali or Jinnah, and called him an embezzler of funds collected for the 'Satyagraha'. A Pathan had almost killed him by hitting hard on his head. He had also been invited to convert to Islam by his client who had employed him originally to plead his cases. But as in India later on, he had turned the other cheek every time. His 'non-violence' vis-à-vis the Muslims in South Africa has not been examined so far.

29. Nathuram Godse: *Why I Assassinated Gandhi*, pp. 43–44.
30. Nathuram Godse: *Why I Assassinated Gandhi*, pp. 44–45. Moplah: Muslim from Kerala, where a huge pogrom of Hindus took place in 1922; see below, ch. 4.
31. V.P. Bhatia: 'The ghost of Rahmat Ali', *Organiser*, 18 September 1994, quoting Tagore as interviewed in *Times of India*, 18 April 1924.
32. Nathuram Godse: *Why I Assassinated Gandhi*, p. 46. His sequence is mixed up.
33. Stanley Wolpert: *Jinnah of Pakistan*, p. 69. Pandal: ceremonial pavilion.
34. Nathuram Godse: *Why I Assassinated Gandhi*, pp. 45–46.
35. ibid, pp. 47–48.

4

# Gandhi's Responsibility for the Partition

Nathuram Godse proceeds to a more detailed survey of Gandhi's contributions to the growth of Muslim separatism:

'70. I shall now describe briefly the enormous mischief done by the slogans and the nostrums which Gandhiji prescribed and followed, in pursuance of his policy, and the fatal results that we now know. Here are some of them.'[1]

## GANDHI'S KHILAFAT CAMPAIGN

In 1918, the Ottoman Empire, which had fought on the German side in World War I, stood defeated and dismembered. All that remained was rump-Turkey with western Armenia (cleansed of Armenians in 1915), Ionia (cleansed of Greeks in 1922) and northwestern Kurdistan (reconquered from the Kurds and French). The Caliph was still in office, but was totally discredited and no longer master of the Islamic holy places, lost to Arab rebels and British (largely British-Indian) intervention troops. Indian Muslims started a mass agitation demanding that the British restore the Caliphate, starting with the return of their conquests in West Asia, including Palestine, to the Caliph.

At its Calcutta and Nagpur sessions in autumn 1920, the Congress approved an initiative already taken by Gandhi, viz. to start a Non-Cooperation Movement on 1 August 1920 demanding Swarajya (home-rule) within one year. In order to forge Hindu-Muslim unity, Gandhi tried to enlist the Muslim movement for the Khilafat in his own movement. Or rather, the sequence is that he first suggested Non-Cooperation to the Khilafatist leaders, and then extended the idea to the Hindus and Congress. It meant in effect that his own volunteers would be campaigning for the dual purpose of achieving home-rule and restoring the Caliphate. Godse invokes the dramatic failure of Gandhi's stratagem:

'70 (a). Khilafat. (...) The Indian Muslims' devotion to the Khilafat was strong and earnest and they believed that it was Britain that had brought about the downfall of the Sultan and the Khilafat. They therefore started a campaign for the revival of the Khilafat. In the moment of opportunism, the Mahatma misconceived the idea that by helping the Khilafat Movement he would become the leader of the Muslims in India as he already was of the Hindus and that with the Hindu-Muslim unity thus achieved, the British would soon have to concede Swaraj. (...) Gandhiji miscalculated and by leading the Indian National Congress to identify itself with the Khilafat Movement, he quite gratuitously introduced a theological element which has proved a tragic and expensive calamity. (...) When failure came, the Muslims became desperate with disappointment and their anger was visited on the Hindus. Innumerable riots in various parts of India followed, the chief victims being the Hindus everywhere. The Hindu-Muslim unity of the Mahatma became a mirage.'[2]

The cooperation between the Congress and the Khilafat Movement was profoundly misconceived. Had the Congress leadership shed its principled superficiality vis-à-vis Islamic doctrine, it would have realized that nationalism and Khilafat are two mutually exclusive notions: the Caliphate is, by definition, transnational, and is considered to command the loyalty of all Muslims over and above the non-Islamic state where they may happen to live. To propagate Khilafatist solidarity among the Indian Muslims was the surest way to estrange them from Indian nationalism.

The logical course would have been to impress upon the Muslims that the long-ailing Caliphate had become a thing of the past with the dismemberment of the Ottoman Empire in 1918, and certainly after the abolition of the Khilafat institution by Atatürk in March 1924, so as to free them for involvement in the struggle of their real motherland, India. But there is no evidence at all that Gandhi or any other Congress leader ever properly informed him of what the notion Khilafat represents in Islamic doctrine, even though Gandhi did understand that it was essentially a religious matter.

Apart from this specifically Islamic angle, it was a strange sight to see an Indian nationalist movement focus its energies for three years on a struggle taking place in distant Turkey. Was this a commendable instance of international solidarity between peoples involved in parallel anti-colonial struggles? Hardly. First of all, it was a one-way solidarity, for the West Asian Muslims showed no interest in India's freedom struggle: the Turks had enough internal problems, and the Arabs knew better than to offend their British allies who had just freed them from Ottoman rule. Secondly, it is a strange anti-colonialism which aims at the revival of what had been, in essential features, a colonial empire. Not only the Christian nations of the Balkans, but even the Arab Muslims had fought to free themselves from Caliphate rule. From whichever angle you look at it, the Congress involvement in the Khilafat agitation was highly irrational.

The Khilafatist involvement of Gandhi's Congress has, with the benefit of hindsight, to be judged a disaster, a trigger of unprecedented rioting and communalization of the polity. Could an Indian decision-maker in 1919 reasonably have foreseen that the

Turks themselves would abolish the Caliphate? Could a different leadership have prevented the movement from turning destructive and anti-Hindu? Godse may be forgiven for not treating these academic questions, but they remain valid questions though they do help only peripherally in determining the extent to which Gandhi may be considered guilty of the resulting disaster. His guilt lay mainly in his refusal to ponder a much simpler question: can Muslims who fight for the restoration of the Empire of Islam have their heart in the struggle for the freedom of India?

## THE MOPLAH REBELLION

When Gandhi unilaterally called off the Non-Cooperation Movement because it had turned violent (February 1922), he threw his volunteers into desperation. Many had left their jobs or studies in order to participate in the historic movement aimed at forcing the British to concede home-rule to India. The Muslims especially felt betrayed by Gandhi and took out their anger on the Hindus in general. However, it is not only the failure of the movement which led to communal rioting. One of the greatest outbursts of communal violence was actually part of the movement itself when it was still going strong.

In August 1921, exactly a year after the start of Non-Cooperation, time for which Gandhi had promised results, the Moplah Muslim community of Kerala installed its own version of home-rule, viz. Khilafat rule. A Khilafat kingdom was declared under one Ali Musaliar. It took the British several months to suppress this rebellion, and meanwhile pogroms were conducted against the local Hindus, involving murder, rape and forcible conversion to Islam. Godse comments:

'70 (b). Moplah Rebellion. Malabar, Punjab, Bengal and N.W. Frontier Province were the scene of repeated outrages on the Hindus. The Moplah rebellion, as it was called, was the most prolonged and concentrated attack on the Hindu religion, Hindu honour, Hindu life and Hindu property (...). The Mahatma, who had brought about all this calamity on India by his communal policy, kept mum. He never uttered a single word of reproach against the aggressors nor did he allow the Congress to take any active steps whereby repetition of such outrages could be prevented. On the other hand, he went to the length of denying the numerous cases of forcible conversions in Malabar and actually published in his paper, *"Young India"* that there was only one case of forcible conversion. His own Muslim friends informed him that he was wrong and that the forcible conversions were numerous in Malabar. He never corrected his misstatements, but went to the absurd length of starting a relief fund for the Moplahs instead of their victims; but the promised land of Hindu-Muslim unity was not yet in sight.'[3]

We may add, at this point, a more recent comment (1993) on the Moplah Rebellion and its political digestion by Gandhi's Congress, by a Hindu historian. In his book *Aryan Invasion Theory and Indian Nationalism*, Shrikant G. Talageri insists that 'Halfway through, the Khilafat agitation was converted into a jihad against Hindus. (...) If the Khilafat agitation was ghastly and horrifying, the secularist response to it was a hundred times more ghastly and horrifying. (...) The Congress suppressed all reports about the atrocities perpetrated by the Moplahs against the Hindus, and Congress leaders condemned the British authorities for taking measures to quell the rioters.' Further, he insists that 'the Mahatma went out of his way to refer to the Moplah murderers as "my brave Moplahs", and expressed admiration for their religious fervour. After 1947, Moplah rioters were classified as freedom fighters and made eligible for pensions paid by the Government of Independent India. And every year, to this very day, the Khilafat Movement is commemorated by a massive procession in Bombay, in which many Leftists and secularists participate along with Muslims.'

However, Godse exaggerates in asserting that Gandhi 'never

uttered a single word of reproach against the aggressors.' The post-Khilafat pogrom of Hindus in Kohat (NWFP) did elicit his stern reproach of local Muslim leaders. While hardly even-handed, Gandhi did try to be fair on some occasions; but the Moplah rebellion was not one of them.

## CALL FOR AN AFGHAN INVASION

The following point concerns an episode which, more than any other prior to 1947, indicates very serious confusion in Gandhi's mind: his openly declared sympathy (though not active involvement, as alleged in a Hindu nationalist publication, titled *Gandhi and Gandhism Unmasked: Was Gandhi a Traitor?* by Brahma Datt Bharti, in which the author argues at great length that the Mahatma was really and personally involved in the Afghan intrigue) with a Muslim appeal to the Amir of Afghanistan to invade British India. Neither a loyalist nor a nationalist could accept the welcoming of a foreign invasion. The only reason why this episode hardly affected Gandhi's stature was the downright nonsensical and hence inconsequential nature of the whole project.

The Amir, Amanullah Khan, had actually invaded the NWFP of British India in 1919, but the British never felt threatened by this 'Third Afghan War', though, after swiftly suppressing it, they gave up their control over Afghanistan's foreign policy in the Anglo-Afghan Treaty of 1921, signed in Kabul. After that diplomatic success, it would have been irrational for the Amir to provoke the British, except in case of an impending collapse of British colonial power (did Gandhi miscalculate that a British abdication was around the corner?)—but in that case, India could well do without the dubious 'help' of a petty feudal ruler like Amir Amanullah. Godse's comment:

'70 (c). Afghan Amir Intrigue. When the Khilafat Movement failed, the Ali Brothers decided to do something which might keep alive the Khilafat sentiments. Their slogan was that whoever was the enemy of the Khilafat was also the enemy of Islam, and as the British were chiefly responsible for the defeat and the dethronement of the Sultan of Turkey, every faithful Muslim was in solemn duty bound to be a bitter enemy of Britain. With that object, they secretly intrigued to invite the Amir of Afghanistan to invade India and promised every support. There is a long history behind this intrigue; the Ali Brothers never denied their share in the conspiracy. The Mahatma pursued his tactics of getting Hindu-Muslim unity by supporting the Ali Brothers through thick and through thin. (...)

'70 (c) (continued). Even with regard to the invasion of India by the Amir, the Mahatma directly and indirectly supported the Ali Brothers. This is proved beyond the shadow of doubt. The late Mr. [Srinivasa] Shastri, Mr. C.Y. Chintamani the editor of *The Leader* of Allahabad and even the Mahatma's life-long friend, the late Rev. C.F. Andrews, told him quite clearly that his speeches and writings amounted to a definite support to the Ali Brothers in their invitation to the Amir of Afghanistan to invade India. The following quotations from the Mahatma's writing in those days should make it clear that he had forgotten his own country in his one consuming desire to please the Muslims and had become a party to the invasion of his motherland by a foreign ruler. The Mahatma supported the invasion in the following words:

> I cannot understand why the Ali Brothers are going to be arrested as the rumours go, and why I am to remain free. They have done nothing which I would not do. If they had sent a message to the Amir, I also would send one to inform the Amir that if he came, no Indian so long as I can help it, would help the Government to drive him back.

The vigilance of the British broke the conspiracy; nothing came out of the Ali Brothers' grotesque scheme of the invasion of India and Hindu-Muslim unity remained as far away as before.'[4]

There are other aspects to the Afghan connection of the Khilafatist fever which deserve consideration. Thus, a demythologizing light is thrown upon the motives of the 'nationalist Muslim' leader Maulana Abul Kalam Azad by the conclusion he drew from the doctrine that the British, in destroying the Caliphate, had become the enemies of Islam. To Azad, like to many Ulema, this meant that British India was a Dar-al-Harb, 'land of strife', i.e., a land controlled by infidel enemies of Islam, where Muslims had the duty either to wage jihad and overthrow the infidel regime or to emigrate to an Islamic state. Since British power was still too strong, Muslims had to emulate the decision of the Prophet to flee Pagan Mecca to Muslim-dominated Medina in AD 622, and therefore, the influential Maulana called on the Indian Muslims to migrate to Afghanistan.

Thousands heeded his call, sold everything or simply left it behind, but found Afghan society to be inhospitable, incomprehending and hostile. Stricken by poverty, famine and religious anguish, they had to return to India in desperation. Some of them died on the way to and from Afghanistan. The man who had brought this misfortune on them with his obscurantist scheme was to become the leading Congress Muslim, Education Minister in Nehru's Cabinet and one of the most powerful men in India after Independence.

This way, the Khilafat crisis was an eye-opener that showed just who was who in Muslim and pro-Muslim India. Unlike Nehru, who did not take religion seriously and cultivated the company of fairly enlightened Muslims, Gandhi built up medieval obscurantists like the Ali Brothers and Maulana Azad. If he attracted the unjust suspicion of involvement in a hare-brained intrigue with the feudal Amir, he really brought it on himself by associating with such shady characters.

## GANDHI'S ATTACK ON THE ARYA SAMAJ

The next point in Godse's statement concerns the Arya Samaj, the Hindu reform movement whose solution for India's communal problem was Shuddhi, the reconversion of the Muslim community to the Vedic religion. In this respect, it was Gandhi's antipode, for the Mahatma believed that everyone should remain inside his parental religion and that all religions were equally good. Muslims opposed the Arya Samaj and countered its Shuddhi with the Tabligh ('propaganda') movement to strengthen the Islamic commitment among nominal (often culturally still very Hindu) Muslims, and with assassinations of Arya Samaj leaders. Though the Arya Samaj had supported the Khilafat Movement, it became an obvious target for Muslim fanatics once this phase of Hindu-Muslim cooperation was over.

In this conflict, Gandhiji was definitely not on the side of the Arya Samaj. He called Swami Shraddhananda, initiator of the Shuddhi movement, 'intrepid and brave', 'irritating', 'hasty and ruffled' and 'pugnacious', though not 'past praying for'.[5] He strongly denounced the project of converting people, even former Hindus, to Hinduism. On the other hand, he equally condemned Khwaja Hasan Nizami's pamphlet Dai-i Islam, which called for conversion of Hindus to Islam by all means fair and foul.[6] As we already pointed out, it is not true that Gandhi absolutely failed to criticize Muslims; this is one case where he did. However, when Shraddhananda criticized Maulana Abdul Bari for openly advocating the killing of apostates (targeting specifically the Muslim Shuddhi converts to Arya Hinduism) in *The Collected Works of Mahatma Gandhi,* and quoted by J.T.F. Jordens in *Swami Shraddhananda,* Gandhi minimized the seriousness of Abdul Bari's statements, and actually praised him by referring to him as a simple child of God and a friend.

This gives another look into Gandhiji's mentality. What was the difference between Gandhi's 'friend' Abdul Bari on the one hand, and the accursed 'fanatics' Shraddhananda and Nizami on the other? It is that the former advocated actual violence, while the latter two were only verbally polemical c.q. deceitful. Gandhi could be very harsh on people who only fought with words, but his tongue became very sweet when mentioning or addressing muscled violence-mongers like the Moplahs or Abdul Bari.[7] This extra respect for ruthless people is also well-known among Western intellectuals, who used to venerate Stalin and Mao. At any rate, this partiality angered Godse, especially because the violence Abdul Bari had called for did actually take place:

'70 (d.) (i). Attack on Arya Samaj. Gandhiji ostentatiously displayed his love for Muslims by a most unworthy and unprovoked attack on the Arya Samaj in 1924. He publicly denounced the Samaj for its supposed sins of omission and commission; it was an utterly unwarranted, reckless and discreditable attack, but whatever would please the Mohammedans was the heart's desire of Gandhiji. The Arya Samaj made a powerful but polite retort and for some time Gandhiji was silenced, but the growing political influence of Gandhiji weakened the Arya Samaj. (...)

'70 (d.) (ii). Gandhiji's attack did not improve his popularity with the Muslims but it provoked a Muslim youth to murder Swami Shraddhanandaji within a few months. The charge against the Samaj that it was a reactionary body was manifestly false. Everybody knew that far from being a reactionary body, the Samaj had been the vanguard of social reforms among the Hindus. The Samaj had for a hundred years stood for the abolition of untouchability long before the birth of Gandhiji. The Samaj had popularised widow remarriage. The Samaj had denounced the caste system and preached the oneness of not merely the Hindus, but of all those who were prepared to follow its tenets. Gandhiji was completely silenced for some time, but his leadership made the people forget his baseless attack on the Arya Samaj and even weakened the Samaj to a large extent. (...)'[8]

The time-lapse between Gandhi's attack on Swami Shraddhananda and the latter's assassination (23 December 1926) was actually longer than Godse assumes here, viz. more than two-

and-a-half years. J.T.F. Jordens in *Swami Shraddhananda* insists that
there was also no causal relation between Gandhi's attack and the
murder, which was apparently triggered by the Swami's acquittal in
a court case for alleged abduction brought by a Muslim whose wife
and children had run away from his home and sought conversion
from the Swami. Nor was the Arya Samaj 'a hundred years' old
in 1926; it was founded in 1875, six years after Gandhi's birth.
Nonetheless, the allegation that Gandhi was less than even-handed
in his criticism of Hindu preachers of conversion and Muslim
preachers of murder of converts was supported by many. One of
these was Ambedkar, who held it against Gandhi that he had not
even condemned the murder of Swami Shraddhananda and other
Arya Samaj leaders.

One of Ambedkar's many criticisms of Gandhiji was this: 'He
has never called the Muslims to account even when they have
been guilty of gross crimes against Hindus.' He cites, among
other examples (like the Moplah rebellion), the series of murders
of people who had criticized Mohammed and the Quran: Swami
Shraddhananda, 'who was shot by Abdul Rashid on 23 December
1926 when he was lying in his sick bed'; Lala Nanak Chand, a
prominent Arya Samajist; Rajpal, the editor of the book *Rangeela
Rasool* ('The playboy prophet', gossip on Prophet Mohammed's sex
life, in reaction to a similar Muslim publication on Sita), 'stabbed
by Ilamdin on 6 April 1929 while sitting in his shop'; Nathuramal
Sharma, 'murdered by Abdul Qayum in September 1934 (...) in the
Court of the Judicial Commissioner of Sind where he was seated
while awaiting the hearing of his appeal against his conviction
under Section 195, Indian Penal Code, for the publication of a
pamphlet on the history of Islam.'[9] That is 'only a short list, and
could easily be expanded.'

Dr Ambedkar points out that, while the murderers were
tried by British judges, the Muslim leadership gave its full moral
support to the murderers: 'The leading Muslims, however, never

condemned these criminals. On the contrary, they were hailed as religious martyrs (...) Mr Barkat Ali, a barrister of Lahore, who argued the appeal of Abdul Qayum (...) went to the length of saying that Qayum was not guilty of murder of Nathuramal because his act was justifiable by the law of the Koran. This attitude of the Muslims is quite understandable. What is not understandable is the attitude of Mr Gandhi.'[10]

The Mahatma has often been accused of Muslim appeasement. Ambedkar makes that criticism his own, as highlighted by J.T.F. Jordens in *Swami Shraddhananda*. Ambedkar was of the view that Gandhi had been very punctilious in the matter of condemning all acts of violence. However, Gandhi had never protested against such murders. The Muslims never condemned these outrages, neither did Gandhi ever ask the leading Muslims to condemn them. He kept silent over them. Such an attitude only showed that Gandhi was anxious to preserve Hindu-Muslim unity and did not mind sacrificing a few Hindu lives for that.

Note also how Gandhi clean forgot his earlier closeness to Swami Shraddhananda. It was Shraddhananda to whom he had sent his two sons to be looked after and educated at Gurukula Kangri near Haridwar, when he was in South Africa. It was Shraddhananda whom he had met at the Gurukul soon after his return to India. And it was Shraddhananda (not Tagore, as is often claimed) who was the first to decorate him with the honorific of 'Mahatma', which he wore throughout his life. The least he should have done was to renounce the title bestowed on him by the Swami when he felt so estranged with the latter as to embrace his murderer as brother.

## GANDHI AND THE SEPARATION OF SINDH

Among subsequent concessions to the Muslim League, one that was to contribute materially to the creation of Pakistan was the partition of the Bombay Presidency, essentially along communal lines: in

1931, the Muslim-majority region of Sindh (though including some Hindu-majority districts) was separated and made into a new province. This new province became one of the constituent provinces of Pakistan:

'70 (e). Separation of Sindh. By 1928, Mr. Jinnah's stock had risen very high and the Mahatma had already conceded many unfair and improper demands of Mr. Jinnah at the expense of Indian democracy and the Indian nation and the Hindus. The Mahatma even supported the separation of Sindh from the Bombay Presidency and threw the Hindus of Sind to the communal wolves. Numerous riots took place in Sindh-Karachi, Sukkur, Shikarpur and other places in which the Hindus were the only sufferers and the Hindu-Muslim unity receded further from the horizon.'[11]

Yet, the harvest of this policy was meagre, and there was no increase in Muslim participation in the Freedom Movement:

'70 (f). League's Good Bye to Congress. With each defeat, Gandhiji became even more keen on his method of achieving Hindu-Muslim unity. Like the gambler who had lost heavily, he became more desperate increasing his stakes each time and indulged in the most irrational concessions if only they could placate Mr. Jinnah and enlist his support under the Mahatma's leadership in the fight for freedom. But the aloofness of the Muslims from the Congress increased with the advance of years and the Muslim League refused to have anything to do with the Congress after 1928. (...)'[12]

Increasing Hindu-Muslim tension was only one reason for the increasing estrangement between the Congress and the League. The adoption by the Congress of a resolution demanding 'total independence' (Poorna Swaraj, 26 January 1930), leaving the old guard's demand of 'Dominion Status' within the British Empire far behind, was quite incompatible with the League's pursuit of a British-friendly policy. The Muslims, as represented by the League, did not want to follow the mainly Hindu Congressites in this next step towards freedom. What they cared for was not some abstract ideal of total independence for India, but merely whichever arrangement served their own communal interests best, and under the circumstances this implied a continued British participation in Indian affairs. Gandhi's gestures failed to cause any 'change of heart' in them.

## THE ROUND TABLE CONFERENCE

According to Godse, none of Gandhi's concessions made the League one bit more conciliatory. This was proven once more in the three rounds of the Round Table Conference (1930–32) hosted by the British Government. Here is Godse's account:

'70 (g). Round-Table Conference and Communal Award. (...) at the Karachi Congress of 1931 it was decided to send Gandhiji alone as the Congress Representative to the Second Session of the Round Table Conference. Anybody who reads the proceedings of that Session will realise that Gandhiji was the biggest factor in bringing about the total failure of the Conference. Not one of the decisions of the Round Table Conference was in support of democracy or nationalism and the Mahatma went to the length of inviting Mr. Ramsay MacDonald to give what was called the Communal Award, thereby strengthening the disintegrating forces of communalism, which had already corroded the body politic for 24 years past. (...)

'Gandhiji himself put an axe on the communal unity on which he had staked so much for the previous fifteen years. (...) Those elected on the communal franchise would be naturally communal-minded and would have no interest in bridging the gulf between communalism and nationalism. The formation of a parliamentary party on political and economic grounds thus became impossible. (...) Almost everywhere Hindus became victims of communal orgies at the hands of the Muslims. People became perfectly cynical about any possibility of unity between Hindus and Muslims, but the

Mahatma kept on repeating his barren formula all the time.'[13]

Even authors more sympathetic to Gandhi have admitted that Gandhi and the Congress played their cards awfully bad at this critical juncture, first by not knowing whether to participate, then by showing up (in the sole person of Gandhi) without any proper negotiation strategy, even failing to valorize the Congress's status as the only multi-communal and pan-Indian organization. In the *Struggle For Freedom*, R.C. Majumdar states that the followers of Christ only understood the language of strength or force, hence Gandhi's Christian meekness and humility fell flat on them. His conduct in the Conference was another example of his inability to carry on negotiations with trained politicians.

## CONGRESS GREED FOR OFFICE

In 1937, after constitutional reforms giving India a large measure of self-government, the Congress formed provincial governments in more than half of British India. Godse knew from experience that, in the Bombay Presidency at least, it had used this newfound power to thwart the initiatives of the HMS. But his critique of these governments concerns a different point:

'70 (h). Acceptance of Office and Resigning in Huff. (...) [The Congress] decided to accept office in July, 1937; in doing so it committed a serious blunder in excluding the members of the Muslim League from effective participation in the Cabinet. They only admitted into the Cabinet such Muslims as were Congressmen. This was the right policy for a country with citizen franchise and without communal representation, but having accepted communal electorate and communal franchise and other paraphernalia of separatism, it became untenable to keep out the members of the Muslim League who represented the bulk of the Muslims in every province where they were in a minority. The Nationalist Muslims who became Ministers were not representatives of the Muslims in the sense in which the Muslim League members were, (...) the rejection of Muslim League members as Ministers gave Mr. Jinnah a tactical advantage which he utilised to the full and in 1939, when the Congress resigned Office in a huff, it completely played in the hands of the Muslim League and British Imperialism.'[14]

Here, Godse supports the more League-friendly version of the Partition history, viz. that the Congress showed its selfishness and bad faith by grabbing power for itself instead of sharing it with the League, as it should have, given the spirit if not the letter of British India's communal arrangement. However, the Congress used to rationalize this attitude with the plea that it counted Muslims in its ranks as well, that it was not a Hindu party, and that the selfishness was on the part of the League as it wanted to grab all Muslim-allotted seats and jobs for its own cadres.

The abdication of the Congress Ministries in protest against British India's declaration of war against Germany (decided on without the approval of the Indian representative bodies being asked) is not evaluated from a nationalist or democratic viewpoint here, but from a tactical angle, and in that respect it is correctly judged to have been a terrible mistake. As we shall see, it antagonized the British unnecessarily and left the political field to the Muslim League so that it could promote its own separatist project.

## GANDHI CONCEDES PARTITION

The next point, numbered 70 (i), does not mention an instance of Gandhi's alleged appeasement policy, but merely states that the Muslim League took advantage of World War II, endearing itself to the British by cooperating in the war effort and positioning itself for future showdowns with the Congress; while Gandhi's Congress was in two minds, failed to take the opportunity, and ended up leaving the centre stage of Indian politics to the Muslim League.

It must be borne in mind that different tendencies within

the Congress and evolving world circumstances led to sections of the Congress taking every possible attitude towards World War II successively or even at the same time. Gandhi himself was full of contradictions. Louis Fischer in *The Life of Mahatma Gandhi* maintains that whenever the Congress rejected Gandhi's pacifism and volunteered to aid the British, he did not interfere. But he objected whenever the Congress agreed with him and wanted to hinder the war effort. Until he called for the Quit India sabotage campaign (August 1942), that is, and for that one he later felt guilty and repented. This way, he was twisting and turning into total irrelevance.

At the Lucknow session of the Congress in April 1936, Jawaharlal Nehru had stated in his presidential address: 'Every war waged by imperialist powers will be an imperialist war whatever the excuses put forward; therefore we must keep out of it.'[14] When war broke out in September 1939, the party-line which crystallized after some debate was that the Congress supported Britain's war aims if these amounted to the defence of democracy everywhere, but would not cooperate with the British war effort unless the choice about India's participation was left to Indians. In protest against Viceroy Lord Linlithgow's unilateral decision to commit India to the war effort, the Congress resigned its provincial governments.

This stand caused the Congress to be increasingly isolated. Most other parties, including the Liberals and the HMS, the nominally independent Princes and, after June 1941, also the Communists, did support the war effort. Indian society cooperated whole-heartedly and enjoyed a booming economy as India became the main production centre for the British war effort. The Muslim League had a field day. Congress leaders became unhappy about their increasing irrelevance, and therefore, were willing to make concessions if these could only bring them to centre stage again.

In these circumstances, the mission of Sir Stafford Cripps (early 1942), though not achieving its objective of involving the

Congress in the war effort, did get the Congress leadership across the threshold of effectively conceding the principle of Partition. This was not yet Partition in its historic form, but a far-reaching autonomy for the provinces regarding the Indian Dominion to be constituted, and this would allow the Muslim-dominated (or any other) provinces to form separate Dominions. Godse correctly saw this as the substance of the Partition scheme:

'70 (j). Cripps' Partition Proposal Accepted. The Congress did not know its own mind as to whether it should support the war, oppose or remain neutral. All these attitudes were expressed in turn one after the other; (...) The war was carried on without let or hindrance till 1942. The Government could get all the men, all the money, and all the material which their war efforts needed. Every Government loan was fully subscribed.

'In 1942, came the Cripps Mission (...) with a clear hint of partition of India in the background. Naturally the Mission failed, but the Congress even while opposing the Mission's proposals yielded to the principle of partition (...) At a meeting of the All India Congress Committee held in April 1942 at Allahabad, the principle of partition was repudiated by an overwhelming majority (...) but Maulana Azad, the so-called nationalist Muslim, was then the President of the Congress. He gave a ruling a few months later that the Allahabad Resolution had no effect on the earlier resolution of the Working Committee which conceded the principle of Pakistan however remotely. The Congress was entirely at the end of its wits. (...)'[16]

Shortly after the failure of the Cripps Mission, Gandhi effectively conceded Partition even in front of his own support base. Writing in his own paper, he mused, 'If the vast majority of Muslims regard themselves as a separate nation having nothing in common with the Hindus and others, no power on earth can compel them to think otherwise. And if they want to partition India on that basis, they must have the partition, unless Hindus want to fight against such a division.'[17] In his defeatist mood, it simply did not occur to him that he might use his tried and tested pressure tactics on the Muslim League, viz. the fast unto death.

In fact, Gandhi had already accepted the perspective underlying the Partition demand as soon as the Muslim League had officially adopted it, in the spring of 1940. In the 6 April 1940 issue of *Harijan*, he averred that he knew of no non-violent method that would compel the obedience of eight crore Muslims to the will of the rest of India, no matter how powerful a majority the rest may represent. He further added that the Muslims should have the right of self-determination that the rest of India possessed because the nation was a joint family, and any member could claim a division. Saying that 'the Muslims' have a right of 'self-determination' amounts to accepting that they as a collectivity constitute the kind of entity which may be the subject of self-determination, i.e., a nation. This statement gives the impression that in spite of his stated objections to Jinnah's Two-Nation Theory, Gandhi had already interiorized it.

## FAILURE OF 'QUIT INDIA'

The grand finale of this trail of concessions was Partition amid bloodshed. However, when World War II broke out, this outcome was still not inevitable, with the Congress having far more democratic legitimacy than the Muslim League, and holding important trump cards, including a number of provincial governments. But the Congress and Gandhi played their cards very poorly, abdicating their government positions and antagonizing the British uselessly, so that the Muslim League could fill the vacuum.

'70 (k). "Quit India" by Congress and "Divide and Quit" by League. Out of sheer desperation, Gandhiji evolved the 'Quit India' Policy which was endorsed by the Congress. (...) But in less than three months, the whole movement was throttled by the Government with firmness and discretion. (...) Mr. Jinnah openly opposed the "Quit India" Movement as hostile to the Muslims and raised a counter slogan "Divide and Quit." That is where Gandhiji's Hindu-Muslim unity had arrived.'[18]

Godse had already dealt with this topic before in para 66. To recapitulate: in August 1942, Gandhi forced his often unwilling supporters to start a mass campaign of agitation and sabotage in order to press the demand for immediate decolonization. Enthusiastic youngsters followed their own lights in improvizing acts of defiance in the service of Mother India. The result was chaotic, often violent, but not exactly threatening to British power. The movement was efficiently suppressed, leaving the Congress discredited among the British and the moderate nationalists (as being a disloyal partner in politics even in wartime) as well as among its own militant supporters (as being incapable of conducting a successful mass movement and realizing even a fraction of its demands).

Perhaps, however, there was one beneficial, though unintended, side effect to the Quit India Movement—it wiped an abject compromise proposal off the table. Gandhi and many in the Congress leadership were still reluctant to accept the idea of dividing the country along communal lines, and increasingly irrational emergency solutions calculated to appease the Muslim League were floated. The ultimate appeasement offer was to keep India united by handing power entirely to the Muslim League. Maulana Azad made this proposal, and Gandhi approved it on 6 August 1942, confirming it again in a letter dated 8 August, 'the Congress will have no objection to the British Government transferring all the powers it today exercises to the Muslim League on behalf of the whole of India.'[19]

But Gandhi did not await any reply and started the Quit India Movement for immediate independence on 8 August. This made the British quite deaf to any 'proposals' by Gandhi and the Congress, including the far-fetched idea of handing India over to the Muslim League.

## GANDHI'S HINDUSTANI

Power equations are illustrated by symbols and cultural policies. Language had been an important bone of contention between Hindus and Muslims since the late nineteenth century, especially in UP and Bihar, where the controversy was between Hindi in the native Devanagari script and its Persianized variety Urdu, written in the Arabic script. Gandhi rejected the choice for Hindi as free India's national language (a choice which was nonetheless made, after his death, by the Constituent Assembly), and favoured a mixture, open to both Urdu and Hindi styles and written in both scripts, which he called Hindustani. Since many Urdu speakers called their language Hindustani, and since Urdu was a mixture (of Hindi and Arabicized Persian) itself, this mixed language named Hindustani was reasonably suspected to be Urdu under another name:

'70 (l). Hindi versus Hindustani. Absurdly pro-Muslim policy of Gandhiji is nowhere more blatantly illustrated than in his perverse attitude on the question of the National Language of India. By all the tests of a scientific language, Hindi has the most prior claim to be accepted as the National Language of this country. In the beginning of his career in India, Gandhiji gave a great impetus to Hindi, but as he found that the Muslims did not like it, he became a turncoat and blossomed forth as the champion of what is called Hindustani. (...) It is a bastard tongue and a crossbreed between Hindi and Urdu and not even the Mahatma's sophistry could make it popular; but in his desire to please the Muslims, he insisted that Hindustani alone should be the national language of India. (...)

'All his experiments were at the expense of the Hindus. His was a one-way traffic in his search of Hindu-Muslim unity. The charm and the purity of the Hindi language was to be prostituted to please the Muslims, but even Congressmen, apart from the rest of India, refused to digest this nostrum. For practical purpose, Hindustani is only Urdu under a different name, but Gandhiji could not have the courage to advocate the adoption of Urdu as against Hindi, hence the subterfuge to smuggle Urdu under the garb of Hindustani. Urdu is not banned by any nationalist Hindu, but to smuggle it under the garb of Hindustani is a fraud and a crime.'[20]

The claim that Hindi is a more 'scientific' language than Urdu possibly refers to the script: logically ordered and phonetically unambiguous in the case of Devanagari, as against the haphazard order and phonetic ambiguity of the Arabic alphabet used in Urdu. It can also be 'scientifically' verified that Hindi had a better claim to the status of link language: it was spoken by many more people than Urdu, and that part of its vocabulary which differentiated it from Urdu was largely shared with most other Indian languages. The distinctive vocabulary of Urdu was Arabic or Persian; the corresponding Hindi terms were native, either desi (local) or tadbhava (Sanskrit-evolved) words which it often had in common with neighbouring languages like Bengali or Gujarati, or tatsama words (integrally adopted from Sanskrit) which were understood by all cultured Indians and used widely even in the Dravidian languages. So, there were good objective grounds for preferring unadulterated Hindi as India's link language.

## GANDHI ON NATIONAL SYMBOLS

Gandhi also intervened in controversies pertaining to symbols with an allegedly communal dimension. The first of these was the choice of the song 'Vande Mataram' as national anthem, or at least as the marching song of the freedom movement. The song's lyrics were taken from Bankim Chandra Chatterji's historical novel *Anandamath* ('Abbey of Bliss'), set against the background of a Hindu freedom fight against Muslim power. Muslims objected to this connotation, as well as to the 'idolatrous' idea of celebrating the Motherland as divine person:

'70 (m). Vande Mataram Not to Be Sung. The infatuation of

Gandhiji for the Muslims and his incorrigible craving for Muslim leadership without any regard for right and wrong, for truth or justice, and in utter contempt for the sentiments of the Hindus as a whole was the high watermark of the Mahatmic benevolence. It is notorious that some Muslims disliked the celebrated song of Vande Mataram and the Mahatma forthwith stopped its singing or recital wherever he could. (...) The right way to proceed would have been to enlighten the ignorant and remove the prejudice, but that is a policy which during the thirty years of unbounded popularity and leadership Gandhiji could not muster courage to try. (...)'[21]

We now know what followed. In the Constituent Assembly, Nehru successfully lobbied to have Vande Mataram replaced with Rabindranath Tagore's song Jana Gana Mana.

Likewise, Gandhi set the trend of avoiding references to Shivaji, the seventeenth century Hindu freedom fighter against the Moghul empire.

'70 (n). Shiva Bavani Banned. Gandhiji banned the public recital or perusal of Shiva Bavani, a beautiful collection of 52 verses by a Hindu poet in which he had extolled the great power of Shivaji and the protection which he brought to the Hindu community and the Hindu religion. The refrain of that collection says: "If there were no Shivaji, the entire country would have been converted to Islam." (...)'[22]

Even the Congress's own design of a national flag had to give way to the merest expectation of Muslim objections:

'70 (y). Removal of Tricolour Flag. The tricolour flag with the Charkha on it was adopted by the Congress as the National Flag out of deference to Gandhiji. (...) When the Mahatma was touring Noakhali and Tippera in 1946 after the beastly outrages on the Hindus, the flag was flying on his temporary hut. But when a Muslim came there and objected (...), Gandhiji quickly directed its removal. All the reverential sentiments of millions of Congressmen towards that flag were affronted in a minute, because that would please an isolated Muslim fanatic (...).'[23]

Another story could be told about the choice of the Congress tricolour flag as national flag in preference to the saffron flag. the Congress had first opted for the saffron flag, which had been waved by earlier freedom fighters including Shivaji, but it quickly backtracked, fearing that Muslims would object. So before they could even express any objection, they were given a new flag of which they could call one third their own, viz. the green strip, as broad as the saffron strip symbolizing Hinduism.[24]

## GANDHI ON COW SLAUGHTER

The most symbolic issue of all concerned the cow and the slaughter of cows.

'70 (x). Gandhiji on Cow-Slaughter. Gandhiji used to display a most vehement desire for the protection of the cow. But in fact he did no effort in that direction. (...) An extract from his speech in this connection is reproduced below:

"Today Rajendra Babu informed me that he had received some fifty-thousand telegrams urging prohibition of cow-slaughter by law. (...) why are so many letters and telegrams sent to me? They have not served any purpose. No law prohibiting cow-slaughter in India can be enacted. How can I impose my will upon a person who does not wish voluntarily to abandon cow-slaughter? India does not belong exclusively to the Hindus. Muslims, Parsees, Christians, all live here. The claim of the Hindus that India has become the land of the Hindus is totally incorrect. This land belongs to all who live here. (...)"'[25]

Though Godse does not comment any further on the cow-slaughter issue, an outsider may remark that Gandhi's position on India being the country of non-Hindus as well does not logically imply that the Indian government has no right to prohibit cow-slaughter. Most sacred objects are sacred to only a part of the population of any country; yet, most governments do prohibit the profanation of all places of worship, graveyards, flags, etc.

Moreover, democratic governments take decisions by majority, not by consensus. If a majority of greenery-minded people enacts a prohibition on cutting down forests, then the minority of eco-skeptics will have to abide by it and respect the trees which it would rather chop down. Similarly, if a cow-revering majority wants to enact a prohibition on cow-slaughter, there is nothing undemocratic about expecting the minority to renounce beef. A problem would arise if any minority was under a religious obligation to eat beef, but that is not the case.

Gandhi created a seemingly insoluble moral problem ('How can I impose my will?'), but real-life politics deals with this kind of decision-making every day; 'imposing the majority's will' is the very stuff democratic politics is made of. Gandhi, of all people, was hardly in the position to treat 'imposing his will' as a moral problem: his own role in Indian politics largely consisted in 'imposing his will', often not on minorities, but on democratic majorities, overruling the will of the people with that of his own 'inner voice'.

## GANDHI'S FRIENDSHIP WITH SUHRAWARDY

The Muslim League mounted pressure for Partition by means of street violence, so as to impress upon everyone the impossibility of governing India against the will of the Muslims, and also to polarize the situation and provoke Hindu retaliation against random Muslims so as to influence wavering and recalcitrant Muslims about the absolute necessity of a separate Muslim state. The greatest instance of this premeditated communal violence was the Direct Action Day (16 August 1946) in Calcutta, commonly known by its characterization in a Statesman headline: 'the Great Calcutta Killing', with 6,000 mortal victims.

Bengal Chief Minister H.S. Suhrawardy was not only politically responsible for the remarkable police inaction, but as a Muslim League leader, he had also organized the agitation. Few things had angered Godse and his fellow conspirators as much as Gandhi's friendship with Suhrawardy:

'70 (o). Suhrawardy Patronised. (...) On the 16th of August 1946 (...) there broke out in Calcutta an open massacre of the Hindus which continued for three days unchecked. (...) At the time, it was considered that the Government which could permit such outrages on its citizens must be thrown out (...). Gandhiji, however, went to Calcutta and contracted a strange friendship with the author of these massacres; in fact he intervened on behalf of Suhrawardy and the Muslim League [and] publicly described Suhrawardy as a martyr.'[26]

Godse and many Hindutva authors since have been indignated at Gandhi's describing Suhrawardy as a shaheed, an Islamic martyr. This may be based on a misunderstanding: Shaheed just happened to be the man's second given name. All the same, Gandhi's friendship with Suhrawardy remains yet another case of a middle-class intellectual infatuated with an unscrupled muscle-man.

Young parents are told that they should teach their children good behaviour by rewarding it, and that they unwittingly teach wrong behaviour if they pay more attention to ill-behaved children in order to appease their tantrums. Gandhi was one such bad parent who rewarded the ill-behaved and punished the well-behaved. He was harsh on the polemical but non-violent Swami Shraddhananda, and kind to the Swami's murderer, about whom he stated in public: 'Abdul Rashid is my brother.' In settling his succession, he spurned his loyal and obedient friend Sardar Patel, and favoured the conceited and un-Gandhian Anglo-secularist Jawaharlal Nehru. His dealings with Suhrawardy were also read by the Muslim agitators as a sign of deference to Muslim aggression, an encouragement to continue on the chosen path of provocation and violence.

## HINDU AND MUSLIM PRINCES

Before Independence, large parts of India were not under direct British administration but were ruled by native princes. Some were models of progress and enlightened governance, e.g., Mysore, while others were feudal backwaters exploited by useless decadent royalty. But the operative division among the princes in the present context is of course between Hindu rulers such as the Maharaja of Kashmir (who had to deal with a popular Muslim Opposition leader, Sheikh Abdullah) and Muslim rulers such as the Nizam of Hyderabad (who had to deal with an oppositional Hindu movement). Godse compares Gandhi's hostile attitude vis-à-vis several Hindu princes with his neutrality vis-à-vis Muslim princes:

'70 (p). Attitude towards Hindu and Muslim Princes. Gandhiji's followers successfully humiliated the Jaipur, Bhavnagar and Rajkot states. They enthusiastically supported even a rebellion in Kashmir State against the Hindu prince. This attitude strangely contrasts with what Gandhiji did about the affairs in Muslim States. (...) In a recent casual Hindu-Muslim clash in Gwalior, because the Mussalmans suffered some casualties, Gandhiji came down upon the Maharaja with a vitriolic attack wholly undeserved.'[27]

70 (v). Ill Advice to Kashmir Maharaja. About Kashmir, Gandhiji again and again declared that Sheikh Abdullah should be entrusted the charge of the state and that the Maharaja of Kashmir should retire to Benares for no other reason than that the Muslims formed the bulk of the Kashmir population. This also stands out in contrast with his attitude on Hyderabad where although the bulk of the population is Hindu, Gandhiji never called upon the Nizam to retire to Mecca.'[28]

This hardly needs any comment, except that in a way, it confirms Gandhi's identification with the Hindu side. Combined with his penchant for self-flagellation, this made him treat the Hindus much harsher than the Muslims.

## INTERMEDIATE STEPS TOWARDS PARTITION

Meanwhile, around Gandhi, other Congress leaders were making their own tryst with destiny and with Pakistan, but not without the Mahatma's blessings:

'70 (q). Gandhiji on Fast to Capacity. In 1943, while Gandhiji was on fast to capacity (...) Mr. C. Rajagopalachari smuggled himself into Gandhiji's room and hatched a plot of conceding Pakistan, which Gandhiji allowed him to negotiate with Jinnah. Gandhiji later on discussed this matter with Mr. Jinnah in the latter part of 1944 and offered Mr. Jinnah virtually what is now called Pakistan. (...)

'70 (r). Desai-Liaqat Agreement. In 1945 came the notorious Desai-Liaqat Agreement. (...) Under that agreement, the late Bhulabhai Desai, the then leader of the Congress Party in the Central Legislative Assembly at Delhi, entered into an agreement with Mr. Liaqat Ali Khan, the League leader in the Assembly, jointly to demand a Conference from the British Government for the solution of the stalemate in Indian politics (...) Mr. Desai offered equal representation to the Muslims with Congress at the said Conference (...) The proposal had, it was then revealed, the blessings of the Mahatma and was in fact made with his previous knowledge and consent. With the full agreement of the Congress Party, 25% of the people of India were treated as if they were 50% and the 75% were brought down to the level of 50%.'[29]

It was neither the first nor the last time that Gandhi and the Congress accepted over-representation of the Muslim community or of the Muslim League. As we have seen, even a division of 100 per cent Muslim and 0 per cent Hindus in the projected first Cabinet of free and undivided India had been considered by Gandhi and Azad. The Congress always took Hindus for granted, and Hindus inside the Congress failed to put up a protest commensurate with the injustice being perpetrated. This time, Gandhi pretended ignorance of the Desai-Liaqat Agreement when Nehru (who was already positioning himself for becoming free India's first Prime Minister and therefore opposed scenarios favouring Jinnah) denounced it after being released from jail later in 1945.

## THE CABINET MISSION PLAN

Next, the Cabinet Mission Plan conceded the Muslim demands in a different way: provincial autonomy would be very large (excluding only Defence, Foreign Affairs and Communications) and include the right to form groups, so that Muslim-majority provinces could form a de facto Pakistan within India.[30] The League accepted the plan; the Congress first rejected, but later accepted it. Godse comments:

'70 (s). Cabinet Mission Plan. Early in the year 1946, the so-called Cabinet Mission arrived in India. (...) while firmly championing unity, the Mission introduced Pakistan through the back-door. (...) The Congress Party was so utterly exhausted by the failure of 'Quit India' that after some smoke-screen about its unflinching nationalism, it virtually submitted to Pakistan by accepting the Mission's proposals.'[31]

For a provisional assessment of Godse's argument up to this point in his chronological survey, we may refer to B.R. Nanda, an avowed admirer of Gandhi, who admits in *Gandhi and His Critics* that 'from the acceptance of separate electorates in the Lucknow Pact in 1916 to the acquiescence in the Communal Award in 1933, and finally to the Cabinet Mission Plan in 1946, it was a continual retreat in the face of Muslim pressure.'

Though Nanda keeps supporting Gandhi on this point, he also insists that some of the Hindu leaders in the Congress that opposed this trail of concessions tended to be niggardly, yielding to Muslim demands step by step.

Incidentally, the Cabinet Mission Plan illustrates the British desire to keep India united. The plan was defensible as a way of preventing the full secession of the Muslim-majority provinces from the rest of the subcontinent. To a large extent, the provinces would be self-governing, but not to the extent of allowing Muslim majorities there to ride roughshod over the minorities. And very importantly from the British angle, India's economic networks would remain intact, e.g., the jute industry of which a part was located in Muslim-majority East Bengal and a part in Hindu-majority West Bengal. In the event, it was Jawaharlal Nehru who caused the failure of this last-ditch attempt at keeping India substantially united. Apart from his personal ambitions, his socialist convictions made him prefer a strongly centralized state. By declaring that the plan was only tentative and that everything remained possible, including an eventual choice for a state structure with far less provincial autonomy, he made Jinnah turn away from the whole negotiating process in disgust. From that point onwards, Jinnah's every move, even when in seeming co-operation with the Congress, was aimed at realizing the Partition.

## GANDHI AND THE PARTITION

In September 1946, a provisional government led by Jawaharlal Nehru was installed at the Centre. The League refused to join it because the Congress refused to concede to it a monopoly of Muslim posts in the Cabinet. But a few months later, the League decided to join the government in order to wreck it from within. The League used its position to thwart government work and drive the Congress leadership to desperation, increasing the pressure on it to concede Partition. In June 1947, the Congress and Gandhi formally accepted the Partition plan:

‘70 (t). Congress Surrenders to Jinnah. By the following year, the Congress Party abjectly surrendered to Mr. Jinnah at the point of bayonet and accepted Pakistan. (...) The thread running throughout this narrative is the increasing infatuation which Gandhiji developed for the Muslims. He uttered not one word of sympathy or comfort for millions of displaced Hindus; he had only one eye for humanity and that was the Muslim humanity. (...) I was shocked by all these manifestations of Gandhian saintliness.

'70 (u). Ambiguous Statement about Pakistan. In one of his articles, Gandhiji while nominally ostensibly opposed to Pakistan, openly declared that if the Muslims wanted Pakistan at any cost, there was nothing to prevent them from achieving it.'[32]

Here, reference is apparently to one of the statements from the April 1940 issue of the *Harijan*, already quoted, most notably that the Muslims must have the right of self-determination that the rest of India had, that India was a joint family and any member might claim a division. After Gandhi conceded the principle, nothing could stop its implementation:

'70 (w). Mountbatten Vivisects India. (...) All the time from the 2 September 1946, the so-called national government (...) was in office, but the Muslim League members who were 50% of the Congress did everything in their power to make the working of a Coalition Government impossible. (...) the more they became disloyal and treasonable to the Government of which they formed a part, the greater was Gandhiji's infatuation for them. Lord Wavell had to resign as he could not bring about a settlement. He had some conscience which prevented him from supporting the partition of India. He had openly declared it to be unnecessary and undesirable.'[33]

In the make-believe world of Nehruvian secularism, it is an unquestioned dogma (nowadays also mouthed by Hindu nationalists) that Partition was forced upon the unwilling Hindu-Muslim brothers by the scheming British colonialists. But this is completely untrue. Viceroys Lord Linlithgow and Lord Wavell had made it quite clear to the Muslim League that they would never countenance partitioning the Indian empire which their forebears had built up so skilfully. India was a coherent unit, historically but also in the actual practice of the modern economy which had developed under British rule (as symbolized by its well-rounded railway system); it would only be destructive to sever certain parts from that organic whole.

Partition was an Indian Muslim initiative, and if certain British politicians ultimately approved of Partition, it was only after listening to the Muslim League's siren song for years, or more often, after being impressed with the violence the League was able to generate, concluding that Partition would be the lesser evil. One such lesser-evil theorist was the next and final Viceroy, who presided over the implementation of the Partition plan, though in practice he was quite ineffective, willingly or unwillingly, in stemming the tide of violence set in motion by the League:

'But his retirement was followed by the appointment of Lord Mountbatten. (...) Rivers of blood flowed under his very nose. (...) This is what Gandhiji had achieved after thirty years of undisputed dictatorship (...) Hindu-Muslim unity bubble was finally burst and a theocratic and communal state dissociated from everything that smacked of united India was established with the consent of Nehru and his crowd, and they have called it "Freedom won by them at sacrifice"—whose sacrifice?'[34]

Concerning Gandhi's role in this episode, less can be said about what he did than about what he failed to do. Even his followers like B.R. Nanda, in *Gandhi and His Critics*, admits regarding Gandhi's 'most potent weapon', that he used it against those who admired and loved him, but never against his opponents. For instance, he did not use this weapon in order to compel the Muslim League to give up its demand for Pakistan. Indeed, breaking a solemn promise, he failed to stake his life for the sake of India's unity.

## NOTES

1. Nathuram Godse: *Why I Assassinated Gandhi*, p. 50.
2. ibid, pp. 50–51.

3. ibid, pp 51–52.
4. ibid, pp. 52–53.
5. *The Collected Works of Mahatma Gandhi*, vol. 24 (Ahmedabad 1967), p. 145, also quoted by J.T.F. Jordens: *Swami Shraddhananda*, p. 145.
6. Gandhi writing in Young India, 29 May 1924 and 26 June 1924, cited in J.T.F. Jordens: *Swami Shraddhananda*, p. 148.
7. *Collected Works of M.K. Gandhi*, vol. 24, p. 146, also quoted by J.T.F. Jordens: *Swami Shraddhananda*, p. 148.
8. Nathuram Godse: *Why I Assassinated Gandhi*, pp. 53–54.
9. Related in J.T.F. Jordens: *Swami Shraddhananda*, p. 156.
10. Mohammed himself had several poets who had criticized and satirized him, stabbed to death by assassins. On chasing the Jews from Khaybar, he first singled out some well-known critics for punishment. On entering Mecca, which surrendered on condition that no one who refrained from armed resistance would be troubled, he rounded up a number of well-known critics for execution. This authoritative example set by Mohammed himself explains the Salman Rushdie affair and related assassinations and murder attempts, as shown in S.R. Goel, ed., *Freedom of Expression: Secular Theocracy Versus Liberal Democracy*. (KE)
11. Nathuram Godse: *Why I Assassinated Gandhi*, p. 55.
12. ibid, pp. 55–56.
13. ibid, pp 56–57.
14. ibid, pp. 58–59.
15. Quoted in R.C. Majumdar: *Struggle for Freedom*, p. 624.
16. Nathuram Godse: *Why I Assassinated Gandhi*, pp. 61–62.
17. *Harijan*, 18 April 1942.
18. Nathuram Godse: *Why I Assassinated Gandhi*, pp. 62–63.
19. Quoted in R.C. Majumdar: *Struggle for Freedom*, pp. 695–696. This would have realized Maulana Azad's objective of turning the whole of India into a Muslim-dominated state: he cleverly used the Muslim League's demands in order to pressurize Gandhi into ever larger concessions to Muslim interests.
20. Nathuram Godse: *Why I Assassinated Gandhi*, pp. 63–64.
21. ibid, p. 65.
22. ibid, pp. 65–66.

23. ibid, pp. 5–76.
24. The story the Congress flag committee (of which Jawaharlal Nehru and Maulana Azad were members) is told by K.R. Malkani in his *The Politics of Ayodhya and Hindu-Muslim Relations*. The tricolour flag was initially rejected as communal, with the Sikhs being dissatisfied that they were not represented on it with a colour of their own, while solid saffron with a blue Charkha (spinning wheel, later replaced with the chakra, the wheel representing the pan-Indian reign of the chakravarti or 'wheel-turner') was welcomed as non-communal.
25. Nathuram Godse: *Why I Assassinated Gandhi*, p. 5.
26. ibid.
27. ibid.
28. ibid.
29. ibid.
30. See (especially for point 15 of the Plan, defining the division of powers) R.C. Majumdar: *Struggle for Freedom*, p. 736.
31. Nathuram Godse: *Why I Assassinated Gandhi*, pp. 71–72.
32. ibid, pp. 2–73.
33. Nathuram Godse: *Why I Assassinated Gandhi*, p. 3; emphasis added.
34. ibid, emphasis added.

5

# Godse's Verdict on Gandhi

## GANDHI'S CHARACTER

Godse continues his analysis by zooming in even more closely on Gandhi's role and responsibility in the political equation which led to the Partition. His intention is to trace Gandhi's fateful mistakes one by one, and to show how they inexorably prepared the ground for Partition. At the same time, he tries to show how Gandhi's mistakes conformed to a pattern that betrayed a peculiar type of personality:

'68. This section summarises the background of the agony of India's Partition and the tragedy of Gandhiji's assassination. Neither the one nor the other gives me any pleasure to record or to remember, but the Indian people and the world at large ought to know the history of the last thirty years during which India has been torn into pieces by the Imperialist policy of the British and under a mistaken policy of communal unity.

'(...) virtually the non-Muslim minority in Western Pakistan have been liquidated either by the most brutal murders or by a forced tragic removal from their moorings of centuries; the same process is furiously at work in Eastern Pakistan. One hundred and ten millions of people have become torn from their homes, of which not less than four millions are Muslims, and when I found that even after such terrible results, Gandhiji continued to pursue the same policy of appeasement, my blood boiled, and I could not tolerate him any longer. (...)'[1]

By 'one hundred and ten millions' is probably meant 'one hundred and ten lakhs', i.e., eleven million, a reasonable estimate of the number of persons displaced by the Partition. By any standard, this wave of refugees amounted to a terrible failure of Gandhi's policies, yet the Mahatma is not known to have criticized his own policy decisions in terms of their role in the escalation towards Partition.

'69. The accumulating provocation of 32 years culminating in his last pro-Muslim fast goaded me to the conclusion that the existence of Gandhiji should be brought to an end immediately. On coming back to India [from South Africa], he developed a subjective mentality under which he alone was to be the final judge of what was right and wrong. If the country wanted his leadership it had to accept his infallibility; if it did not, he would stand aloof from the Congress and carry on in his own way. Against such an attitude there can be no half way house; either the Congress had to surrender its will to his and had to be content with playing the second fiddle to all his eccentricity, whimsicality, metaphysics and primitive vision, or it had to carry on without him.'[2]

By Gandhiji's 'metaphysics' and 'primitive vision', Godse means the seemingly irrational concepts like 'soul force' and the 'inner voice', which Gandhiji routinely invoked, and which took the place of cool strategy. 'Eccentricity' refers to Gandhiji's gimmicks, such as his half-naked dressing habits, which were all the more bizarre given that Gandhiji, unlike most Indians, had worn cumbersome Western suits, ill-adapted to the Indian or African climate, for decades.[3] Winston Churchill, a man of the world who was comfortable with ethnic peculiarities, considered the 'half-naked faqir' Gandhi as outlandish even for an Indian.

'Whimsicality' seems to refer to the lack of strategic consistency in his policies, which drifted from one extreme to another, e.g., from abject collaboration with the British to head-on confrontations; from letting intra-Congress democracy take its own decisions (e.g., the election of Subhas Bose as Congress president) to challenging those very decisions by means of ostentatious fasts; from boycotting the 1931 census count to accepting power divisions based on the resulting census figures; from promising to stake his own life for the prevention of Partition to meekly accepting the Partition on the plea that 'the people' had chosen it. A glaring example of Gandhi's whimsical policy shifts is his changing the course of the Civil Disobedience Movement of 1930–31. The agreed aim of this mass agitation was complete independence, nothing less. Yet Gandhi threw the movement into disarray by suddenly formulating far more modest demands. These were mostly conceded and included in an entirely individual pact between himself and Viceroy Lord Irwin (March 1931): promise of future parleys on constitutional reform, release of prisoners, restoring confiscated property.

R.C. Majumdar, the leading historian of the freedom movement, reports in the *Struggle for Freedom* that the Pact had caused a great disappointment to many. Subhas Chandra Bose had summed up the main points of opposition which received general approval at the Youth Congress. Later, Gandhi used a quintessentially Gandhian explanation in a statement that apportioned the victory to both parties. Majumdar also insists that when Jawaharlal Nehru saw the terms of the Pact, he was disappointed. He questioned if it was for this pact that the people of India had behaved so gallantly for a year and if all their brave words and deeds would end in this manner. He said that in his heart he felt a great emptiness as though something precious had gone, almost beyond recall.

Majumdar nonetheless credits Gandhi with one undeniable long-term gain, viz. the Viceroy's readiness to treat Congress as an equal negotiation partner for the first time. A few weeks later, Congress at its Karachi session also ended up approving the step which Gandhi had unilaterally taken, though 'the resolution of the Congress endorsing the Pact is a curious example of self-delusion and an attempt to mislead the people' (obscuring the Pact's continued acceptance of British control over vital matters like defence, foreign affairs and finance).[4] Gandhi had to force a reluctant Nehru to sponsor the resolution; the self-delusion and attempt to mislead were Gandhi's own input. The Congress delegates' ultimate submission to Gandhi's will cannot alter the fact that Gandhi had undemocratically overruled the will of Congress, whimsically imposing an unexpected new direction on the freedom movement.

## OTHER VOICES ON GANDHI'S CHARACTER

Shocking as some of Godse's qualifiers may sound; Godse was not the only one to describe Gandhi as something of a mental case. During Gandhi's initial years as Congress leader, prominent spokesmen of the Moderate wing of the nationalist movement called him 'fanciful' (V.S. Srinivasa Sastri) and 'a madman, mad and arrogant' (Dinshaw E. Wacha), while Annie Besant characterized Gandhi's 1920 mass agitation (Non-Cooperation, co-opted into the Khilafat Movement) as 'a channel of hatred'.[5] Though Majumdar describes Gandhi's dealings with the Muslim League in the 1940s in more restrained language, he still believes that it was difficult to follow the rather contradictory trends of his thought.

Another historian opines: 'with Lenin he shared a quasi-religious approach to politics, though in sheer crankiness he had much more in common with Hitler (...) One of his favourite books was Constipation and Our Civilization, which he constantly reread. (...) His eccentricities appealed to a nation which venerates sacral oddity. But his teachings had no relevance to India's problems. (...) His food policy would have led to mass starvation. In fact

Gandhi's own ashram (...) had to be heavily subsidized by three merchant princes.'And Gandhi was expensive in human life as well as money. The events of 1920–21 indicated that though he could bring a mass-movement into existence, he could not control it. Yet he continued to play the sorcerer's apprentice, while the casualty bill mounted into hundreds, then thousands, then tens of thousands, and the risks of a gigantic sectarian and racial explosion accumulated. This blindness to the law of probability in a bitterly divided sub-continent made nonsense of Gandhi's professions that he would not take life in any circumstances.'[6]

This is how the French musician and ideologist Alain Daniélou, a confidant of the traditionalist leader Swami Karpatri, characterizes Gandhi: 'an enigmatic character, sly and acetic, ambitious and devout, one of those gurus who exert an incredible magnetism on the crowds and often lead them to disaster (...) a sentimental religiosity coupled with a lack of scruples (...) During his lifetime, no one could stop his fateful influence. It will take a long time before the victims of his charisma, in India as well as in the West, dare to make an account of his actions.' By virtue of his Bania (merchant) caste background, Gandhi's religion consisted in 'extreme puritanism, the strictest vegetarianism, the total absence of metaphysical concerns and philosophical culture, and, conversely, the grossest religious sentimentalism' in which 'icy puritanism masks dishonesty.'[7]

In his autobiography, Daniélou is even more outspoken. He claims that he found Gandhi to be truly repulsive and hence avoided contact with him and his entourage as much as possible. He describes Gandhi as a thin little man who was puritan and full of complexes. He seemed the kind of a revolutionary who would create an idealism in order to attract crowds, but then would later identify this ideal with their own persons and with their secret desire for absolute power. He repeats the old taunt that it takes a lot of money to afford Gandhi, his ascetic lifestyle (with his third-class train wagon specially accommodated for him), and claims to know that even Rabindranath Tagore 'detested the ambitious and wrong-headed Gandhi' as 'a very dangerous man'.[8]

The sharpest criticism of Gandhi nowadays comes from the so-called Dalit movement, actually only a fringe of genuine Dalit (i.e., Scheduled Caste) politics, along with its allies in Islamist and American Black Muslim circles. They highlight lesser-known facts, such as Gandhi's sharing the white view of blacks in South Africa—the Mahatma conceived the betterment of the position of the Indians in Natal as essentially lifting them up from equality with the blacks (whom he deemed lustful and lazy) to equality with the whites, without questioning the inequality of black and white.[9]

A very knowledgeable critic of the Mahatma is Jodhpur University philosopher M.M. Kothari, whose book *Critique of Gandhi* contains a sober survey of the claims made for Gandhi and matching them against the record. This includes a look into some of the morbid aspects of the Great Soul's personal behaviour, such as his 'testing his chastity' by sleeping with under-age girls. There is no point in duplicating Prof. Kothari's many insightful observations here, except for his general verdict on Gandhi's main claim to fame, his mixing of saintly asceticism with a political struggle: 'Hinduism in its most perverted forms was preached and practised by Gandhi. He tried to obliterate the distinction between the life of a monk and the life of a householder by making ordinary people behave like monks. He wanted India to have a monkish economy, a monkish politics, a monkish foreign policy and a monkish defence policy. Consequently, under the leadership of Gandhi, India acquired a great heart but lost its head.'[10]

It is entirely pertinent that Gandhi mixed the norms of a monk's life into his conception of the householder's or the politician's life. A telling example, which he himself also put into practice, was that he wanted married couples to live as if they were unmarried, i.e., to abstain from sex, as counseled by Saint Paul to his Christian flock living in expectation of Jesus' impending Second Coming, but entirely contrary to Hindu tradition. The genius of Hinduism is, among other things, that it recognizes difference, starting with different norms for different stations in life or different occupational groups, and of course, including the difference between a monk and a layman. The abstinence which is a virtue in a monk is not a virtue at all in a husband.

The economy of a kingdom may well be conducted according to different principles than the economy of a monastery; just as a twentieth century economy had every right to differ from a medieval one with its spinning-wheels. The Buddha may have stood against the robber and killer Angulimala with nothing but his soul-force, but he never asked the kings he encountered on their way to battlefields to replace their armies with mere soul-force. From the viewpoint of Hindu tradition as well as that of common sense, it was dangerous and nonsensical to transplant the ascetic's taste for self-mortification to the political field of Indian-British or of Hindu-Muslim relations, where Gandhi always wanted people to sacrifice their lives. Gandhi's mixing of 'saintly' posturing into the hard business of politics is precisely what evoked admiration in many; but it was one of his most fundamental mistakes. This was not so much 'Hinduism at its most perverted', for unlike most of Gandhi's other vices (and virtues), this one was actually profoundly un-Hindu.

## GANDHI AND THE LEADER PRINCIPLE

Godse was particularly piqued at Gandhiji's practice of what amounted to the Leader Principle, to use the term popularized by the contemporaneous vogue of Fascism:

'69 (continued). He alone was the judge of everyone and everything; he was the master brain guiding the civil disobedience movement; nobody else knew the technique of that movement; he alone knew when to begin it and when to withdraw it. The movement may succeed or fail; it may bring untold disasters and political reverses but that could make no difference to the Mahatma's infallibility. 'A Satyagrahi can never fail' was his formula for declaring his own infallibility and nobody except himself knew who a Satyagrahi was. Thus Gandhiji became the judge and the counsel in his own case. These childish inanities and obstinacies coupled with a most severe austerity of life, ceaseless work and lofty character made Gandhiji formidable and irresistible. Many people thought his politics were irrational but they had either to withdraw from the Congress or to place their intelligence at his feet to do what he liked with it. In a position of such absolute irresponsibility, Gandhiji was guilty of blunder after blunder, failure after failure and disaster after disaster. No one single political victory can be claimed to his credit during 33 years of his political predominance. (...)'[11]

Here again, Godse exaggerates. Gandhi must be given credit for some victories on other battlefields, as with his Salt March breaking the British monopoly on the salt trade, or with his controversial fast forcing Dr Ambedkar to sign the Poona Pact (preventing the Scheduled Castes from being classified as a community separate from the general Hindu category, September 1932). He is often credited with victory on the major battlefield, viz. achieving independence by non-violent means. The latter widespread assumption must be taken with a pinch of salt, for other factors were at least as decisive, e.g., the American pressure on Britain to decolonize, the exhaustion of the colonial powers by World War II, the Navy mutiny of February 1946 (small by itself but an indication that the British could no longer trust their Indian troops), et al.

Nevertheless, it cannot be denied that the Congress movement under Gandhi's leadership had contributed substantially to the achievement of freedom. On two central points, however, Gandhi met with total failure: India paid for its independence with Partition, and this process was the very opposite of non-violent.

On earlier occasions too, Gandhi's whimsicality brought about serious political reverses. When he halted the Non-Cooperation movement after the killings of Chauri Chaura, he gave a mighty blow to the political aim of the movement, viz. home rule, and also caused more, rather than less violence to take place. Even Congress leaders strongly committed to non-violence believed it was wrong to halt such a large movement aimed at such a momentous political goal for the sins of a few activists in one locality. Those with foresight could also tell that even purely from the viewpoint of non-violence, Gandhi's decision was wrong, as the general frustration among the activists, and especially among the Muslims, would lead to far more violence. By contrast, if the movement had stayed on course, Gandhi could have used the shock of Chauri Chaura to discipline his followers into a more scrupulous adherence to non-violence. But no better counsel could prevail over Gandhi's autocratic charisma.

## DID GANDHI WIN INDIA'S INDEPENDENCE?

The remainder of Godse's statement is mostly a rewording of the same argument, hammering especially at Gandhi's irrationality and at the irresponsibility of his non-violence. The first point to follow, however, is an attempt to set the record straight on the respective merits of different groups of people in the Indian freedom struggle. The common notion that Gandhiji achieved independence by his non-violent campaigns is judged as follows:

'71. (...) there was never a more stupendous fiction fostered by the cunning and believed by the credulous in this country for over a thousand years. Far from attaining freedom under his leadership, Gandhiji has left India torn and bleeding from a thousand wounds.'[12]

'85. (...) I am therefore surprised when claims are made over and over again that the winning of freedom was due to Gandhiji. My own view is that constant pandering to the Muslim League was not the way to winning freedom. It only created a Frankenstein

(...) permanently stationing a hostile, censorious, unfriendly and aggressive neighbour on what was once Indian territory. About the winning of Swaraj or freedom, I maintain that the Mahatma's contribution was negligible. But I am prepared to give him a place as a sincere patriot.'[13]

Godse then describes the freedom struggle against Muslim rule and against the British encroachment under the Marathas and Sikhs, the 'War of Independence' of 1857 (that is what Savarkar called the Mutiny), and the violent acts of the revolutionary nationalists in the first decades of the twentieth century. According to Godse, this armed struggle had definitely contributed to India's independence from Britain, as we shall see in the subsequent paragraphs.

## GANDHI VERSUS BOSE

One leader who took to armed struggle when the opportunity presented itself was Congress leftist, Subhas Chandra Bose:

'85 (continued). In my opinion, S.C. Bose is the supreme hero and martyr of modern India (...) advocating all honourable means, including the use of force when necessary, for the liberation of India. Gandhiji and his crowd of self-seekers tried to destroy him.'[14]

This is Godse's version of the intra-Congress conflict between Gandhi and Bose after the latter's election as Congress President:

'78. (...) In actual practice, however, Bose never toed the line that Gandhiji wanted during his term of office. And yet, Subhas was so popular in the country that against the declared wishes of Gandhiji in favour of Dr. Pattabhi Sitaramayya, he was elected president of the Congress for a second time with a substantial majority even from the Andhra Desha, the province of Dr. Pattabhi himself. This upset Gandhiji beyond endurance and he expressed his anger in the Mahatmic manner full of concentrated venom by stating that the success of Subhas was his own defeat and not that of Dr. Pattabhi. (...) Out of sheer cussedness, he absented himself from the Tripura Congress session, staged a rival show at Rajkot by a wholly mischievous fast, and [it was] not until Subhas was overthrown from the Congress gaddi that the venom of Gandhiji became completely gutted.'[15]

Godse's Red Fort trial had been preceded by another Red Fort trial, viz. that of three of Bose's lieutenants in the Azad Hind Fauz ('Free India Army') or Indian National Army (INA), which Bose had formed under Japanese tutelage from among British-Indian Army prisoners in Singapore in 1943. The British had refrained from passing the normal harsh sentence for desertion and treason on them when they saw the immense popularity which the INA enjoyed, basking in Bose's reflected glory (even Jawaharlal Nehru, who had opposed Bose tooth and nail, offered to serve as their lawyer). The Naval Mutiny of 1946 was a symptom that Bose's defiance and willingness to take up arms against the British had penetrated the armed forces. The then Prime Minister Clement Attlee was later to declare that this ominous development was decisive in Britain's decision to decolonize India.

In fairness to Gandhi, it must be said that there were other objections to Subhas Bose besides his political differences with Gandhi. K.M. Munshi, who was Home Minister in the Government of Bombay Province at that time, had conveyed a message to Gandhi from the Governor of Bombay that, according to intelligence reports, Bose was on a secret visit to Bombay and had contacted the German Consul.[16] In view of Bose's well-known admiration for Fascist Italy and Nazi Germany, along with the Soviet Union, Gandhi was right in suspecting Bose of conspiring with a third party, which to British and world opinion would turn the Congress into a stooge of Hitler, and thus damage the freedom movement. Nowhere does Gandhi testify that he opposed Bose for this very reason, but it would not have been in the interest of the Congress to reveal such a reason, so the causal connection between the secret service reports and Gandhi's intense opposition to Bose remained a secret at that time. There was no personal dislike on either side; the opposition was purely ideological. Gandhi admired Bose for his courage and spirit of sacrifice. Conversely, Bose's Axis-collaborationist Azad Hind Radio was the first to name Gandhi as the 'Father of the Nation'.

## CREDIT TO THE REVOLUTIONARIES

'86. The real cause of the British leaving this country is threefold and it does not include the Gandhian method. The aforesaid triple forces are:

'86 (i). The movements of the Indian Revolutionaries right from 1857 to 1932, i.e., up to the death of Chandra Shekhar Azad at Allahabad; then next, the movement of revolutionary character, not that of Gandhian type, in the countrywide rebellion of 1942; and an armed revolt put up by Subhas Chandra Bose, the result of which was a spread of the revolutionary mentality in the Military Forces of India; are the real factors that have shattered the very foundations of the British rule in India. And all these effective efforts to freedom were opposed by Gandhiji. (...)'[17]

'77. (...) And the more the Mahatma condemned the use of force in the country's battle for freedom, the more popular it became. This fact was amply demonstrated at the Karachi session of the Congress in March 1931: in the teeth of Gandhiji's opposition, a resolution was passed in the open session admiring the courage and the spirit of sacrifice of Bhagat Singh when he threw the bomb in the Legislative Assembly in 1929. (...) To sum up, the share of revolutionary youth in the fight for Indian Freedom is by no means negligible and those who talk of India's freedom having been secured by Gandhiji are not only ungrateful but are trying to write false history.'[18]

In Godse's view, Congress reaped where the revolutionaries had sown. It may reasonably be argued that the British concessions to the Congress leadership were motivated, at least in part, by the British fear of an escalation of the revolutionary violence if the non-violent alternative was not rewarded with some successes (just as the concessions made by Akbar and other lenient Muslim rulers to the Hindus had largely been necessitated by Hindu armed resistance). Then again, the record of the revolutionary tendency was far from impressive, and the British managed to put it down quite effectively. Some of its veterans, like Sri Aurobindo, renounced it for both moral and strategic reasons. Its share in bringing about freedom was greater than Gandhians admit, but far smaller than Godse asserted.

## CREDIT TO THE MODERATES

At the other end of the political spectrum within the freedom movement was a less spectacular tendency which had contributed to the achievement of independence: the Moderates. Godse lauds their contribution to Britain's abdication, and pits them against Gandhi:

'86 (ii). So also a good deal of credit must be given to those who, imbibed with the spirit of patriotism, fought with the Britishers strictly on constitutional lines on the Assembly floors and made a notable progress in Indian politics. The view of this section was to take a maximum advantage of whatever we have obtained and to fight further on. This section was generally represented by late Lokmanya Tilak, Mr. N.C. Kelkar, Mr. C.R. Das, Mr. Vithalbhai Patel brother of Hon'ble Sardar Patel, Pandit Malaviya, Bhai Parmanand, and during last ten years by prominent Hindu Sabha leaders. But this school of men of sacrifices and intelligence was also ridiculed by Gandhiji himself and his followers by calling them as job hunters or power seekers, although they often resorted to the same methods.'[19]

Godse alleges that in his differences with the Moderates and their strictly constitutional methods, Gandhi was led by contempt for democracy and parliamentary politics:

'73. Even the constitutional movements carried on by the Moderates in the Congress registered some progress towards Freedom. In 1892, the British Government was obliged to extend the then Legislative Councils. This was followed up by the Morley-Minto Reforms in 1909 when for the first time the elected representatives of the people secured the right to participate in the work of the Legislatures both by their voice and by their votes. Twelve years later (...) the Montagu-Chelmsford Reforms conceded partial Provincial Autonomy and also increased the number of elected members (...) and in 1935 came the complete Provincial Autonomy and substantial Central responsibility which covered every subject except foreign policy, army and to some extent finance. Gandhiji had no love for parliamentary bodies. He called them prostitutes and always urged their boycott. (...) The Act of 1935 was of course seriously defective, more especially because of the numerous and vexatious safeguards granted to the British vested interests and the premium it placed on Communalism.

'74. (...) Even then it is reasonably certain that if the Act had not been boycotted under Gandhiji's leadership, India would have long since reached the status of a Dominion which we are now supposed to be enjoying after losing one-third of Indian territory.'[20]

A political leader often has to make a choice between settling for a moderate success and spurning it for a risky attempt at achieving either a bigger prize or nothing at all. By wanting complete independence at once, the Extremists hardened British hearts against any Indian aspirations and delayed the more limited concessions for which the Moderates worked. Godse's point is that these limited concessions were sometimes of crucial importance, and that the speed with which they were achieved determined whether an enemy force would get the time to build up and vitiate them. In practice, in 1935, the Muslim League was not very strong yet, and if the Congress had been more consistent and cooperative in its dealings with the British, it might have influenced the 1935 Government of India Act in such a way as to achieve a large autonomy for India, positioning it for independence, and to endow it with the political structure of a firm pan-subcontinental union, thus precluding a drift towards Partition at the time of complete independence. Briefly, India would have been as good as independent before the Partition demand could have built up momentum.

In defence of Gandhi, it must be said that in 1935, Partition was not very prominent on the agenda yet, so that no leader was calculating his moves in terms of avoiding it. Another defect in Godse's critique is that he neglects to analyze what was wrong with Gandhi's specific contribution, viz. mass agitation. For all we know, the effect of literally millions taking to the streets in protest against colonial rule (and the publicity given to it by American journalists) definitely helped in impressing upon the British the strength of India's refusal to remain a colony.

## THE INTERNATIONAL CONTEXT

Godse's third factor of India's independence, after the armed struggle and the constitutional methods, is the international context:

'86 (iii). There is also one more, but nonetheless important reason for the Britishers which made them part with power, and that is the advent of Labour Government and an overthrow of Mr. Churchill, superimposed by the frightful economic conditions and the financial bankruptcy to which the war had reduced Britain.'[21]

British historians have criticized Churchill for persisting with the war effort even when Hitler offered peace in 1940. Hitler wanted to incorporate parts of Central and Eastern Europe in his Reich and securely dominate the rest of continental Europe; but he had no designs whatsoever on the British Empire, which he admired as a model of Aryan domination over the inferior races of mankind. They imagine that the Empire might have continued in the event of an Anglo-German peace treaty. Instead, Churchill chose to persist with the war and got Britain bankrupt in a matter of months, making it totally dependent on American support. Though the Empire would only be dismantled in subsequent decades, Britain effectively ceased to be a superpower by 1941, losing the capability of maintaining its empire against American pressure and native self-assertion.

Of course, the situation in Britain was merely one of the international circumstances which contributed to the abdication from the Raj. Other factors include the drift towards decolonization caused by the creation of the League of Nations mandate territories (instead of colonies, thus theoretically already decolonizing the former German colonies and Ottoman provinces) after World War I; and most of all, the anti-colonial pressure exerted by the new post-1945 superpowers, the USA and the USSR. But Godse is right to point out very generally the importance of extra-Indian factors for which Gandhi could not take any credit.

Godse's skepticism regarding Gandhi's decisive role in achieving independence is supported by historians, e.g., Paul Johnson mentions American pressure and the 'collapse of the will to rule' in England as the decisive foreign factors. He explains: 'Gandhi was not a liberator but a political exotic, who could have flourished only in the protected environment of British liberalism. (...) All Gandhi's career demonstrates was the unrepressive nature of British rule and its willingness to abdicate.'[22]

'Unrepressive' is a highly relative judgement and might not be shared by the many ordinary freedom activists who fell under British bullets, but compared with contemporaneous levels of repression in the Soviet Union, the British Empire was very liberal and unrepressive indeed. Gandhi in person had to suffer little more than polite incarcerations under medically supervised conditions. His methods would have failed completely if used against a ruthless totalitarian regime.

## GANDHI'S IRRATIONALITY

Godse becomes sarcastic when speaking about the eccentric policies which made Gandhi's public image, e.g., his extolling the charkha (spinning-wheel) and his invocations of his 'inner voice'. There can be no doubt that in terms of production output, the spinning-wheel remained a marginal contributor.

'87. (...) The charkha after 34 years of the best efforts of Gandhiji had only led to the expansion of the machine-run textile industry by over 200 per cent. It is unable even now to clothe even one per cent of the nation.'[23]

More importantly, Godse contrasts Gandhi's exhibitionistic reliance on his 'inner voice' and on the satyagrahi's 'soul force' with Jinnah's rational and practical approach:

'89. (...) Mr. Jinnah had also openly demanded Pakistan. (...) He has deceived no one (...) His was the behaviour of an open enemy. (...)

'90. Gandhiji had seen Mr. Jinnah many a time and called upon him. Every time he had to plead with him as "brother Jinnah". He even offered him the premiership of the whole of India, but there was not a single occasion on which Mr. Jinnah had shown any inclination even to co-operate.

'91. Gandhiji's inner voice, his spiritual power and his doctrine of non-violence of which so much is made, all crumbled before Mr. Jinnah's iron will and proved to be powerless.

'92. Having known that with his spiritual power he could not influence Mr. Jinnah, Gandhiji should have either changed his policy or should have admitted his defeat and given way to others of different political views to deal with Mr. Jinnah and the Muslim League. But Gandhiji was not honest enough to do that. He could not forget his egoism or self, even for national interest. There was, thus, no scope left for practical politics while the great blunders— blunders as big as the Himalayas—were being committed.'[24]

These inconsistencies add to Godse's view of Gandhi as a charlatan:

'99. In Gandhiji's politics, there was no place for consistency of ideas and reasons. Truth was what Gandhiji only could define. His politics was supported by old, superstitious beliefs such as the power of the soul, the inner voice, the fast, the prayer, and the purity of mind.'[25]

'105. I thought it rather a very unfortunate thing that in the present 20th century such a hypocrite should have been regarded as the leader of the all-India politics. (...)'[26]

Here, Godse is on Savarkar's wavelength: a modern rationalist. This may come as a surprise to those who equate Hinduism with superstition and hence Hindu extremism with extreme superstition. For someone who is widely regarded as a Hindu extremist, Godse actually goes very far in dismissing fasts, prayers and even 'purity of mind' as so much nonsense. It would have been more typically Hindu to acknowledge the value of these practices, but keep them separate from public life.

As the late philosophy Professor Kedar Nath Mishra (Benares Hindu University) explained to me, the one decisive reason why people rooted in genuine Hinduism have never accepted Gandhi as a saint, was his exhibitionism with private matters, both pertaining to spiritual practices and to far more mundane facts of life. A sannyasi normally refuses to mention any information about his pre-sannyas life; Gandhi, by contrast, wrote an autobiography giving all the details, *The Story of My Experiments with Truth* (1927). And on a daily basis, he would inform his ashram inmates and the readership of his several periodicals about his own sins, lapses, bowel movements and struggles with his celibacy vows. On those occasions, he sounded like a Catholic Christian making his confession, but then before the public instead of in secret to a priest.

## GANDHI'S NON-VIOLENCE REVISITED

Godse then proceeds to demolish Gandhi's non-violence as extremely skewed to the disadvantage of the Hindus, using quotations from Gandhi's 1947 speeches, e.g.:

'93. (...) extracts given below from Gandhiji's post-prayer speeches:

'93 (a). (...) Hindus should never be angry against the Muslims even if the latter might make up their minds to undo even their existence. If they put all of us to the sword, we should court death bravely (...) We are destined to be born and die, then why need we feel gloomy over it? (...) (6th April 1947)

'93 (b). The few gentlemen from Rawalpindi who called upon me (...) asked me, what about those who still remain in Pakistan. I asked them why they all came here (to Delhi). Why they did not die there? I still hold on to the belief that one should stick to the place where we happen to live even if we are cruelly treated and even killed. Let us die if the people kill us, but we should die bravely with the name of God on our tongue. Even if our men are killed, why should we feel angry with anybody, you should realise that even if they are killed they have had a good and proper end. (...) (23rd September 1947)

'93 (c). (...) If those killed have died bravely they have not lost anything but earned something. (...) They should not be afraid of death. After all, the killers will be none other than our Muslim brothers. Will our brothers cease to be our brothers after change of their religion? (...)' (no date given for this last quote)[27]

The instances can be multiplied, e.g., when meeting Hindu refugees from West Punjab, Gandhiji told them to return to their homes, even if this meant certain death: 'If all the Punjabis were to die to the last man without killing, the Punjab will. become immortal. Offer yourselves as nonviolent, willing sacrifices.'[28]

The lightness with which Gandhi calls on people to give up

their lives is simply stunning. At the same time, it is shockingly un-Hindu. Hindu scriptures envisage a long life of one hundred years as the normal span for humans. Hindu prayers as well as blessings by Gods, sages and elders also entertain a long life of health and happiness. On the other hand, Hinduism approves of not only dying but also killing in defence of one's life and honour; it doesn't reject the use of force in facing the aggressor. However, the more important problem (not analyzed by Godse) with Gandhi's advocacy of dying rather than fighting back is its lack of political rationale: what is the use of non-violence if it simply means surrendering to the killer?

During Gandhi's non-violent agitations against the British, the whole idea was that political success could be achieved by non-violent means. The sacrifices made by the satyagrahi, like those made by a soldier in the war, were expected to help achieve a specific political goal. His first non-violent campaigns in South Africa undeniably helped the Indians there in securing certain civil rights. By 1947 however, Gandhi's conception of non-violence had drifted to the point of advocating surrender and death for the victim, and an open field of willing victims for the aggressor. There is no longer any reference to the achievement of some public good (the undoing of Partition?) in exchange for the death of Hindus at the hands of Muslims in Pakistan.

INEFFECTIVENESS OF NON-VIOLENCE

Another example of Gandhi's strange interpretation of non-violence is given in the following paragraph:

'134. The practice of non-violence according to Gandhiji is to endure or put up with the blows of the aggressor without showing any resistance either by weapon or by physical force. Gandhiji has, while describing his non-violence, given the example of a "tiger becoming a follower of the creed of non-violence after the cows allowed themselves to be killed and swallowed in such large numbers that the tiger ultimately got tired of killing them." It will be remembered that at Kanpur, Ganesh Shankar Vidyarthi fell victim to a murderous assault by the Muslims of the place on him. Gandhiji has often cited this submission to the Muslims' blows as an ideal example of embracing death for the creed of non-violence. I firmly believed and believe that the non-violence of the type described above will lead the nation to ruin (...)'[29]

Undeniably, Godse is on the same wavelength as the state leaders of every single country; no state runs its defence policy on Gandhian principles, and every state reserves the right to use force in self-defence. At the individual level too, almost every human being would claim the right to use force in self-defence, and the laws of most countries recognize this right. On the issue of non-violence, not Godse but Gandhi was the fanatic.

As for the tiger parable: a tiger who has eaten his fill does indeed 'get tired of killing', so he goes to sleep; but after waking up well-rested, with the beef inside well-digested, he starts killing all over again. Thousands of generations have passed, and still there is no tiger who trades in his meat for vegetables. The animal kingdom is a bad place to look for examples of the effectiveness of Gandhian non-violence. The only chance which non-violence and 'turning the other cheek' have against armed aggression is to stir the aggressor's conscience, that product of human civilization.

## INCONSISTENCY OF GANDHI'S NON-VIOLENCE

Apart from being extreme and irrational, Gandhi's non-violence was also not applied consistently. Godse has no problem digging up a few examples of Gandhi's cooperation in violent operations, notably two of the size of a World War. Gandhi's recruitment efforts for the British Army in World War I have already been discussed, and as for World War II:

'97. He first gave out the principle that no help should be given by India to the war between England and Germany. (...) But the wealthy companions and followers of Gandhiji added enormously to their wealth by undertaking contracts from the Government for the supply for the materials of war. (...) Not only that, but Gandhiji had given his consent to taking up the contract for supplying blankets to the Army from the Congress Khadi Bhandar.'[30]

In spite of the disastrous Bengal famine of 1943, India generally fared well under the war circumstances. Indeed, after the United States, India was probably the country that gained most from World War II in economic terms. The war effort generated many jobs, and at the end of it all, Britain had incurred an astronomical debt vis-à-vis its premier colony; for years to come, its payment was to finance Nehru's socialist development policies. It is quite true that Indian industrialists, including prominent Gandhians, did excellent business with the British war machine.

'98. Gandhiji's release from jail in 1944 was followed by the release of other leaders also, but the Government had to be assured by the Congress leaders of their help in the war against Japan. Gandhiji not only did not oppose this but actually supported the Government proposal.'[31]

In 1944, India was still a colony and the freedom of its native leaders to determine policy was limited. But after Independence, e.g., during the Pakistani invasion of Kashmir in autumn 1947, there were no excuses left for compromising on the principle of non-violence. Yet:

'101. The problem of Kashmir followed very closely that of Pakistan. (...) Pt. Nehru consulted Gandhiji about sending military help to Kashmir and it was only on the consent of Gandhiji that Pt. Nehru sent troops for the protection and defence of Kashmir. (...)'

'103. Had Gandhiji [had] a firm belief in the doctrine of non-violence, he should have made a suggestion for sending Satyagrahis instead of the armed troops and tried the experiment. (...) It was a

golden opportunity for Gandhiji to show the power of his Satyagraha
(...)

'104. But Gandhiji did nothing of the sort. (...) Gandhiji was
reading the dreadful news of the Kashmir war, while at the same
time fasting to death only because a few Muslims could not live
safely in Delhi. But he was not bold enough to go on fast in
front of the raiders of Kashmir, nor had he the courage to practise
Satyagraha against them. All his fasts were to coerce Hindus.'[32]

This is the strongest point of Godse's argumentation: there is
just no denying that Gandhi refrained very strictly from pressurizing
Muslims such as those in the Khilafat leadership, the Muslim League
or, later, the Pakistani authorities. Moreover, in the Kashmir crisis,
when he was in a position to dictate state politics at last, he refused
to put his non-violent methods to the test against a real army.

## THE LIBERATION OF HYDERABAD

Godse goes beyond this assessment of Gandhi's past performance,
and claims that the death of Gandhi helped to solve a problem
which Gandhi was sure to create or perpetuate had he lived after
30 January 1948, viz. the communal situation in the Muslim-
dominated princely state of Hyderabad, where Kasim Rizvi's Razakar
militia terrorized the Hindus:

'133. (...) It is not at all necessary to refer to the atrocious
misdeeds perpetrated by the Nizam's Ministers and the Razakars.
Laik Ali, the Prime Minister of Hyderabad, had an interview with
Gandhiji during the last week of January 1948. It was evident from
the manner in which Gandhiji looked at these Hyderabad affairs
that Gandhiji would soon start his experiments of non-violence
in the State of Hyderabad and treat Kasim Razvi as his adopted
son just as Suhrawardy. It was not at all difficult to see that it was
impossible for the Government in spite of all the powers to take
any strong measures against a Muslim State like Hyderabad so long

as Gandhiji was there (...) for Gandhiji would have gone on fast unto death and Government's hands would have been forced to save the life of Gandhiji.'

'135. (...) I felt that Indian politics in the absence of Gandhiji would surely be practical, able to retaliate, and would be powerful with armed forces. No doubt my own future would be totally ruined, but the nation would be saved from the inroads of Pakistan. (...)'

'138. The problem of the State of Hyderabad which had been unnecessarily delayed and postponed has been rightly solved by our Government by the use of armed force after the demise of Gandhiji.'[33]

We will never know how Sardar Patel's police action liberating Hyderabad from Muslim terror would have fared had Gandhiji lived. It is known for sure that Nehru was against using force in Hyderabad; there were greater chances that Gandhi would have gone the same way. But it is also possible that like in Kashmir, the Mahatma would have refrained from interfering with the Government's military solution. Then again, he had a special stake in keeping Kashmir inside India which did not apply to Hyderabad, viz. that it was a Muslim-majority state and Gandhi was interested in keeping inside India as many Muslims as he could. He also preferred Sheikh Abdullah to the Hindu King of Kashmir, and the Sheikh supported India's armed intervention for reasons of his own (his career prospects in Pakistan weren't very good because of his personal enmity with Jinnah, while in a state dominated by reputedly weak Hindus, he expected to gain maximum autonomy, esp. from Nehru, a Kashmiri Brahmin who had a soft spot for his ancestral land). So, political calculations overruled non-violence in the case of Kashmir; it is uncertain whether the same would have been the case in Hyderabad had Gandhi still been alive.

## BECAUSE I LOVED INDIA MORE

The last part of Godse's statement (112–150) chronicles his own involvement in the Hindutva movement, already discussed, and the train of events which led him to his decision to assassinate Gandhi. Let us hear the most important passages:

'136. There now remains hardly anything for me to say. If devotion to one's country amounts to a sin, I admit I have committed that sin. If it is meritorious, I humbly claim the merit thereof. I fully and confidently believe that if there be any other court of justice beyond the one founded by mortals, my act will not be taken as unjust.'

'139. I am prepared to concede that Gandhiji did undergo sufferings for the sake of the nation. He did bring about an awakening in the minds of the people. He also did nothing for personal gain, but it pains me to say that he was not honest enough to acknowledge the defeat and failure of the principle of non-violence on all sides. (...) But whatever that may be, I shall bow in respect of the service done by Gandhiji to the country (...) and before I fired the shots I actually (...) bowed to him in reverence. But I do maintain that even this servant of the country had no right to vivisect the country (...) There was no legal machinery by which such an offender could be brought to book and it was therefore that I resorted to the firing of shots at Gandhiji as that was the only thing for me to do.'[34]

The argument is similar to the one given by Caesar's killer, Brutus, in Shakespeare's Julius Caesar: I killed him 'not because I loved Caesar less, but because I loved Rome more.' The former Gandhian activist Nathuram Godse thought that Gandhi had become an obstacle to the well-being of the nation to which both of them were devoted. In that case, the interests of the nation had to be put before the lives of its servants.

## GODSE'S FAREWELL

Nathuram Godse's farewell may be quoted here without comment:

'140. (...) So strong was the impulse of my mind that I felt that this man should not be allowed to meet a natural death so that the world may know that he had to pay the penalty of his life for his unjust, anti-national and dangerous favouritism towards a fanatical section of the country. I decided to put an end to this matter and to the further massacre of lakhs of Hindus for no fault of theirs. May God now pardon him for his egoistic nature which proved to be too disastrous for the beloved sons of this Holy Land.'[35]

'147. May the country properly known as Hindusthan be again united and be one and may the people be taught to discard the defeatist mentality leading them to submit to the aggressors. This is my last wish and prayer to the Almighty.'

'149. It is a fact that in the presence of a crowd numbering 300 to 400 people I did fire shots at Gandhiji in open daylight. I did not make any attempt to run away; in fact, I never entertained any idea of running away. I did not try to shoot myself, it was never my intention to do so, for it was my ardent desire to give vent to my thoughts in an open Court.

'150. My confidence about the moral side of my action has not been shaken even by the criticism levelled against it on all sides. I have no doubt honest writers of history will weigh my act and find the true value thereof on some day in future.

'Akhand Bharat Amar Rahe!

'Vande Mataram!'[36]

## NOTES

1. Nathuram Godse: *Why I Assassinated Gandhi*, pp. 48–49.
2. ibid, p. 49
3. The somewhat irreverent term 'gimmick' is applied to Gandhi's tactics

by Sir Algernon Rumbold, as quoted in B.R. Nanda's *Gandhi and His Critics*, p. 71.

4. R.C. Majumdar: *Struggle for Freedom*, p. 487.

5. Quoted in Stanley Wolpert's *Jinnah of Pakistan*, p. 69. Even Wolpert himself sometimes describes Gandhi's political evolution in psychiatric terms, e.g.: 'His commitment to recruiting for the war' (World War I), which yielded him 'congratulations of so many imperialists for having abandoned non-violence to curry favour with a viceroy', made him feel 'wretched' and would 'drive him to severe mental breakdown before the end of 1918' (p. 55).

6. Paul Johnson: *Modern Times*, pp. 470–472. Following Ved Mehta (*Mahatma Gandhi and His Apostles*, p. 56), Johnson quotes one of Gandhi's ashram guests (apparently Sarojini Naidu) as saying: 'It costs a great deal of money to keep Gandhiji living in poverty.'

7. Alain Daniélou: *Histoire de l'Inde*, p. 364. Himself a socialist, Daniélou notes that 'this character with his ascetic appearance always had the unconditional support of the great Indian capitalists' and that 'his social reforms always ended up benefiting the merchant bourgeoisie.' For similar reasons, the Communists used to call Gandhi the 'cleverest bourgeois scoundrel'.

8. A. Daniélou: *Le Chemin du Labyrinthe*, p. 193.

9. E.g. Fazl-ul-Haq: *Gandhi, Saint or Sinner?* argues at some length that in his South-African period, Gandhi, then a British loyalist, shared the British prejudices about blacks. A rebuttal of sorts is provided by R.V. Ramdas: 'Zulus as Gandhiji saw them', *Organiser*, 29-1-1995, quoting Gandhi's book *Satyagraha in South Africa* as expressing admiration for the Zulus' qualities of character and physique. But there is no real contradiction here: the British too admired the martial and other qualities of their favoured subject peoples (Sikhs, Gorkhas, et al.), yet reserved the right to rule only to themselves as they deemed all others less fit to rule themselves, i.e., inferior in respect of political autonomy.

10. M.M. Kothari: *Critique of Gandhi*, Jodhpur 1996, p. iv; also quoted in the anti-Hindu fortnightly *Dalit Voice*, 1 April 1997, p. 23, where the book is praised as 'A must book for every student of India. Extraordinary post-mortem on the "Father of the Nation".'

and demythologized analysis that murder was the solution. There is no necessary relation between criticism and murder. It is an old rhetorical trick of despots to associate criticism of their regime with disorder and crime. Given the despotic nature of the 'secularism' imposed on India by a self-alienated elite group, no one will be surprised to notice that criticism of Gandhi's policy of 'Muslim appeasement' is routinely criminalized by vocal 'secularists', typically with reference to Godse's crime.

In this chapter, we want to give a hearing to some of the criticisms of the Mahatma voiced in various Hindu circles. The reader can judge for himself/herself whether these comments on Gandhi's politics are pregnant with violence. In some cases, they seem rather to contain the kind of insights which might have averted or limited the violence witnessed at the culmination of Gandhi's political career.

## AUROBINDO ON GANDHI

Sri Aurobindo Ghose was one of Gandhi's main Hindu critics. He was very skeptical about Gandhi's idiosyncrasies and mostly about his 'outlandish' positions on serious matters. When questioned about Gandhi's remark that there was little difference between Imperialism and Fascism, Aurobindo commented: 'There is a big difference. Under Fascism, he wouldn't be able to write such things or say anything against the State. He would be shot.'[1]

The point is also pertinent to the general question of the feasibility of non-violent agitation. This had worked against the British to some extent, but to stop a Japanese or Chinese or Pakistani invasion with it would be a different matter. When Aurobindo heard of Gandhi's musings about non-violent national defence, he commented: 'Non-violence can't defend. One can only die by it.'[2] In his young days, Aurobindo had been active in the Bengali revolutionary wing of the freedom movement. Later, when he became a spiritual teacher, he gained an international following, including many people who identified Hindu spirituality with Gandhian non-violence, and who therefore claimed that after his release from prison (1909), he had renounced the option of armed struggle. But from his own words, we can gather that he certainly hadn't swung to the Gandhian extreme.

In 1940, shortly after the Muslim League had passed its Pakistan resolution, Sri Aurobindo heard that Gandhi 'says that if eight crores of Muslims demand a separate state, what else are the twenty-five crores of Hindus to do but surrender? Otherwise, there will be civil war.' On this, Sri Aurobindo commented: 'If you yield to the opposite party beforehand, naturally they will stick strongly to their claims. It means that the minority will rule and the majority must submit. (...) This shows a peculiar mind. I think this kind of people are a little cracked.'[3]

Against Gandhi's saintly but unrealistic policy, which never achieved Hindu-Muslim unity, Aurobindo advocated a policy of realism. As Sudhir Kakar notes, Gandhi 'was a perennial object of the sage's sarcasm.'[4] But Aurobindo's skepticism regarding the Congress policy of making gestures to attract more Muslims dated to well before Gandhi appeared on India's political scene.[5] In 1906 already, Aurobindo remarked: 'The idea that the election of a Mohamedan president will conciliate the anti-Congress Mohamedans is a futility which has been repeatedly exposed by experience.'[6] Making non-negotiated concessions and presents to the Muslims (such as paying the train fare of Muslim delegates who would not have cared to attend Congress sessions otherwise) did not earn Congress any respect among them, not to speak of popularity.

Aurobindo showed that it was possible to be a pragmatic and virile Hindu, that Hinduism need not mean eccentricity and masochism, as some Gandhians (and ever since Gandhi, many outsiders) seemed to think. This distinction is very important in the process of mental decolonization. There is a belief abroad; best articulated by Ashis Nandy, that Gandhi was the true leader of mental decolonization because he refused to emulate the colonial British glorification of masculine values: 'Gandhi was trying to fight colonialism by fighting the psychological equation which a patriarchy makes between masculinity and aggressive social dominance and between femininity and subjugation. (...) Honour, he asserted, universally lay with the victims, not the aggressors.'[7]

This sophisticated psychologist's jargon amounts to devaluing the simple anti-colonial struggle which opposes the colonizer's strength with native strength, the British conquest with a native reconquest of India, the undoing of British victory with native victory, as somehow an emulation of the values promoted by the colonizer. In effect, because the colonizer is by definition a winner, it is wrong for the colonized people to become winners, for this would amount to an emulation of the colonizer.

Aurobindo had no patience with such contrived views. Strength and other martial virtues are by no means un-Hindu and borrowings from the colonial scale of values. It is precisely the colonial view that Hindus are effeminate, passive bystanders when their country was overrun by one invader after another, naturally meek people who stand in need of the virile leadership of the colonizer. The straight fact is that India's history is replete with martial feats and heroism as much as Britain's is, and that Hindu literature, likewise, glorifies bravery and victory.

Both Aurobindo and Gandhi have written spiritualist commentaries on the Bhagavad Gita, but it is only Gandhi who has read the value of absolute non-violence into it, against the very explicit evidence of the text itself (which is partly a refutation of Arjuna's quasi-Gandhian pacifist arguments given in its first chapter).[8] In so doing, Gandhi had, to an extent, interiorized a certain Western view of Oriental disinterest in the world and in worldly virtues. Gandhism, like many other Hindu revivalist teachings (e.g., Swami Vivekananda contrasting the materialist West with the spiritual East), was in a certain measure tainted with the psychological impact of the very colonialism against which he was fighting.

## GODSE'S ACT AS A STRATEGIC MISTAKE

In murdering Gandhi, Godse did not achieve his political objective of keeping India united, nor of turning public opinion and the political class away from the policies which had led to the Partition. In fact, by his single act, he smashed his own windows and those of his entire movement more thoroughly than anyone in living memory has ever done.

Let us first of all note that what actually happened was only the second-worst scenario. If Godse's original murder attempt on 20 January 1948 had succeeded, he would have gained notoriety as the killer of not only Gandhiji, but of many more people, mostly Hindus, as well. The bomb exploded by Madanlal Pahwa on that day did not kill or hurt anyone, and was not meant to. The explosion took place in the garden outside Birla House, and was meant as a signal for the other conspirators, who were present in the audience and in adjoining rooms, to throw their grenades and shoot their pistols, so as to kill everyone near Gandhiji and thus make sure that the Mahatma got killed as well. According to their plan, Digamber Badge was the first to act, but he wimped out at the very last moment.[9] After that, the others kept their weaponry in their pockets and made their escape.

If the conspirators had carried out this original plan to kill the Mahatma by 'carpet-bombing' his meeting, several dozens of Hindus might have been killed or maimed, just like the Hindus in Pakistan. In that case, it is doubtful that Godse would have achieved the popularity which he came to enjoy during his trial (especially among refugee women), and which he still enjoys posthumously among a certain section of the Hindus.

But even in the scenario which actually took place, Godse hurt his own movement far more than any enemy forces ever did. Before the Mahatma was murdered, he was a discredited leader, a proven failure, hated by many millions of Hindus, including millions of Hindu and Sikh refugees. The Hindutva movement was riding a wave of popular support after Congress had failed its promise (on which it had won the Hindu vote in the 1945 elections) of preventing Partition. Overnight, the tide turned completely against the Hindutva forces, and Gandhi was resurrected as a saint and hailed as a martyr whose failures were strictly taboo as a topic of discussion. From the viewpoint of Hindutva strategy, the murder was the worst possible blunder.

For this reason, the erstwhile Jana Sangh leader Balraj Madhok, while remaining true to the old condemnation of the Mahatma as a false Messiah, at the same time denounced the murder on political as much as on moral grounds. He wrote that the murder was 'a very un-Hindu act', which saved the Mahatma from 'the dustbin of history' for which he was headed after the creation of Pakistan, and had crowned the victory of Islamic separatism over Gandhi's Hindu vision of trans-sectarian unity.[10] This then has become the classical Hindutva view of the Mahatma: that Gandhi was a failure headed for the dustbin of history, whose reputation was saved only by his martyrdom at the hands of Nathuram Godse.

## HINDUTVA AND GANDHIAN NON-VIOLENCE

Among the Mahatma's partial followers (there are no 100 per cent Gandhians left), we must certainly reckon the Hindutva activists. Like Gandhi, they believe in the value of religion and oppose the aping of the West and the importation of Western consumerism. Even the main points of disagreement may hide more agreement than commonly believed.

Thus, whereas Gandhi had advocated a strictly non-violent

strategy including an unarmed defence against the impending Japanese invasion, the Hindu parties advocate a strong defence capability. This may end up including weapons of mass destruction, but it starts at any rate with a mentality of preparedness for combat. It would seem that it was this very mentality which Gandhi opposed all his life. Yet, even here the Hindutva movement is more Gandhian than one would expect.

We have already discussed the Mahatma's famous statement: 'There is no doubt in my mind that in the majority of quarrels the Hindus come out second best. But my own experience confirms the opinion that the Mussalman as a rule is a bully, and the Hindu as a rule is a coward. (...) Between violence and cowardly flight, I can only prefer violence to cowardice.'[11] It is this insight which allowed Hindu nationalist militias to fight rearguard actions in the Pakistani territories and save many a helpless and unprepared Gandhian Congressite in his escape to the India dominion in that dreadful summer of 1947.

But the similarity doesn't end there. It is also in Gandhi's extreme pacifism, in his attitude of 'turning the other cheek' to the aggressor, that the Hindutva movement has often put Gandhiji's lessons into practice. True, along with Godse, many RSS orators have mocked some of the more eccentric instances of Gandhian pacifism. Quoting his appeal for willing self-sacrifice to the Jews in Nazi Germany is the easiest way of creating doubts in the minds of Gandhi fans, and RSS critics of Gandhi's ahimsa (non-violence) extremism regularly refer to it. Yet, even in this extremist view of non-violence, the RSS is often a follower of Gandhi.

During the Khalistani separatist struggle in Punjab (1981–93), hundreds of RSS and BJP men were killed by the Khalistanis, yet this did not provoke a single act of retaliation, neither against the actual perpetrators nor against the Sikh community in general. On the contrary, when Congress secularists allegedly killed thousands of Sikhs in 1984, it was the Hindutva activists who went out of their way to save the Sikhs. When in the 1980s, and again from 1996 till the time of this writing, Communist militants started killing RSS men in Kerala, the RSS was very slow to react in kind. The bomb attacks on Hindutva centres in Chennai, the murders of BJP politicians in UP and Mumbai and elsewhere, have not provoked any counter-attacks. Anti-Hindu governments in Bihar and West Bengal have achieved some success in preventing the growth of sizable RSS chapters by means of ruthless intimidation and violence, all without having to fear any RSS retaliation.

The RSS often celebrates its 'martyrs', whom it calls 'shaheed', unmindful of the fact that this is a strictly Islamic term.[12] The word shaheed is related to shahada ('witnessing', viz. to the two truth claims of the Islamic creed: there is no God but Allah, and Mohammed is Allah's prophet), and means 'a witness (to the Islamic faith)', i.e., one who has fallen during Islam's war against the unbelievers. To use this term for an unbeliever killed by the believers is an insult to both sides. Anyway, the main point about this martyr cult lies elsewhere; honouring those who died for the cause is fine, but the thing to note is that the Sangh Parivar never honours those who killed for the cause. Muslim tradition at least honours the kafir-killer (ghazi) along with the martyr (shaheed), but the Sangh Parivar follows Gandhi in choosing to extol dying rather than killing for the cause.

## AMBEDKAR'S SUPPORT TO GODSE'S CRITIQUE

Nowadays, Hindutva activists often use Dr Ambedkar, a leader of the former untouchables, as a shield; he is above criticism, a kind of secular saint, and on some points, he defended the line which would now be denounced as 'Hindu communalist'. Ambedkar is well-known for opposing Mahatma Gandhi's paternalistic views on the liberation and uplift of the untouchables, particularly with his acceptance of the Communal Award giving separate electorates to the untouchables. His bitter dislike of Gandhi became even more intense when Gandhi forced ('blackmailed', according to Ambedkarites) him by means of a five-day 'fast unto death' to abandon the separate electorates in favour of a compromise known as the Poona Pact of 1932, amounting mainly to reservations for untouchables in parliamentary seats and job recruitment.[13] But the rights of the untouchables were not his only point of difference with Gandhi.

The Mahatma has often been accused of Muslim appeasement, most pointedly by Godse, and Dr Ambedkar made that criticism his own. Indeed, his lengthy survey of the evolution of Hindu-Muslim relations ever since Gandhi's appearance on the Indian political scene is in exactly the same scathing tone as Godse's apology, and drives home the same point: that Gandhi was unrealistic and foolhardy in his pursuit of Muslim support at the expense of Hindu lives and interests.

Ambedkar is actually more radical than Godse, who never rejected the possibility of Hindu-Muslim unity but merely Gandhi's handling of this project. He quotes an editorial of the Congressite newspaper *Hindustan* (1926), which draws some lessons from the unrelenting communal violence: 'To talk about Hindu-Muslim unity from a thousand platforms or to give it blazoning headlines is to perpetrate an illusion whose cloudy structure dissolves itself at the exchange of brickbats and the desecration of tombs and temples.'[14] And he comments: 'Nothing I could say can so well show the futility of Hindu-Muslim unity. Hindu-Muslim unity upto now was at least in sight although it was like a mirage. Today, it is out of sight and also out of mind.'[15]

Ambedkar quotes a number of statements by Muslim political and religious leaders showing that Hindu-Muslim co-existence in one independent state is impossible because the Muslims will settle for nothing less than to be the rulers. For instance, Maulana Azad Sobhani is quoted as saying, with a typical pan-Islamic outlook: 'Our big fight is with the 22 crores of our Hindu enemies, who constitute the majority (...) if they become powerful, then these Hindus will swallow Muslim India and gradually even Egypt, Turkey, Kabul, Mecca (...) So it is the essential duty of every devout Muslim to fight on by joining the Muslim League so that the Hindus may not be established here and a Muslim rule may be established in India as soon as the English depart.'[16]

Ambedkar seconds Mrs Annie Besant's warning: 'It has been one of the many injuries inflicted on India by the encouragement of the Khilafat crusade, that the inner Muslim feeling of hatred against "unbelievers" has sprung up, naked and unashamed (...) We have seen revived, as guide in practical politics, the old Muslim religion of the sword (...) In thinking of an independent India, the menace of Mohammedan rule has to be considered.'[17] The point she makes is not that Islamic dreams of world conquest are inevitable; on the contrary, she attributes the revival of such dreams to the contingent impact of Gandhi's maladroit Khilafat campaign.

Ambedkar totally rejected the facile explanation, still repeated by today's Nehruvian secularists (and by Nathuram Godse), that the cause of the communal problem could be found in British 'divide and rule' policies: 'The Hindus say that the British policy of "divide and rule" is the real cause of this failure [of Hindu-Muslim unity]. But time has come to discard the facile explanation so dear to the Hindus (...) What stands between the Hindus and Muslims is not a mere matter of difference, and this antagonism is not to be attributed to material causes. It is formed by causes which take their origin in historical, religious, cultural and social antipathy, of which political antipathy is only a reflection.'[18]

Among the non-Muslim leaders, Ambedkar was probably the only one who accepted the Partition of India before the power shift to the League's advantage of 1939–44 and the bloody events of 1946–47 more or less forced the acceptance of Partition on India's political class. At that point, of course, he was poles apart with the Hindu nationalists. In a lengthy chapter, Ambedkar argued that neither Savarkar nor Mahatma Gandhi had a solution for the problem that Muslims were unwilling to live in peace as a minority in a secular state.[19] He even says that suppression of a minority (which, according to him, was not Savarkar's intention), of which 'the aim is to bring into being one nation', is preferable to having two distinct nations living together in one state.[20]

Ambedkar envisaged Partition as a complete territorial separation of Hindus and Muslims, implying an exchange of population between truncated India and Pakistan. He had worked this out in detail, with blueprints for the transfer of pension rights and property rights. It is quite likely that the implementation of his plan for an orderly division, with an orderly exchange of population, would have saved hundreds of thousands of lives. By contrast, Gandhi's and Nehru's refusal of this exchange, effectively sacrificing the Hindus in Pakistan to the dogma of Hindu-Muslim unity, made them responsible for the deaths of hundreds of thousands of innocent people.

## RAM GOPAL ON THE DEATH OF GANDHISM

In an article which the RSS mouthpiece *Organiser* agreed to publish, retired civil servant Ram Gopal provides a new analysis of Gandhiji, which seems to be increasingly popular in Hindutva circles.[21] Its strength is that it does not choose between Gandhi and Godse, but between certain values which Gandhiji embodied at one point in his career, and Gandhiji's later positions and policies. It claims to criticize Gandhi from a Gandhian angle, always a safer position than to openly assume the 'Godse angle' on Gandhi. While the Sangh Parivar's top leaders may consider it safer to avoid criticizing Gandhiji for some more years, the publication of this article by a non office-bearer in the RSS mouthpiece may indicate a reorientation in the RSS party line.

Ram Gopal starts by noticing that 'Gandhism is dead.' He

quotes recent German visitors to India: 'After their extensive touring here, they said, "In this land of Gandhi, nowhere did we find Gandhism." No one can deny the truth of this statement.'[22] Indeed, today India is a country full of consumerism and violence, where Gandhiji would have felt much less at home than in British India. Now, 'the million-dollar question is: who killed Gandhism?'

Ram Gopal quotes Rafi Ahmed Kidwai, a Muslim confidant of Nehru's, as saying at the end of Gandhiji's cremation: 'Jawaharlal has performed the last rites not only of Gandhi but of Gandhism as well.'[23] This has become the commonplace view: Nehru buried Gandhism, for by his anti-religious outlook, his policy of speedy industrialization, and his maintaining (in spite of pacifist posturing) a sizable standing army, he went against Gandhian principles, and put India as a whole on an entirely non-Gandhian course. The point of Ram Gopal's article is to deconstruct this identification of Nehru as the killer of Gandhism and lay the blame elsewhere: 'An objective analysis of the political events from 1919 to 1947 reveals that Gandhi himself had discarded Gandhism during his lifetime.'

As point of reference defining 'Gandhism' as a political philosophy, Ram Gopal chooses Gandhi's initial political programme, the book *Hind Swaraj* (1909). He summarizes its vision quite accurately in the following points:

'(a) India is one nation; the mere fact that people of many faiths live here does not make India a multi-national country;

'(b) Swarajya (independence) does not mean passing of the political power from the British to Indian hands; it means replacement of the British administrative machinery, the British legislative system and the British judicial system by the indigenous ones, wedded to Hindu culture and Hindu civilization;[24]

'(c) Replacement of English language by Hindi and by other Indian languages;

'(d) Shedding Western culture based on consumerism; and adoption of Indian culture based on non-violence;

'(e) Development of villages and revival of the Panchayati Raj;[25]

'(f) Going back to nature and villages instead of urbanization; and promotion of cottage and small-scale industries, instead of rabid industrialization.'

It is undeniable that India under Nehru's leadership chose the opposite direction on every one of the above six points. Against (f), Nehru opted for speedy industrialization. Against (e), Nehru, along with his first Law Minister, Dr Ambedkar, dismissed the Panchayat (village council) system as a hotbed of reactionary social attitudes, and their opting for industrialization implied an emphasis on urbanization rather than village development. Against (d), the Indian political class had been divided only between the liberal and socialist varieties of materialism, and Indian culture figured in their calculations only as a factual background, and often as the demon to be tamed and destroyed ('the evils of Hindu society'), but never as a guiding principle. Against (c), the Constitutional provision to replace English with Hindi by 1965 was successfully sabotaged by the English-speaking elite, and the importance of English has only increased. Against (b), English institutions and procedures have not been replaced by indigenous counterparts at any point, except that British orderliness has given way to corruption. An attempt in the early 1950s to have civil disputes resolved through panchayats rather than by courts, a fine example of the indigenization of the institutions which Gandhiji had in mind, was quickly scuttled, not because of its failure but because of its success (it was putting the courts out of business). Against (a), the Nehruvian philosophy has always been, and still is, that 'India is a nation in the making', not a nation but a conglomerate of mutually foreign communities brought together under one government by the British. Admittedly, this view accepts India's national unity as a goal if not as a historical given (in contrast with the separatists who deduce that India can never and should never achieve unity), but it differs from Gandhiji's position. The Mahatma's view of Indian national unity as a centuries-old fact is now routinely decried as 'Hindu communalist history falsification'.

## GANDHI, KILLER OF GANDHISM

These six points of difference between Gandhian doctrine and Nehruvian policies are well-known; possibly a few more could be added. Ram Gopal's thesis is that Gandhi started discarding them during his co-operation with the Khilafat Movement, the most important (and fateful) caesura in the history of the Freedom Movement: 'Now Gandhiji and the British government vied with each other in their offers to Muslims in order to win their support. In this attempt, the principles of Hind Swaraj were sacrificed one after another.'[26] Thus, it was at a Khilafat conference (Mumbai, 19 March 1920) that Gandhiji abrogated the principle of non-violence at least for Muslims (in Ram Gopal's interpretation) and dismissed a plea by a Muslim for a Muslim undertaking not to slaughter cows.

In so far as the policy changes vis-à-vis the principles of Gandhi's Hind Swaraj programme were brought about after his death by Nehru and like-minded people from 1948 onwards, Gandhiji remains responsible for them in one crucial respect: it was he and no one else who publicly named Nehru as his successor and put him at the helm, knowing fully well what policies Nehru stood for. In Ram Gopal's words: 'Gandhi chose Jawaharlal Nehru as his successor and took all pains to make him the first Prime Minister, the maker of a new India, knowing fully well that Nehru was opposed to each and every ideal of Gandhism or his Ramrajya. In a letter to Gandhi in January 1928, Jawaharlal had clearly expressed his preference for Marxism as practised in the Soviet Union and pleaded for Western culture. Their only meeting ground was the policy of appeasement towards Islamic fundamentalism. The nagging question is: had Gandhi by 1946–47 succumbed to Jawaharlal's viewpoint? If not, why did Gandhi go out of his way to promote Jawaharlal ignoring the claim of Sardar Patel who was not only senior to him, but was more disciplined and more capable than Nehru?'[27]

The real scenario may well be even more problematic than Ram Gopal suggests. Gandhi ignored not just Patel's qualities and proven Gandhian orientation, he also ignored the well-known preference of the competent political body, the CWC. Because Gandhi knew that the CWC was about to vote for Patel and against Nehru, he prevailed upon Patel (whom he openly called his 'yes man') to withdraw his candidature. Only when Nehru was the single candidate, and moreover the Mahatma's candidate, did he win the CWC's approval. Gandhiji overruled democracy and the established procedure in order to sideline Patel in favour of Nehru.

Why Gandhi's extraordinary enthusiasm for Nehru? Ram Gopal quotes eye-witness Durga Das, Congressman and journalist, about Gandhi's last chance to make Patel (who had passed up the Congress presidency at Gandhiji's bidding) rather than Nehru, already Congress president, the first Prime Minister of free India. In August 1946, when the Viceroy was to invite the Congress President Jawaharlal Nehru to form the interim government at the Centre, Durga Das met Gandhi and told him that the majority of the CWC was in favour of Sardar Patel. In the words of Durga Das: 'He readily agreed that Patel would have proved a better negotiator and organiser and Congress president, but felt Nehru should head the government. When I asked him how he reconciled this with his assessment of Patel's qualities as a leader, he laughed and said: "Jawahar is the only Englishman in my camp."'[28]

In spite of his nativist affectations (loin-cloth, charkha), the record shows that the English-educated barrister M.K. Gandhi, Kaiser-i-Hind medalist for his services to the British Empire in South Africa and World War I, preferred his own kind to a non-anglicized native thoroughbred like Sardar Patel. He persisted in this social nepotism even when it meant putting a man in power who was certain to abandon everything Gandhi reputedly stood for.

Unlike Savarkar, who had always claimed independence as the Indians' birthright, Gandhi was always sympathetic to the British Empire and did not think beyond Dominion Status during most of his life, as shown by his voluntary enlisting in and recruiting for the British war effort against the Boers, the Zulus and Germany during 1899–1918. Thus, speaking to Indian students in London in 1914, he told them that 'if they claimed equal rights as citizens of the British Empire, they must do their bit for Britain, their adopted country, in its hour of trial.'[29] Though his political position got radicalized towards the demand of complete independence from Britain, his cultural Britishness, obscured by Swadeshi campaigns (Salt March, homespun cloth) and Hindu religious rhetoric, remained and bore fruit at the end of his life in his appointing Nehru. Ram Gopal comments: 'The circumstances show that, by 1946, Gandhi had travelled far away from his original theme to which Sardar Patel was committed. In the new political equations, Patel was a misfit. Jawaharlal Nehru was, therefore, the right choice to give a final burial to Gandhism or Gandhi's Hind Swaraj.'

To conclude, Ram Gopal explains that a choice is to be made between the South-African Gandhi of Hind Swaraj and the patron saint of Nehru's first government of truncated free India. The Hindu nationalist choice is obvious: 'Today, when the RSS, the BJP or the Swadeshi Jagaran Manch swear by Gandhi, they have in mind the Gandhi of the pre-1920 era. The Congressmen and others who also swear by Gandhi and ridicule the Sangh Parivar have in mind the Gandhi of the post-1920 period, inherited and amplified by Jawaharlal Nehru.'[30]

So, even when it was becoming feasible to openly repudiate Gandhi, as Bal Thackeray and Mayawati (who, with BJP support, was the Ambedkarite chief minister of Uttar Pradesh) have done in no uncertain terms, the Hindu nationalists have kept on claiming the Gandhian heritage. On the whole, they are more entitled to it, both in its commendable and in its deplorable aspects, than the self-styled secularists in India.

## SITA RAM GOEL ON GANDHI'S MERITS

There is truth in Prof. Madhok's assessment that Gandhi was a failure headed for the dustbin of history, but only if we limit Gandhi's politics to his quest of 'Hindu-Muslim unity.'[31] Obviously, this reduction is questionable. But in the Hindutva spectrum, it is hard to find a fair account of the Mahatma's achievements and failures.

On the one hand, there is the A.B. Vajpayee line which imitates Congress and therefore uncritically exalts Gandhi, e.g., when Vajpayee chose as the ideology of the newly constituted BJP in 1980 a so far undefined 'Gandhian socialism'. In the writings of RSS stalwarts like Deendayal Upadhyaya, Nanaji Deshmukh and Dattopant Thengadi, we find attempts to reactualize Gandhian concepts such as 'trusteeship', the notion that man is responsible for but not the owner of economic goods and the treasures of nature.[32] On the other hand, there are the hardliners who merely despise Gandhi's 'appeasement' policy and its failure to contain Muslim separatism.

It is among non-Sangh Parivar intellectuals that a few contributions have been made towards a sincere analysis of Mahatma Gandhi's life and work from the Hindu viewpoint, without reducing Gandhi's significance to his stand on a single issue; but in those cases, the hard topic of Gandhi's failure on the Hindu-Muslim front is passed over too quickly.

A purely Gandhian message, holding Gandhiji and his achievements up as a source of inspiration for contemporary social activism, is Arun Shourie's book *Individuals, Institutions, Processes: How one may strengthen the other in India today*. However, apart from proving that there is nothing incompatible between Gandhian inspiration and a commitment to Hinduism, this book does not concern us here, as it does not develop a critical analysis of Gandhiji's failures, merely of his achievements.[33]

Likewise, Ram Swarup, author of *Gandhism and Communism* (1954) and *Gandhian Economics* (1977), has upheld Gandhian views on a number of social, economic and cultural issues till the end of his life, but he has not dealt with Gandhi's major failures, at least not in writing. Sita Ram Goel and others have told me independently about Ram Swarup's oft-repeated observation on Godse's murder of the Mahatma: 'Such a big tragedy as Partition had taken place and if nothing had happened, history would have buried the Hindu society as dead. Godse proved before the whole world that Hindu society was still alive.' One comment of his that I have heard myself is that for a man of Gandhi's dramatic stature, dying in bed would not have been appropriate.

The job of evaluating Gandhiji's failures from a sympathizing Hindu angle has so far only been discharged by Sita Ram Goel, who acknowledges the influence of Ram Swarup. As authentic Gandhians with a record of Gandhian service during the last years of the freedom movement, and without any taint of Godseism, Ram Swarup and Sita Ram Goel could address the issue with an undisturbed conscience. To those polemicists who identify Gandhi with secularism, it ought to be a matter for serious reflection that Hindu revivalism has attracted competent thinkers from among Gandhi's young disciples, while secularism has only gathered superficial pamphleteers.

The Hindu revivalist evaluation of Gandhi emphasizes his commitment to the well-being of Hindu society, and treats this as the background which puts Gandhi's defeat in the struggle against Partition in the proper perspective. The chapter on Mahatma Gandhi in Goel's *Perversion of India's Political Parlance* is a sharp rebuttal both to Nathuram Godse's justification for the murder of the Mahatma, and to the numerous attempts to use the Mahatma as a 'secularist' argument against the Hindu cause.

Briefly, this is what it says:

First of all, the Islamic and Communist lobbies who currently invoke the Mahatma's name as a stick with which to beat the Hindu movement had no use for the Mahatma while he was alive. They thwarted his policies and opposed him tooth and nail, and their press attacked him in the crassest language. Even well after his death, Gandhi's philosophy was described by Communist journalist R.K. Karanjia as 'confused and unscientific,'[34] and as 'sentimental and spiritual.'[35]

On the issue of Partition, of course, the Muslim political leadership (along with the Muslim electorate in the 1945–46 elections) and the Mahatma were poles apart; but the Communists supported the Partition plan ideologically as well as strategically. The language which the British-Islamist-Communist combine hurled at Gandhi was the same, down to the detail, as that which is now hurled at the Hindu revivalists. Apart from politics, there were numerous personal attacks on Gandhi from those quarters as well.

Secondly, the Mahatma's first and foremost loyalty was towards Hindu society. If he criticized it, it was for its own upliftment, to force it out of its inertia, to rejuvenate and re-awaken it. The very fact that he criticized the evils of Hindu and not those of Muslim society, a major irritant to the Godse party, proves that he identified with Hindu society and considered Muslim society as not his own, so that interfering in it would be impolite. He was a proud and combative Hindu, whose defence of Hinduism against the claims and allegations levelled by Christianity and by colonialism was very clear and unwavering.[36] So was his opposition to the seeds of separatism which hostile forces tried to sow within Hindu society, via the Tamils, the Harijans and the Sikhs.

Thirdly, in the freedom struggle, it was his strategy that managed to involve the masses. Unlike the HMS, which championed religion but thought and worked in strictly political terms borrowed from Western secular nationalism, the Mahatma understood that the Hindu masses could only be won over by a deeply religious appeal. The ethical dimension of politics which he emphasized, regained for Hinduism a good name throughout the world, and is still highly relevant.[37] Therefore, it is nothing short of morbid to remember the Mahatma only as the leader who failed to stop Islamic separatism, as Godse did and as a minority within the Hindutva movement still does.

## GANDHI'S FAILURE, HINDU SOCIETY'S FAILURE

On the other hand, writes Goel, 'It must be admitted that the failure which the Mahatma met vis-à-vis the Muslims was truly of startling proportions (...) his policy towards Muslims had been full of appeasement at the cost of Hindu society. But nothing had helped. Muslims had continued to grow more and more hostile (...) there must be something very hard in the heart of Islam that even a man of an oceanic goodwill like Mahatma Gandhi failed to move it.'[38]

As for Gandhiji's share in the responsibility for Partition, Goel emphasizes that the failure to prevent Partition can only be blamed on the Mahatma for the period when (and to the extent that) he dictated Congress policy. The political course which had led to Partition had been started before his arrival on the Indian scene. And when he was at the helm, most Congress leaders had equally approved of decisions which we can now recognize as steps on the road to Partition.

For instance, the 1916 Lucknow Pact between Congress and the Muslim League, which legitimized the privileges (separate electorates, one-third representation in the Central Assembly) that the Muslim League had obtained from the British, was signed by Lokmanya Tilak. Till today, pro-Hindutva publications regularly contrast Tilak with Gandhi as an unquestionably staunch Hindu. The involvement in the Khilafat Movement, that giant boost to Muslim separatism, was accepted not only by the Nehrus ('whose support for Islamic causes was always a foregone conclusion'), but also by such Hindu stalwarts as Lala Lajpat Rai and Pandit Madan Mohan Malaviya. Even Swami Shraddhananda spoke at the Jama Masjid in Delhi in support of the Khilafat agitation. For another example, less consequential but highly illustrative, it was when Mahatma Gandhi was in prison in 1922 that Deshbandhu C.R. Das led the Bengal Provincial Congress into signing a Hindu-Muslim pact which permitted Muslims to kill cows during their festivals, but forbade Hindus to play music before mosques.

It is true that the Mahatma did not adapt his policies to the feedback he was getting from reality, viz. that concessions to the Muslim League were never reciprocated but were, instead, followed by new and higher demands. But this stubborn blindness before the grim facts was not Gandhiji's invention. In Goel's opinion, a correct assessment of Muslim separatism would have implied a fundamental critique of Islam, something which the Mahatma rejected completely; he called Islam 'a noble faith', and even when faced with Muslim misbehaviour, he attributed it to non-essential circumstances such as Islam being 'a very young religion.' Right or wrong, Gandhi's positive prejudice towards Islam was not at all a personal idiosyncrasy, but was quite common among Hindu politicians and intellectuals of his day, including the whole spectrum from Nehru to Guru Golwalkar.

Goel strongly rejects Godse's allegation that the Mahatma by himself was the chief culprit for the Partition: 'It is highly doubtful if Hindu society would have been able to prevent Partition even if there had been no Mahatma Gandhi. On the other hand, there is ample evidence that Hindu society would have failed in any case.'[39] The failure of the Mahatma before Islamic separatism was the failure of Hindu society.

Unfortunately, the late Mr Goel has not been able to complete the book he had planned—*From Shivaji to Stalin*—presenting his extensive study of the revolutionary movement in Bengal and elsewhere from 1905 to 1933. However, on the basis of that research, he told me how even Sri Aurobindo had glorified Islam as a great religion and written a whole essay on 'Muhammad the Great Yogi', how he and B.C. Pal had invited the Muslims to join the national movement for 'the greater glory of Islam', how both of them had kept mum on the atrocities committed by Muslims again and again in East Bengal, and how the revolutionary leader Sarala Devi Ghoshal had visited Kabul to invite the Amir of Afghanistan to invade India. The revolutionaries who had been inspired by Shivaji to start with and who took the oath of initiation in front of his statue with Ganga water and tulsi leaves started swearing by Marxism-Leninism after the Bolshevik coup in Russia and joined the Communist Party of India (CPI) in due course.

Meanwhile, Goel observes, they had murdered several hundred Hindus in dacoities, as police officers, as dissidents and as suspected informers, and looted as many Hindu houses in order to finance their revolution. They did take notice of Muslim atrocities and collaboration with the British. They advertised the facts quite frequently among the rich Hindus to collect funds for purchase of arms and providing relief to the victims of Muslim gangsterism. But they used the money thus collected for their own revolutionary purposes, that is, murdering more Hindus and never for meeting the Muslim challenge. Thus, all their talk against Muslims was a pretence, which too was abandoned as they moved away from their Hindu moorings.

## GANDHI AND THE HINDUTVA LEADERSHIP

According to Sita Ram Goel, Gandhi made the mistake of ignoring the ideological dimension of politics, in particular, the political doctrine of Islam. He sees the same mistake being repeated by the Hindu leadership today, except that the latter compares unfavourably with Gandhi in several respects: 'It is amazing as well as painful that the Hindu leadership which has emerged in the post-independence period should fail singularly in learning from the failure of Mahatma Gandhi. Amazing because they are following the same line vis-à-vis Islam and Muslims for which they have criticized the Mahatma rather vehemently. This is painful because they show no sign of the Mahatma's commitment to the culture of Sanatana Dharma. The present-day Hindu leadership cherishes the fond belief that they can manage the Muslims in India and elsewhere by praising Islam, its prophet, and its scripture. They forget that this is exactly what the Mahatma had done, and that this is precisely the reason why he had failed.'[40]

But there is a moral difference: 'The only difference is that while the Mahatma was sincere in praising the "noble faith of Islam", the present-day Hindu leadership speaks "strategically". The strategy is not only serving Islamic imperialism but also compromising Hindu honour.'[41] This then is one of the major inter-Hindu disputes. Goel's criticism of the organized Hindu movement is that it has a 'pickpocket mentality'.

Goel then shifts the comparison from Gandhi to an earlier and similar Hindu failure as staggering as Gandhi's, viz. the way Maratha expansion changed from a Hindu war of liberation against the Moghul Empire into a mindless self-serving movement which ended up bullying its Hindu allies and collaborating with its main enemy: 'The Hindu leadership at present can be easily compared to the Maratha leadeship which came to the fore after the Third Battle of Panipat (1761).[42] Like its predecessor, it has neither knowledge nor appreciation of Hindu spiritual vision, or Hindu culture, or Hindu history, or Hindu social philosophy. Hinduism for it is no more than a political card to be played for getting into power. Hindu culture and Hindu history mean nothing to it except some catch-phrases or patriotic rhetoric for collecting crowds and securing votes.'[43]

In my opinion, Goel exaggerates, for you come across a lot of genuine dedication in Sangh circles. As Ram Swarup told me, 'In 1971, all we had was Indira Gandhi. But she won the Bangladesh war. Now, all we have is this Sangh Parivar. It is no use wishing we had something better; we might as well make the best of it.'[44] But Goel has a point: the Hindutva movement's commitment to Hinduism is not very firm, especially among the leaders. After the foundation of the BJP in 1980, Sangh leaders have started saying quite often that it 'is no more practical to describe ourselves as Hindus (*ab apne apko Hindu kahne se kaam nahin chalega*)'. Small wonder that the BJP Constitution avoids even mentioning the word 'Hindu' as if it was a dirty word. It is only the rival political parties who denounce it as a Hindu party, without realizing that the denunciation helps the BJP to get Hindu votes. When the chips are down, it may well behave like the Congress, which promised to prevent Partition in the 1945 elections when it had already made up its mind to concede Partition: 'As has happened in the case of the Congress, Hindus are once again being taken for a ride.'[45]

The years of the BJP-dominated government (1998–2004) have shown a number of instances of BJP Gandhism. In spite of the continuation of Pakistan's proxy war against India through terrorism, the BJP government has gone out of its way to humour the Pakistanis and take peace initiatives. This is in keeping with K.R. Malkani writing repeatedly for many years that the BJP as an avowed Hindu party alone has the credentials to sign peace with Pakistan, the way US President Nixon as an avowed anti-communist had to sign peace with Communist China. He did not bother to remember that the BJP has never called itself a Hindu party, and that unlike China and the USA which saw a common enemy in the Soviet Union, Pakistan has no enemy against whom it may need India's help; India happens to be its only enemy. When Pakistan reciprocated Prime Minister Atal Bihari Vajpayee's peacenik bus trip to Lahore with a military invasion of the Kargil district of Jammu and Kashmir in 1999, the Indian Army was not allowed to cross the Line of Control and strike at the invaders' bases and supply lines in Pakistan Occupied Kashmir. This raised the death toll among Indian soldiers, the typical Gandhian price for a pose of saintliness, if not for a Nobel Peace Prize. Like the Mahatma, Vajpayee is liberal when it comes to loss of lives. Critical Hindu commentators such as Varsha Bhosle started describing the BJP leader as 'Mahatma Vajpayee'.

## GANDHI VERSUS SECULARISM

Today, Gandhiji is often rhetorically contrasted with the Hindutva movement, and held up as a model of 'secularism', a term which the deeply religious Mahatma never used.[46] But from a weapon in the hands of Hinduism's 'secularist' enemies, Sita Ram Goel turns Mahatma Gandhi into a pioneer of the Hindu revival. Gandhi had repeatedly propounded the following three views which are in stark contrast with those of the Nehruvian establishment:

1.  India is one nation. It is not, as self-glorifying Britons and Nehruvians thought, 'a nation in the making'. It has a common culture known as Sanatana Dharma ('eternal value system', Hinduism), and the adherence to this common heritage transcends the borders between language areas and other divisions which elsewhere would define a nation: 'The English have taught us that we were not one nation before and that it will require centuries before we become one nation. This is without foundation. (...) It was because we were one nation that they were able to establish one kingdom.'[47]

2.  Hinduism is in no way inferior to other religions and ideologies. On the contrary: 'Whatever of substance is

contained in any other religion is always to be found in Hinduism, and what is not contained in it is insubstantial or unnecessary.'[48]

3. Political achievements like independence, national unity and social transformation can only be based on a religious and cultural awakening of Hindu society (it is for this reason that Communists often allege that Communalism started with Gandhi, because he introduced religious language and imagery into politics, e.g., West Bengal CPM Minister Ashok Mitra called Gandhi 'the original sinner' in linking politics with 'Hindu mythology').[49]

These three are viewpoints which the political Hindu movement shares, so it could assert that secularism's claims on the Mahatma are false: 'Mahatma Gandhi stands squarely with Maharshi Dayananda, Bankim Chandra, Swami Vivekananda, Lokmanya Tilak and Sri Aurobindo in developing the language of Indian nationalism. His mistake about Islam does not diminish the lustre of that language which he spoke with full faith and confidence. On the contrary, his mistake carries a message of its own.'[50]

Goel's conclusion puts the Mahatma in the centre of the Hindu revival: 'The one lesson we learn from the freedom movement as a whole is that a religious and cultural awakening in Hindu society has to precede political awakening. The language of Indian nationalism has to be the language of Sanatana Dharma before it can challenge and defeat the various languages of imperialism. The more clearly Hindu society sees the universal truths of Hindu spirituality and culture, the more readily it will reject political ideologies masquerading as religion or promising a paradise on this earth.'[51]

## GANDHI'S FAILURE VIS-À-VIS CHRISTIANITY

At some point, even a loyal Gandhian Hindu like Sita Ram Goel had to become critical of Gandhi's role on India's battlefield of religions, though focusing on elements far outside the field of perception or concern of the Hindutva activists. He has described in detail, and praised, the Mahatma's steadfast opposition to Christian missionaries. A tireless debater, Gandhi argued with them in favour of Hinduism's right to exist, affirming its ability to satisfy his spiritual hunger to the fullest, and dismissing Christianity's claims for sole possession of the key to salvation. And yet:

'But, at the same time, it has to be admitted that Mahatma Gandhi's prolonged dialogue with Christian theologians, missionaries, moneybags and the rest, left the Hindus at home more defenceless vis-à-vis the Christian onslaught than they had ever been before. Whatever laurels the Mahatma may have won abroad, he has proved to be a disaster for the Hindus in India.'[52]

Before the Mahatma appeared on the scene, Hindu society had developed two distinct lines of intellectual defence against the Christian offensive. One of these had been pioneered by Dayananda Saraswati, founder of the Vedic-fundamentalist Arya Samaj, ca 1880. Though quite retrograde in his scripturalism, he was rather modern in his polemic against Christian doctrine, devoting a chapter of his classic *Satyarth Prakash* ('Light of Truth') to criticizing the teachings of Jesus and of the Church as morally questionable, logically untenable or factually untrue. Like Western religious skeptics of his day, he attacked the claims of Christianity head-on. In the normal course of events, Hindus after him should have given increasing sophistication to this approach by drawing on the latest developments in Western scholarship of the Bible and Church history. This way, they would have deprived Christianity of any attractiveness it might have, at least among the educated.

Instead, a softer approach carried the day, largely under the

Mahatma's influence. It had been pioneered by the Brahmo Samaj, founded by Ram Mohan Roy, from ca 1828 onwards. The Brahmo Samaj was quite modern in its general outlook, seeing religion in a universalist perspective, with all religions being ultimately rooted in the same soil of natural human spirituality. However, this modern universalism paradoxically led to the acceptance of self-righteous and irrational theologies like Christianity as being equal with Sanatana Dharma, even in its most updated Brahmoist version ('scientific religion'). Some members of the Brahmo Samaj went quite far in their glorification of Jesus, most notably Keshab Chandra Sen.

Yet, under the circumstances (viz. of Christian domination), this kowtowing to Christ was a paradoxically effective way of blunting the sword of the missionaries: Jesus got incorporated into a reformulated universalist Hinduism, or in a projected universal future religion, as merely one teacher, one guru, perhaps even one avatar, but not as Christianity's unique Saviour. By incorporating a certain veneration of Christ, the doctrinal essence of Christianity, viz. belief in Jesus' unique divinity and salvific mission, was kept at a distance. This attitude has found and retained wide acceptance among those sections of India's English-speaking elite who still identify themselves as Hindu rather than 'secularist'. Through the Theosophical Society and its offshoots, this demotion of Christ and his incorporation into a larger class of World Teachers also became popular among religious seekers in the West.

However, the intellectual lightness and sleight-of-hand of this approach implied that it could only be valid as a special transition arrangement, a solution under emergency circumstances, not an intellectually satisfying final judgement. It should have been discarded at least by the 1950s, when the Niyogi Committee Report focused attention on missionary misbehaviour in the tribal belt of Central India. At that point, India's intelligentsia should have openly started an inquest into the belief system which these missionaries were promoting. Instead, the Hindu mind proved to have been benumbed by the enormous influence of the Mahatma on all thinking about inter-religious relations.

Gandhi had radicalized the Brahmo Samaj approach into a firm doctrine of the equal validity of all religions. Whereas the Brahmoist ideas had only reached the anglicized circles of Bengal, the Mahatma's words penetrated every corner of India. With a new slogan (which many wrongly believe to be ancient Vedic wisdom), he summed up the new creed as sarva-dharma-samabhava, 'equal respect for all religions'. According to Goel, 'No other slogan has proved more mischievous for Hinduism than the mindless slogan of sarva-dharma-samabhava vis-à-vis Christianity and Islam.'[53]

Gandhi's slogan goes against the Hindu tradition that 'had always stood for tolerance towards all metaphysical points of view and ways of worship except that which led to atatayi acara (gangsterism) (...) but that tolerance had never become samabhava.'[54] Hindus had given hospitality to Christians from the fourth century onwards and given them every facility to practise their faith; but this act of kindness and tolerance never implied that they believed in the equality, let alone profound unity, between the Christian creed and the Gita.

Gandhi's original intention was to tell Christians that Hinduism had as much right to exist as Christianity, but the effect was that the missionaries politely ignored this advice while Hindus massively lapped up the converse implication that Christianity had as much right on India as Hinduism, and even that it was equally valid as a way of life and of spiritual liberation. I have encountered the hypnotic influence of Gandhi's slogan numerous times in conversations with educated Hindus and Hindu-born 'secularists': you just cannot discuss the irrationality of Christianity's or Islam's truth claims with many of them, for they immediately invoke the (equally irrational) dogma of equal validity of all religions. This slogan provides aggressive religions with a first line of defence deep inside enemy territory, viz. Hindu society.

A related point raised by Goel is that Gandhi discouraged all critical thinking about religion and promoted the mindless acceptance of all kinds of religious claims, including the idealized image of Jesus which the missionaries promoted. In effect, 'he upheld an unedifying character like Jesus as a great teacher of mankind, and glorified no end the sentimental nonsense that is the Sermon on the Mount.'[55] This was perhaps an instance of the anti-intellectualism which Gandhi, in spite of his sharp debating skills, shared with the RSS ideologues: 'One wonders whether the Mahatma knew what modern research had done to the myth of Jesus. (...) As regards the Sermon on the Mount, it has only to be referred to a Vyasa or a Valmiki or a Confucius or a Socrates, and it will be laughed out of court as bogus ethics devoid of discriminative wisdom.'[56]

No Christian in his right mind ever put the Sermon into practice, for apart from the Gospel, Christian children also read the more robust Pagan authors from Greece and Rome, and of course they also learned directly from the realities of life. 'Blessed are the meek, for they will inherit the earth': everyone knows that it usually means they can call it theirs by being buried in it. That at any rate was what it meant when Gandhi told Hindu refugees from Pakistan to meekly go back and get killed by their Muslim brethren.

A final point made by Sita Ram Goel is that Gandhi raised the status of the missionaries precisely by debating with them: 'Till the Mahatma started advertising the Christian missionaries in his widely read weeklies, Hindus had looked down upon them as an unavoidable nuisance deserving only contempt and ridicule. The Mahatma invested them with unprecedented prestige and made them loom large on the Indian scene. (...) He had done the same when he salvaged the Muslim mullahs from their ghettos and made them look like giants during the infamous Khilafat agitation.'[57]

At first sight, the point about Gandhi giving a platform to the missionaries is only a very minor criticism. Unlike his involvement in the Khilafat Movement, it does not pertain to political errors with large-scale lethal consequences. Also, the missionaries themselves would have continued their aggressive campaigns of propaganda and subversion regardless of what Gandhi said and did. His position did not affect them, but it affected the Hindus, in that it altered their perception of one of the declared enemies of Hinduism in a mildly positive sense. Gandhi's promotion of religious obscurantism, indirectly in his debates with missionaries but very openly in the Khilafat episode, has played an auxiliary role in creating one of the strangest phenomena in the Indian opinion climate: the protection of non-Hindu religions against the light of reason in the name of secularism.

In the West, secularists are people who allow, promote and practise criticism of religion and deconstruction of religion-based myths and social evils. In India, by contrast, secularists protect the medieval Muslim and Christian personal law systems (all while supporting modernizing reforms in Hindu law) against the Constitutional injunction to enact a Common Civil Code. They also shield anti-Hindu legends from historical criticism, e.g., that the apostle Thomas brought Christianity to India and was martyred by Brahmins. While there may not be a discernible direct line of causation linking Gandhi to the specifics of this secular-obscurantist propaganda, he certainly helped to set the general trend.

## NOTES

1. From Aurobindo's Evening Talks, 18 June 1940, in India's Rebirth, p. 219.
2. ibid., p. 220.
3. From Aurobindo's Evening Talks, 28 May 1940, in India's Rebirth, p. 218.
4. Sudhir Kakar: 'Disdain behind Hindu tolerance', *The Times of India*, 25 August 1993.

5. Conversely, Aurobindo also pioneered ideas which would later be associated with Gandhi, e.g., 'passive resistance', explained in Bande Mataram 11 April to 23 April 1907, see R.C. Majumdar: *Struggle for Freedom*, p. 75.

6. Aurobindo (13-9-1906): India's Rebirth, p. 18. Reference is to such occasions as Muslim lawyer Badruddin Tyabji's presiding over the 1887 Congress session in Madras, see R.C. Majumdar: *British Paramountcy and Indian Renaissance*, p. 542.

7. A. Nandy: *At the Edge of Psychology*, p. 74.

8. See esp. Aurobindo: Essays on the Gita, pp. 36–42. Unlike B.G. Tilak, who saw the Gita as a book of action, Aurobindo sees it as a book of yoga, but nonetheless one which recognizes the reality of conflict in worldly affairs.

9. The story is told by Manohar Malgonkar: *The Men who Killed Gandhi*, p. 117. I am in no position to judge a rumour spread by people close to co-conspirator Dr Parchure (and who asked me not to be named) that Godse had originally wanted to direct the popular anger for the murder against the Muslims by the following stratagem: one of the conspirators would get himself circumcised, dress up as a Muslim, shoot Gandhi, and then be shot dead 'in revenge' by another conspirator present. By the time the police would discover the assassin's real Hindu identity, days would have passed and mob violence would have chased many more Muslims out of India.

10. B. Madhok: *Rationale of Hindu State*, p. 68.

11. 'Hindu-Muslim Tension: Its Cause and Cure', Young India, 29/5/1924; reproduced in M.K. Gandhi: *The Hindu-Muslim Unity*, pp. 35–36.

12. Unlike the day-to-day politicians in the BJP, the more clerical Sangh spokesmen in the VHP do use proper Hindi terms, like hutâtma or atmabalidan instead of shaheed. Though terminology is not important in itself, it is a good indicator of the speaker's level of ideological understanding.

13. See Dr Ambedkar: *What Congress and Gandhi Have Done to the Untouchables* (1945).

14. B.R. Ambedkar: *Pakistan*, p. 186.

15. ibid, p. 187.

16. Ambedkar: *Pakistan*, p. 273, with reference to Azad Sobhani's speech published in the Anand Bazar Patrika.
17. Quoted in B.R. Ambedkar: *Pakistan*, pp. 274–275, from A. Besant: *The Future of Indian Politics*, pp. 301–305. Emphasis added.
18. Ambedkar: *Pakistan*, pp. 328–329. Not a matter of 'difference', or in current jargon: not a matter of 'Otherness'.19B.R. Ambedkar: *Pakistan*, pp. 129–194.
20. ibid, p. 144.
21. The article turns out to be a summary and update of ch. 4, 'Mahatma Gandhi', of Ram Gopal's book, *Hindu Culture during and after Muslim Rule*, Delhi 1994.
22. Ram Gopal: 'The last rites of Gandhism', *Organiser*, 6 October 1996.
23. Quoted by Ram Gopal from Durga Das: *India from Curzon to Nehru and After*.
24. Though in Gandhi's writings, the characterization of this civilization as 'Hindu' was always implicitly made, its explicitation was mostly avoided.
25. Panchayati Raj: 'rule by village councils'
26. Ram Gopal: 'Last Rites of Gandhism', *Organiser*, 6 October 1996.
27. Ram Gopal: 'Last Rites of Gandhism', *Organiser*, 6 October 1996. Nehru's letter is quoted in D.G. Tendulkar: Mahatma (vol.1, Mumbai 1951), p. 343.
28. Gopal: 'Last Rites of Gandhism', *Organiser*, 6 October 1996, with reference to Durga Das: *India from Curzon to Nehru and After*, p. 230.
29. Quoted in B.R. Nanda's *Gandhi and His Critics*, p. 116.
30. Ram Gopal: 'Last Rites of Gandhism', *Organiser*, 6 October 1996. Swadeshi Jagaran Manch: 'National self-reliance awakening front', an anti-globalization forum in the margin of the RSS.
31. B. Madhok: *Rationale of Hindu State*, p. 68.
32. See the selection of cursory passages on this topic, M.K. Gandhi: Trusteeship.
33. A defence of Gandhian principles is present somewhere in each of Shourie's works; an explicit defence of Gandhi against the virulent anti-Gandhism of the Ambedkarites (but not pertaining to those

aspects of his career which Godse addressed, hence not discussed here) is given in Shourie: *Worshipping False Gods: Ambedkar and the Facts which Have Been Erased* (1997), especially ch. 5.

34. R.K. Karanjia: *The Mind of Mr. Nehru*, p. 22.
35. ibid, p. 25.
36. About Gandhi's criticism of the missionaries, see S.R. Goel: *History of Hindu-Christian Encounters*, ch. 14.
37. For an example of how Gandhi's strategy of appeal to morality and 'change of heart' is made relevant in an age which is losing even the memory of the idealism and sacrifice of the freedom struggle, see the already-mentioned book by Arun Shourie: *Individuals, Institutions, Processes*.
38. S.R. Goel: *Perversion of India's Political Parlance*, pp. 46–47.
39. ibid, p. 47.
40. ibid, p. 53.
41. ibid, p. 53.
42. Reference is to a development most dramatically illustrated in 1771 when Maratha general Mahadji Scindia, militarily the most powerful man in India, had freed the Moghul emperor from captivity and defeated his (the Moghul's) Pathan rivals, and then prostrated himself before the helpless Moghul, assuming the role of a loyal vassal instead of folding up the decrepit Moghul empire and declaring Hindu sovereignty—the original goal of the Maratha struggle as envisaged by Shivaji a century earlier.
43. S.R. Goel: *Perversion of India's Political Parlance*, p. 53.
44. Speaking to me in Delhi, December 1992, Goel told me that Ram Swarup became a bundle of contradictions when it came to his two pets—Gandhi and the Sangh Parivar. He was often very harsh in criticizing both of them but reached for the jugular of anyone else who criticized them even mildly.
45. S.R. Goel: *Perversion of India's Political Parlance*, p. 53.
46. This is the main position of Gargi Chakravarthy: *Gandhi, a Challenge to Communalism*.
47. M.K. Gandhi: *Hind Swaraj*, ch. 9, quoted in S.R. Goel: *Perversion of India's Political Parlance*, p. 51.

48. M.K. Gandhi: Young India, 8-4-1926, quoted in S.R. Goel: *Perversion of India's Political Parlance*, p. 51. On p. 52, Goel also draws attention to the articles Gandhi wrote against the eruption of anti-Brahminism in Tamil Nadu in 1925, arguing e.g., that 'if Brahmanism does not revive, Hinduism must perish.'

49. Ashok Mitra: 'The Holy War of Myth and Symbol', *Sunday Observer*, 6 October 1996.

50. S.R. Goel: *Perversion of India's Political Parlance*, p. 53.

51. ibid, p. 53.

52. S.R. Goel: *History of Hindu-Christian Encounters* (revised and enlarged edition, 1996), p. 235.

53. ibid, p. 237.

54. ibid, p. 235.

55. ibid, p. 235.

56. ibid, p. 237.

57. ibid, p. 238.

# Conclusion

In 1990, I stayed for a few days at the Gandhi Peace Foundation in Delhi. It was the time of the Ayodhya controversy concerning the mosque structure occupying the birthplace of Rama, the deified hero whose name Gandhiji is said to have uttered with his dying breath. Nearly the whole crowd there—residents and foreign guests alike—were very opposed to the Hindu claim to this sacred site of Hinduism. In fact, most were quite anti-Hindu.

Thus, I heard an Australian and an American discuss the vexing question whether Hinduism can be reformed out of its present 'ugly and inhuman' state or whether it should be annihilated altogether. When an Indian Muslim joined the conversation, they started praising Islam and comparing it to its advantage with Hinduism, e.g., as Westerners accustomed to a woman's right to an income of her own, they set different standards ad hoc to evaluate the position of Muslim women: 'Muslim women are better off than Hindu women: not being allowed to go out to work, they at least don't have to combine working for money with homemaking.' In fact, they praised Islam to the point that the Muslim started looking embarrassed from having to gracefully accept all those compliments.

The most persistent impression I got there was one of moral smugness (what the French call 'arrivisme'), of Gandhians feeling morally superior and securely in a position to pass judgement on others, particularly on Hindus. Their opinions were very conformistic, and in this they definitely failed their master, for the Mahatma at least did dare to go against dominant opinion once in a while. Their holier-than-thou attitude was likewise a few notches below the standards which Gandhiji set for himself, for he at least listened to his adversaries and sometimes displayed a certain understanding of their positions even when opposing them. He at least had a feeling for the problematic nature of most controversies, which are not simply black-and-white, much in contrast with the blanket condemnation of Hindutva by such Gandhians as Kamalapati Tripathi and B.N. Pande, then in the news for opposing the Ayodhya movement. When the Mahatma was critical of his own failures (admittedly rarely), it was not a pose but a genuine churning of his conscience.

That smugness was already affecting Gandhi's followers at the time of the murder. While in custody, Nathuram received a letter dd. 17 May 1949 from Ramdas Gandhi, son of the Mahatma. It was a polite letter extolling the worldwide cry for peace and admonishing Godse to repent. In his reply dd. 3 June 1949, Nathuram complimented Ramdas for writing in the spirit of his father's teachings, much in contrast with the abuse he received from declared Gandhians who showed nothing of their hero's self-control and pacifism: 'I do not consider that they were written by any disciple of your father.'[1] He also apologized for the human suffering he had caused: 'I express my utmost regrets as a human being for your sufferings due to the death of your father by my hands.'[2]

Godse also explained that thus far he saw no reason for repentance, and that Gandhian gestures such as sparing him the death penalty would have no effect on his self-judgement. But he was willing to be convinced by reason, and therefore, he invited Ramdas and a small delegation of Gandhians to come over for a personal talk. Only: 'The condition of the talk must be that we must stick to truth alone.'[3]

In has Jr's reply dd. 13 June 1949, Ramdas announced that he was seeking Nehru's permission to visit Godse in the company of Vinoba Bhave and Kishorlal Mashruwala, a visit which unfortunately never materialized. In this letter, we see the smugness appearing in Ramdas Gandhi's irritated remark: 'I think you should not have stipulated the condition, "we should speak in consonance with truth", because I think that condition was not only unnecessary in my case but also unnecessary in the case of any close associates of my father.'[4]

As a matter of courtesy, Godse in his final reply admitted that he 'should not have stipulated that "truth alone should be spoken",' that he had had no intention of hurting Gandhi Jr's feelings (meaning his ego), but that unfortunately, he himself had met 'many so-called votaries of the creed of "Truth" who "in actual life bother the least about that creed."'[5] In fact, Godse had been entirely right in warning against the tendency to settle for more comforting options than 'sticking to truth alone' concerning Gandhi's record.

The tendency to obscure prickly questions about the Mahatma was strongly in evidence among his devotees. Over the decades, we have seen Gandhians failing to take a critical look at their guru's mistakes, preferring instead to emulate and radicalize him in his self-deluded views of Islam, as in B.N. Pande's whitewash of Islam's destructive record in India or Vinoba Bhave's selective reading of the Quran.[6] Even at a distance of decades, people invoking Gandhi's name still evade the hard questions raised by Godse in his speech.

Numerous contemporaneous and later observers shared Nathuram Godse's criticism of Gandhiji's character and politics to a large extent. To summarize:

1. Gandhi's non-violent agitation had but a limited action radius: he only used it on people with whom he shared a number of cultural and moral premises, viz. Hindus and liberal Britons.

2. The political success of Gandhi's non-violent action was

much more limited than is generally assumed (though more important than Godse was willing to admit), for other internal and external factors have decisively contributed to India's independence.

3. In his policy of non-violence, Gandhi was erratic, and like a gentle surgeon, he made some stinking wounds which demanded a high toll in human lives.

4. Gandhi made all sorts of appeasement gestures to please the Muslim League and the Muslim lobby inside Congress. He made his concessions to them in the name of the Hindus, but never negotiated a mature quid pro quo in which similar concessions were made by the Muslims.

5. Gandhi flattered the Muslims and their religion endlessly. With that, he did not convey the opinion of his Hindu constituents, and it was a strategic mistake in that it made the Muslim leaders more arrogant and less willing to compromise.

6. Gandhi resolutely refused to learn anything from the feedback which political reality was providing: though the policy of unilateral and unconditional concessions yielded no rapprochement between Hindus and Muslims, he continued it all the same.

Some will defend Gandhi's policy on these points, e.g., on Hindu-Muslim relations, they will maintain that one should go to the utmost in one's generosity, that one should not do any quid pro quo calculation in the exercise of virtue. But virtue, as Aristotle taught, is always a balance between extremes which are not virtues, e.g., courage taken to the extreme of foolhardiness ceases to be a virtue. In Gandhi's case, generosity taken to the extreme of self-undoing, with ordinary Hindus paying the price, was no longer a virtue. This then is one of the hard questions with which Gandhians, including all those who use Gandhi's name as a political trump argument till today, will have to come to terms at last. They should come out of their smugness.

Hindutva activists, by contrast, will have to face the problematic aspects of Godse's act. The thoughtful ones among them have already been forced to do this. Unlike the Gandhians, their hero did not get a halo of saintliness, so they could not bask in his reflected glory and dispense with the trouble of critically rethinking the event. The unthinking ones, those who go on mindlessly pontificating about 'teaching Muslims a lesson' and all that, should gather their wits at last and ponder the adverse effects of Godse's act, viz. the enormous harm done to the Hindutva movement itself and to larger Hindu interests. Finally, they should spare a thought for the value of every human life, of Muslims as well as Hindus, even that of a fallible human being like the Mahatma.

## NOTES

1. Nathuram Godse: *Why I Assassinated Mahatma Gandhi*, p. 128.
2. ibid, p. 129.
3. ibid, p. 129.
4. ibid, p. 130.
5. ibid, p. 132.
6. Vinoba Bhave: *The Essence of the Quran*, 1962; B.N. Pande: *Islam and Indian Culture*, 1985.

# Appendix 1

# Sangh Parivar, the Last Gandhians

(The following text was published as chapter 6 of our book, *BJP vis-à-vis Hindu Resurgence*, Voice of India, Delhi, 1997, and shows how the BJP, frequently labelled as 'Godse's heirs', is in a way the most Gandhian political party in India. *Sangh Parivar*, 'family of the RSS', the array of semi-independent organizations linked with the Hindu nationalist movement RSS, including the BJP.)

When in 1980, the secularist tendency led by Nana Deshmukh and Atal Bihari Vajpayee imposed 'Gandhian socialism' on the newly founded BJP as its official ideology, all the establishment secularists laughed at this transparent attempt to acquire a new secular identity.[1] 'This party is neither Gandhian nor socialist,' they said. The party was in fact more socialist than it would like to admit after liberalization became the new orthodoxy, certainly more socialist than the non-socialist 'cleverest bourgeois scoundrel' Gandhi ever was, but we can agree that it was less socialist than was normative in 1980. What interests us more, is whether the BJP, always accused of having historical links with Gandhi's assassin, can legitimately be called Gandhian.

Our view is that within the present political spectrum, the BJP is definitely and by far the most Gandhian party. The former socialists and populists, who had inherited part of the Gandhian legacy through Jayaprakash Narayan, have become nothing but casteist interest groups steeped in coercive tactics and crime; there is nothing Gandhian about them anymore. Congress, of course, presided over the betrayal of every single Gandhian policy under Nehru's Prime Ministership, and its level of morality and dedication to the nation is nothing that Gandhi would be proud of.

By contrast, the BJP, or rather the Sangh Parivar as a whole, is definitely a Gandhian movement in many respects. The Sangh Parivar supports economic self-reliance (swadeshi) coupled with cultural self-reliance. The Sangh workers shun luxury and move around by public transport, in the lowest-class compartments. In communications as well as in their martial arts practice (with the stick), they are deliberately settling for older technology, quite comparable to Gandhi's choice for living in the past with his charkha. Sangh whole-timers practice the typically Gandhian mix of politics and asceticism (including sexual abstinence). The Sangh protests against Miss World flesh shows, the promotion of meat consumption by American fast food chains, the unnecessary and disruptive promotion of tooth paste at the expense of indigenous methods of dental hygiene, and other instances of dumping India's heritage in favour of undesirable and/or foreign alternatives. This earns Sangh activists haughty smirks from the elite, but that itself is yet another point in common with Gandhi and his spinning-wheel.

In some respects, the RSS follows Gandhi even where Gandhi was decidedly un-Hindu. The seeming unwillingness to use the most modern technology and media (which is gradually being superseded by modernizing efforts originating largely in NRI circles) is Gandhian enough, but is unwarranted from a Hindu viewpoint. The ancient Hindus in the Indus-Saraswati civilization were in the vanguard of humanity in science and technology; Gandhi had his retro-mania from Christian romantics like Thoreau and Tolstoy. The combination of social work with celibacy is characteristic of certain Roman Catholic monastic orders, but is foreign to Hindu tradition, where a clean separation is maintained between, on the one hand, the self-supporting worldly society, which takes care of its needy and in which every able-bodied young man is expected to start a family, and on the other hand the circles of celibate sadhus from whom no worldly service is required because their spiritual practice is contribution enough.

Three central aspects of the Sangh's work are typically Gandhian, and are also the key to its success. One is its grass-roots work, its impressive record in actual social service, which is far larger and more deserving of a Nobel Prize than Mother Teresa's heavily foreign-financed operations. Like for Mahatma Gandhi, politics for the Sangh is but one aspect of a much larger social programme carried out by the citizens' own initiative and effort. This creates a much closer rapport with the masses, a movement with much stronger roots than purely political movements like the Hindu Mahasabha.

The second Gandhi-like aspect of the Sangh's success is its religious dimension. Though the BJP insists on its secular character, many of the Sangh-affiliated organizations and individuals are not that shy about their Hindu moorings, and this is precisely one of the reasons why they strike a chord of confidence among the people. Tilak, Aurobindo and Gandhi made the independence movement into a mass movement by giving it a religious dimension; it is for the same reason that the Sangh has become a mass movement firmly rooted in the general population, a pool of Hindu commitment on which the BJP can draw at voting time.

The third Gandhian trait in the Sangh's style of functioning is the moral dimension which it gives to its politics. The BJP advertises itself as a disciplined party free of corruption. When during the 1996 Lok Sabha election campaign, Narasimha Rao's men tried to implicate L.K. Advani in a financial scandal, the public reacted with a sincere disbelief: he may be a communalist, but we never saw any sign of corruption in him. Our own experience confirms that in general, the workers of the Sangh-affiliated organizations are sincerely dedicated to the well-being of their country and society without expecting personal benefits in return.[2] Of late, this reputation has been corroded by scandals involving the BJP (though it remains the cleanest party by far), and even RSS grassroots recruitment is feeling the effect of the general spread of consumerism in Hindu society. Traditionally, Hindus have held self-abnegation as practised by Sangh workers in high esteem, but many members of the new generation ('yuppie' or 'goonda') merely find it funny; the RSS-Gandhian ethos has now become an upstream effort defying the spirit of the times.

The kinship between the Sangh and Gandhi is real enough in these positive aspects, but it is just as palpable in some negative respects. To start with a small but nasty point, Gandhi thought his own position (call it the 'Gandhian sampradaya'/'sect') represented the whole of Hinduism, both at the political and the religio-philosophical level, and strongly resented alternative centres of Hindu mobilization. Though calling himself a Hindu, he claimed the leadership of the whole nation and not just of the Hindus, though the British secularists and the Muslims never conceded this more-than-Hindu identity to him (certainly a parallel with the Bharatiya rather than Hindu Janata Party). When the Muslim League became a formidable challenger to Gandhi's claim, it would have been in the nations and his own interest to let the Hindu Mahasabha counterbalance the League's influence; Moderates normally use the presence of radicals as a useful bargaining-chip. But Gandhi and his Congress wanted the whole Hindu cake to themselves.

The same intolerance of or at least annoyance with rivals for the Hindu constituency is in evidence in the Sangh. In surveys of Sangh history, there is remarkably little reference to the Hindu Mahasabha and other Hindu organizations. Especially glaring is the RSS reluctance to acknowledge the role of Babarao Savarkar (elder brother of V.D. Savarkar and an outstanding revolutionary in his own right). It was Babarao who had drafted the original RSS pledge and included the term Hindu Rashtra in it. He had suggested the saffron RSS flag. He had merged his own Tarun Hindu Sabha as well as Sant Panchelgaonkar Maharaj's Mukteshwar Dal into the fledgling RSS. He was responsible for bringing into the RSS such luminaries as Bhalji Pendharkar, the noted film director and later the Dadasaheb Phalke Award winner Kashinath Pant Limaye who became the provincial head of the Maharashtra RSS, Babu Padmaraj Jain and others. Babarao toured extensively for the RSS in spite of his failing health. Both Hedgewar and Golwalkar had great respect for Babarao. Yet *The RSS Story* by K.R. Malkani does not even mention Babarao's name. In fact, some narrow-minded RSS leaders from Pune had tampered with the chapter on Babarao's contribution (written by P.N. Gokhale) that deals with Babarao's contribution to the growth of the RSS. Similarly, no acknowledgement is made of the help which the RSS received from the Arya Samaj and the Hindu Mahasabha everywhere.

During the 1989 elections, when the BJP had an electoral alliance with the Janata Dal, Balraj Madhok stood as a candidate for the reconstituted Bharatiya Jana Sangh against the Janata Dal candidate in Lucknow. Most Hindutva people were eager to work for Madhok, 'one of us', against the JD secularist officially supported by the BJP. When Madhok looked sure to win the election, Vajpayee hurried to Lucknow to discipline the BJP workers; he could not tolerate that a non-BJP man would enter the Lok Sabha in spite of his proven merit for the Hindu cause.

In a way, the Sangh attitude mirrors that of mendacious secularists who always label anyone speaking up for the Hindus as an 'RSS man'; they identify the Hindu cause with the Sangh. Generally they do not see beyond the confines of the Sangh and are practically unaware that there are conscious Hindus outside the Sangh.

A typical Gandhian flaw in BJP functioning, the result of mixing self-denial (a personal discipline) with politics (a public affair), is the absence of any healthy sense of quid pro quo. Gandhi always sacrificed Indian or Hindu interests without asking anything in return, hoping that this would soften the heart of the beneficiary and put him in the right mood to give something back at his own initiative. Thus, after the outbreak of World War I, 'Indian political leaders, "moderate" as well as "extremist", were unanimous that the people of India should support the British cause against the Germans, but only for a price: the promise of home rule after the war. Gandhi was almost alone in rejecting the idea of a political bargain with the British; he cherished the hope that in return for unconditional support, a grateful and victorious Britain would give India her due when the war was over.'[3] As it turned out, the British took Gandhi's services (recruiting Indian volunteers to die a useless and horrible death in the war against Germans who had done the Indians no harm) but, except for an embarrassing medal of loyal service to the British Empire, they gave him nothing in return. In the real world, politicians bargain for a tangible quid pro quo and don't count on gratitude.

This Gandhian idiosyncrasy has set a trend in Indian foreign policy. In his infamous 1954 'Panch sheel' treaty with China, Nehru conceded China's claim to Tibet but extracted no Chinese acceptance of India's established borders in return. In the Indo-Pak wars, Indian successes on the battlefield were squandered in Nehru's vainglorious attempt to posture as an apostle of internationalism (bringing in the UNO in the Kashmir dispute, 1948), or as an occasion to show off India's sportsmanship (ceding the territory conquered in 1965), or in return for a meaningless declaration of good intent (releasing the Pakistani prisoners for a never-kept promise to keep the Kashmir issue bilateral in 1971). In 1996, India parted with a large percentage of the Ganga water supply in an empty show of generosity to Bangladesh, effectively hurting its own agriculture and shipping industry, without even asking anything in return—not that Bangladesh treat the Hindu minority correctly, not that it restore the Chakma lands to its Chakma refugees, not that it take back its illegal Muslim migrants, not that it close its borders to separatist guerrilla groups terrorizing India's northeast.

In this habit of making unilateral gestures to undeserving enemies, Gandhi had no followers more imitative than the BJP. This party always sells out its principles and pays homage to everything and everyone its enemies cherish, without ever exacting even a promise (let alone a real bargain) in return. No matter how many concessions A.B. Vajpayee offered during his 13-day tenure as Prime Minister in search of a majority, no matter how hard he kicked his Kashmiri refugee supporters in the groin by promising to preserve Art. 370, no matter how sincerely he condemned the Ayodhya demolition, he did not get a single undertaking from a non-'communal' parliamentarian to support the government during the confidence vote. No matter how deep the BJP leaders crawl in the dust begging for certificates of good secular conduct from their enemies, this has never yielded them anything except contempt. But so far, everything indicates that they can be counted upon to continue in the same direction.

## NOTES

1. We omit discussion of the lack of an agreed meaning for the term 'Gandhian socialism'. An insider told me that during one of the constituent meetings of the budding BJP, a vote was taken on whether the ideology should be 'integral humanism' or 'Gandhian socialism'; the latter won with a small majority, but to please everyone, it was then decided that 'Gandhian socialism' is actually the same thing as 'integral humanism'. The incident reveals the lack of ideological *sérieux* in the BJP. Similar illustrations of this weakness include K.N. Govindacharya's 1996 enthusiasm for 'social engineering', a term dear to totalitarian regimes, by which he meant simply the induction of more Backward Caste candidates in the elections.

2. It is a different matter that this personal modesty is often combined with

a lack of collective Sangh modesty: many Sangh workers are extremely touchy about criticism of the Sangh, even when they don't mind criticism of Hinduism or India.

3. B.R. Nanda: *Gandhi and his Critics*, OUP, Delhi, 1993, p. 116.

# Appendix 2

# Gandhi in World War II

(From K. Elst: *The Saffron Swastika: On the Notion of Hindu Fascism*, Voice of India, Delhi, 2001, p. 506–21.)

## 1. GANDHI AND HITLER

During World War II, Mahatma Gandhi shifted his tactical position regarding the war effort several times, as we shall see shortly. However, his fundamental moral outlook on the war remained constant, and was one which wouldn't gain him many friends today. Gandhians, at any rate, are conspicuously averse to discussing their hero's wartime declarations, such as his working hypothesis that 'Hitler is not a bad man', or his advice that the British give Hitler all he wanted, 'your land but not your souls', or his post-war assessment that the victors had tried every lie and 'broken every moral principle' in their conduct of the war. And yet, Gandhi had a point.

Gandhi merely spoke for international majority opinion in 1940 when he wrote: 'The Germans of future generations (...) will honour Herr Hitler as a genius, as a brave man, matchless organizer and much more.'[1] In the same article, he did acknowledge that Hitler stood for naked aggression, but: 'Hitlerism will never be defeated by counter-Hitlerism. It can only breed superior Hitlerism raised to the nth degree. What is going on before our eyes is a demonstration of the futility of violence as also of Hitlerism.' Gandhi didn't believe in containing Hitler by military means.

Consequently, he applauded France's decision to offer an armistice rather than fight a hopeless battle against the German powerhouse: 'I think French statesmen have shown rare courage in bowing to the inevitable and refusing to be party to senseless mutual slaughter. (...) The cause of liberty becomes a mockery if the price to be paid is wholesale destruction of those who are to enjoy liberty.'[2] The alternative was tried out in Poland, which could have avoided war by conceding the German demands concerning Danzig and the West-Prussian corridor (reuniting Germany with East Prussia). While it may be questioned that these demands were reasonable, they were probably more so than spilling the blood of six million Poles (divided fifty-fifty between Catholics and Jews), only to achieve the subjection of Poland to Soviet domination.

Gandhiji's approval of the French ceasefire was a defeatist position, and as such certainly open to criticism, but still considerably more reasonable than his advice to the Hindus of Punjab during the Partition massacres in 1947, when they were threatened not just in their liberty but in their lives. He told them repeatedly to stay home and get killed by their Muslim brethren rather than flee to Delhi, because: 'If all the Punjabis were to die to the last man without killing, the Punjab would become immortal.' Larry Collins and Dominique Lapierre rightly connect this saintly advice with its wartime precedents: 'As he had counseled the Ethiopians, the Jews, the Czechs and the British, so he now counseled his enraged Hindu countrymen: "Offer yourselves as non-violent, willing sacrifices."'[3] And yet, look at the contrast in today's perception of Gandhi's stances in that critical pre-independence decade. His position during the Partition massacres is frequently held up as a shining contrast of humanism against the barbarity of the non-defeatist Hindu nationalists (though mostly without giving embarrassing details like the advice just quoted). At the same time, his less extreme and less lethal plea in favour of the French armistice, humiliating but not suicidal, is systematically treated as a blot on the Mahatma's fair name and kept out of view. Non-violent conflict resolution is an ancient path perfected by diplomats not with dramatic Gandhian gestures but with patient deliberation, human understanding and a nose for the common ground on which a compromise can be based. If we leave out the Mahatma's masochistic idiosyncrasies, a serious case could be made, if only as a retrospective thought experiment, for a non-violent conflict resolution between Germany and its Polish and Anglo-French opponents in 1939–40.

In recent years, there has been some debate about the suggestion of leading British historians (to various degrees, A.J.P. Taylor, Alan Clark, Maurice Cowling, Andrew Roberts, Niall Ferguson, John Charmley, and most controversially David Irving) who deplore Churchill's determined belligerence as a decisive factor in Britain's decline. The idea is that peace with Hitler might have favoured the continuation of the British Empire. Almost as an aside, some of them intimate that this would have made possible the avoidance of the Holocaust, viz. through an agreed resettlement policy for the European Jews.[4] Along similar lines, American right-wing leader Pat Buchanan has argued that his country should have stayed out of war because there were no American interests at stake.[5]

British or American national interests are not my (or Gandhiji's) kind of consideration in deciding this question, but I would agree that there was an excellent reason to avoid or stop this war or contain it at minimal magnitude, viz. the immense suffering it was sure to cause. Another good reason was that the war gave Stalin a chance to extend his power over another dozen countries, in the longer term making possible the Communist take-over of China and other countries as well, thus bringing about many more massacres.

Yet, in the British historians' debate, the dominant opinion turned out to be that the prospect of leaving Hitler in power was simply 'too horrible to countenance'. In other words, that getting Hitler out of the way was worth fifty million lives.

In particular, it is argued that anything and everything had to be done to stop the Holocaust. The only debate considered valid is whether the war could have been conducted differently so as to rescue more Jews. It is forcefully asserted that the best and only rescue for the Jews was for the Allies to win the war.[6] But that is obviously unconvincing, for the war was won by the Allies, yet the Holocaust did take place. Moreover, it is entirely a matter of hindsight, absolutely not reflected in the wartime sources, that the stake of the war was the fate of the Jews: 'The Allies certainly did not wage World War II for the sake of saving the Jews from annihilation. We can now denounce that as shameful (...) but at that time their concern was winning the war, and that for a number of other reasons. Somehow we have started to find the genocide ever more important, as if that was what the war was about.'[7]

Most war leaders, like Churchill or Charles de Gaulle, don't even mention the fate of the Jews in their memoirs. This does not disprove the Holocaust, as negationists might deduce, it merely illustrates that generals are callous to the suffering of ordinary people, which they deem inconsequential to their one goal: victory. Moreover, knowing that anti-Jewish sentiment was widespread, the Western leaders kept news about the specifically anti-Jewish thrust of Nazi repression from the public precisely to avoid the impression that the war was being fought for the sake of the Jews. Also, the war leaders themselves were in a position to know better than anyone that the war was not a reaction to but rather a trigger of the Holocaust, which started only two years after Britain's declaration of war on Nazi Germany. Hitler had openly announced in 1939 that if the Jews were to inflict a war on Germany, they would dearly pay for it. Not that any of the anti-German war leaders was Jewish, but everyone knew that Hitler would blame the hidden Jewish hand anyway. Specifics apart, it is common knowledge that a declaration of war tends to endanger those communities in enemy territory which are suspected of siding with the aggressor. In case the British leaders had forgotten this, they should have been alerted by the fate of the German inhabitants of Poland, who became hostages of the Poles after the German invasion, and of whom perhaps fifteen thousand were killed in pogroms in a matter of days (Hitler put the death toll four times higher). The massacre was stopped by the swift Polish defeat, but surely the British war leaders cannot have expected to overrun Germany in an equally brief campaign? With our benefit of hindsight, we could uncharitably put it this way: the British government unintentionally yet knowingly sacrificed the Jews in Axis-held territory by declaring war on Germany.

Stalin's entry into the war didn't help the Jews either. He had killed tens of thousands of Jewish Bolsheviks during the great purges, and definitely didn't want the salvaging of the Jews to become the aim of war. His policy of using Jews for hateful tasks of repression directly led to the enthusiastic participation of East-Europeans in SS-supervised massacres of Jews. He had even delivered large numbers of German-Jewish (along with German Communist) refugees to the Nazis, under a secret clause to the Hitler-Stalin Pact of 1939.[8] Saving the Jews' lives, though not their continued presence in the German Reich, was perfectly possible, but only in a non-war scenario. Until 1941, the Nazi leadership hoped to eliminate the Jews from Europe by deporting them elsewhere: Siberia (a plan taken up by Stalin, who created a Jewish territory in the Manchurian region of Birobijan), Uganda, Madagascar or Palestine. Let it be clear that I am not in favour of the deportation of a community which had contributed so much to European societies, but obviously exile would have been a lesser evil as compared to death. Who would know better than the wandering Jew that as long as there's life, there's hope, even if it requires migrating?

If the Allied powers had been so concerned about the Jews that they waged war to save them (quod non), why didn't they negotiate some such resettlement plan? The unintended result of their failure to do so was that the SS worked out a crueler manner of eliminating the Jews from Europe. Even when the Holocaust had started, it remained theoretically possible to stop it by concluding a peace treaty with Nazi Germany, but the Allies chose to fight for total victory without regard for the fate of the millions of Jews who had become the hostages of the Nazis. It is said that the Jewish guerilla leader and later Israeli Prime Minister Yitzhak Shamir hated the United States precisely for this reason: 'Shamir believed that, because Roosevelt had refused to come to terms with Hitler, the United States was partially responsible for the Holocaust.'[9]

Let us consider the argument that the prospect of leaving Hitler in power was too horrible to countenance. From 1933 onwards, German policies against the Jews were discriminatory and obnoxious, pushing them into exile while also locking up political opponents. But there was no mass killing, so that the stray killing of Jews during the Kristallnacht pogrom (9 November 1938, official death toll 96) came as a shock to German public opinion, even though it was still infinitesimal when compared with Stalin's massacres of millions (yet nobody was or is saying that leaving Stalin in power was 'a prospect too horrible to countenance'). The fact is that the vast majority of the victims of Nazi policies of oppression, deportation, enslavement and deliberate extermination fell during a period of war, in circumstances caused, or rendered possible, by the war.

This may be contrasted with the case of Communist massacres. Most victims of Communism fell during peacetime repression or during civil wars which the Communists themselves had started: Russia after 1917, China in 1945–50 (and even during the supposedly united efforts with the Nationalists against the Japanese in 1937–45), or Angola after decolonization in 1975 when the

Soviet-oriented MPLA refused to share power with the other liberation movements. Camp systems processing tens of millions of prisoners functioned for decades in peacetime, e.g.: 'the Chinese Communist labor reform camps (laogaidui) have been in existence for over forty years, and in every respect—in terms of scope, cruelty, and the number of people imprisoned—they rival the Nazi and Soviet systems.'[10]

To be sure, the war which made the Nazi 'special treatment' of the Jews possible had also been started by the Nazis, viz. with the invasion of Poland. Yet, National-Socialist guilt for the outbreak of the war was much less solid than Communist guilt for the October Revolution and all that ensued. Like in World War I, there was an escalation of hostilities with different actors. Poland was not altogether innocent of the German invasion, for emboldened by the Anglo-French pledge of support, it refused to correct its oppressive policy vis-à-vis its German minority. It fell to Britain and France to declare war on Germany and turn a local conflict into a world war. It was Germany which occupied Norway, but then it was only one day ahead of a British plan to do the same. In 1940, Hitler's peace offers were turned down by Churchill. And before Germany declared war on the USA, the Americans were already attacking German ships and giving financial and material support to warring Britain. Moreover, even assuming exclusive German guilt for the war, the Allies still could have taken steps towards a peaceful resolution of the conflict, especially when their war fortunes improved, but they totally rejected the idea. So, Gandhi had a point when he refused to give the Allies credit for better war morals.

But Gandhi went even farther than to distribute the guilt more evenly: he kept on believing that Hitler had a human side which could be addressed and awakened. In 1939–45, it was already non-conformistic to acknowledge that there could be good Germans. Today, it is still eccentric to concede that one or other individual Nazi was actually a human being. One who did get that recognition was Oskar Schindler, who saved hundreds of Jews by employing them in his factory, and whose story became famous through Steven Spielberg's film Schindler's List. Another one was John Rabe, who saved hundreds of thousands of Chinese during the Japanese 'rape of Nanjing' in 1937. He was a German businessman in China and a loyal Nazi Party member, and it was these Nazi credentials which gave him the chance to do some good: 'After all, he has only to wave his swastika armband under the nose of a vicious Japanese soldier to stop him in his tracks', and so, when all the foreigners and rich Chinese had fled Nanjing, 'Rabe stays on to face unimaginable horrors and doesn't leave until some sort of order has been restored and the people clinging to his coat-tails—he had 600 of them in his own garden—are able to leave the Safety Zone without being massacred. (...) without the Good German's initiative the evil would have been on a far more massive scale.'[11]

The line between good and evil runs through every man, not between class and class, not between nation and nation. But in 1944, even the anti-Nazi conspirators who plotted Hitler's death weren't considered as good enough Germans. The Allied war leaders were fighting against Germany, not against some hazily defined subsection called Nazis. They didn't want to trouble themselves with nuances, and demanded the unconditional surrender of Germany, even in case a non-Nazi government would take over.[12] It may be noted that the German conspirators against Hitler thought of circumventing the demand of 'unconditional surrender' by appealing to the authority of the Pope. From the viewpoint of Roman Catholic 'just war' theory, developed from Saint Thomas Aquinas onwards, a peaceful solution was obviously preferable to an unnecessary continuation of the war. A war can only be 'just' if it is, among other conditions, economical with violence, i.e. if its aims cannot be achieved by peaceful means. In this case, the retreat from the occupied countries and the release of all prisoners by a post-Nazi regime would have been more economical with violence than the continuation of the war, hence preferable. Yet, if a post-Nazi regime had arisen and offered peace, the Allies were determined to reject it, just as they had rejected Rudolf Hess's strange peace mission in 1941, and just as they had rejected Hitler's own peace offers in 1940.

Restraints on war were already an ancient value in Hindu Civilization, which is one reason why Gandhi could never muster any enthusiasm for the Allies' all-out war against the Axis powers. But in his attitude to Hitler as an individual, I discern more of the Christian influence on the Mahatma: just as Jesus was depicted as braving the disapproval of decent society by dealing with all manner of despised and hated people (foreigners, tax collectors, public women), Gandhi was willing to assume a basic human quality even in Hitler. And of course, though no reputation-conscious Gandhian will come forward to say it aloud; Gandhi would not have been Gandhi if he hadn't extended his faith in man's capacity for compassion and self-correction to even Adolf Hitler. So, he wrote a letter to Hitler advising him to try the way of non-violence. Hitler didn't care to send a reply, though his war policy was reply enough. While it was in principle possible to bring out the humane side in every human being including Hitler, the Mahatma was not the man to achieve such a feat. Nonetheless, it was probably meritorious and certainly quintessentially Gandhian that he tried.

In the absence of a true sage capable of kindling the peace-loving spark in Hitler by mystic means, it still remained possible to save and maintain the peace in Europe by time-tested regular means. It was done during the Cold War. As long as nobody had the strength and the will to stop him, Stalin gobbled up country after country in Europe and East Asia in 1944–50; but after the Anglo-Americans moved to support the counter-insurgency effort in Greece and the international community (with Indian participation) showed its seriousness about containing Communist expansionism in Korea, the rate of Communist expansions sharply declined, and Communism was contained until it imploded. It is from this kind of combat-ready position, exuding readiness to throw a predator-state back the moment it makes a wrong move, that the Allies might have contained Nazi Germany as well: peace through strength.

Of course, such an armed but non-violent solution would not have been a Gandhian solution. Containment of Germany by non-fascist governments (like Léon Blum's Front Populaire in France) was too Gandhian: they were pacifistic and cut down on defense expenditure. The British Labour Party even wanted to dismantle the Royal Air Force. So, Hitler felt confident when he attacked the democracies, anticipating little resistance and little will to fight. With Gandhi in charge, France would simply have abolished its army and traded its artillery in for spinning-wheels, a defence policy which wouldn't have impressed Hitler very much. With a Savarkar in charge, by contrast, the countries threatened by Nazi Germany might have built up their strength and dissuaded the Nazis from attacking them. Maybe, just maybe, that would have led to some self-introspection in Nazi Germany, to a swastika version of glasnost and perestroika, to the return of normalcy.[13]

## 2. 'QUIT INDIA' AND THE IMPENDING AXIS VICTORY

For India, the entry of the Soviet Union and Japan into the war in 1941 changed the situation in terms of ideology c.q. strategy. For the first reason, the Communists changed the party-line and, along with Nehru, started supporting the British. For the second reason, Gandhiji, who had first been inclined to support the British, was reckoning with a Japanese victory when he announced the Quit India agitation. The minutes of the preceding Allahabad session of Congress make it clear that impending British defeat was widely taken for granted, which partly explains the vehemence of the British crackdown on the 'traitorous' Quit India activists. Though in mid-1942 the Germans were facing the first setbacks, the Japanese were still going from victory to victory, and especially the surrender of Singapore (February 1942) had impressed on most Indians the inevitability of a British defeat.

Gandhiji's reasoning was that the Japanese were essentially waging war on the colonial powers (which category included the United States, given its possessions in the Pacific), not on the Asian nations. This was not correct, as Japan had attacked the Chinese Republic and Thailand, but it certainly agreed with the Japanese propaganda of a brotherly 'Greater East-Asian Co-Prosperity Sphere'.

Nonetheless it was a reasonable proposition that native Indians guarding their motherland would better be able to deal with the Japanese than the British occupation forces, either by preventing further hostilities or by offering 'non-violent resistance' in case the Japanese did invade India. It was in view of an impending Japanese invasion that in August 1942, the British were called upon to make haste and 'quit India'.

Altogether, Congress policy under Gandhi and Nehru was quite confused: Nehru was influenced by the Soviet party-line, while Gandhi dreamed of dissuading Hitler by non-violent means. Most Congressmen were indignant when the Viceroy agreed to involve India in the war effort without consulting the Indian leaders, but many disagreed with the Congress leadership's decision to boycott the British administration by retreating from the Provincial Governments. After the attack on the Soviet Union, Nehru became an enthusiastic supporter of the Anglo-Soviet war effort, but failed to win a majority for his new position in the Congress leadership. After the Japanese entry into the war, Gandhi ordered a semi-violent agitation against the British. The Congress leadership was locked up and released only in 1943–44, on condition of their lending support to the war effort. This way, in the period 1939–45, Congress took, in succession or even at the same time, practically all possible positions vis-à-vis the war. By contrast, the Hindu Mahasabha's position was crystal-clear—supporting the British war effort and gaining military experience and a foothold inside the British-Indian Army. In geostrategic terms, Gandhi, along with Congress Socialists like Jayaprakash Narayan, had become a fence-sitter: in the worldwide polarization, he refused to side with either camp. Trying to be 'above' the ongoing conflict is perhaps a typical attitude of pacifists, but unless one is slightly more powerful (or vastly more clever) than the two contenders, it is not usually a very profitable position. It is certainly more rewarding to be on the side of the winner. And a cool consideration of the military equation in Asia would have suggested that Japan, in spite of its impressive successes, had little chance of conquering and keeping Burma and India, where its forces would be over-extended and unable to defeat the British—at least if the British were supported by the Indian people. Perhaps the Indian people themselves were holding the balance, tipping it in favour of the Japanese or the British—depending on their own active loyalty. In these circumstances, however, it was not the Hindutva movement but a leftist Congress faction which opted for collaboration with the Axis.

## NOTES

1. M.K. Gandhi in *Harijan*, 22-6-1940, quoted in Nirad Chaudhuri: *Thy Hand, Great Anarch*, p. 536.

2. M.K. Gandhi: 'How to combat Hitlerism', *Harijan*, 22-6-1940. It may be noted that by and large, the population of France, and likewise that of Belgium, heaved a sigh of relief and expressed its gratitude when their Government ceased fire. The French Parliament voted in favour of the armistice. With World War I in mind, many preferred German occupation (also because the German soldiers gave a first impression of discipline and restraint, not plundering or raping) to the prospect of endless and wasteful warfare. Of course, the national mythology of these countries doesn't like this fact to be highlighted, but the population agreed with Gandhiji that liberty was not worth the wholesale destruction of their own nations.

3. Larry Collins and Dominique Lapierre: *Freedom at Midnight*, Avon 1976 (1975), p. 385. For a discussion of his advice to the Jews, and the reaction of some Jewish intellectuals, vide Dennis Dalton: *Mahatma Gandhi: Nonviolent Power in Action*; Columbia University Press, New York 1993, pp. 134–138.

4. Vide e.g., John Charmley: *Churchill, the End of Glory*, Hodder and Stoughton 1992; or, for a non-symphatizing mention of Churchill revisionism (also criticized, at the time of Charmley's publication, by historian Norman Stone), vide e.g. Gertrude Himmelfarb: 'The company he kept', *New York Times Book Review*, 16-7-1995, a review of Andrew Roberts: *Eminent Churchillians*, Simon & Schuster, New York 1995.

5. Pat Buchanan: *A Republic, Not an Empire*, Regnery Publ., 1999. Likewise Joseph Sobran: 'The friends of Uncle Joe', *Sobran's* monthly, February 2000, pp. 2–6.

6. That is the main thesis of William D. Rubinstein: *The Myth of Rescue*, Routledge, 1997. He is right within his assumption, viz. that the war was inevitable or even necessary. From a certain point onwards, it was at any rate a reality, and within those circumstances, the Allies did what they could. Rubinstein makes a convincing case against those who allege that the Allies refused Jewish refugees (most pre-1940 refugees were easily allowed into the USA, Britain and other countries), that they failed to bomb the railways to Auschwitz (the Germans were very efficient at repairs), etc. No plan could have saved one Jew more, except an agreement with the Nazi regime, or support to its overthrow from within, but both these alternatives were excluded by the Allied insistence on unconditional surrender.

7. Max Arian: 'Bombarderen met woorden', *De Groene Amsterdammer*, 9-6-1999.

8. Arkadi Vaksberg: 'Quand Staline livrait des juifs à Hitler', interview recorded by Guillaume Malaurie, *Le Vif/L'Express*, 2-1-1998. Vaksberg quotes Molotov, after his nomination as Soviet Foreign Minister, as saying to his predecessor Litvinov in 1939: 'We are here to disperse the synagogue.' A crown witness of Stalin's policy of returning refugees from Germany was Margarete Buber-Neumann, wife of Communist

leader Heinz Neumann: he was shot by the Soviets; she was imprisoned in Karaganda, then handed over to the Nazis and locked up in Ravensbrück. She survived the war and testified at Viktor Kravchenko's trial (Paris 1949) and in a book: *Prisonnière de Staline et d'Hitler* (Seuil, Paris).

9. J.O. Tate: review of Gordon Thomas: *Gideon Spies: The Secret History of the Mossad*, in *Chronicles*, October 1999, p. 25. Shamir's alleged hate for the USA is mentioned as explanation for his okaying the transmission of American military secrets and technology to Communist countries.

10. Wu Hongda (Harry Wu): *Laogai, the Chinese Gulag*, Westview, Boulder 1992, p. xii. In 1960, Wu had been locked up for 19 years as a 'counterrevolutionary rightist element'. In 1994 he estimated that there were still 10 million people doing slave labour in Laogai camps.

11 Andrew Barrow: 'The nicest of Nazis', *Spectator*, 6-2-1999, a review of Erwin Wickert, ed.: *the Good German of Nanking: the Diaries of John Rabe*, Little, Brown, 1999. Rabe died in Germany in 1950, after living through the Soviet rape of Berlin, his diaries were discovered only in 1996.

12. Churchill said about the overtures from German conspirators against Hitler: 'Our attitude towards all such inquiries or suggestions should be absolute silence'; quoted in Thomas Powers: 'The conspiracy that failed', *New York Review of Books*, 9-1-1997, from Marie Vassiltchikov: *The Berlin Diaries* 1940–45, Knopf, p. 187.

13. I am of course aware that writers who speculate on the 'what if' of Nazi history, 'invariably overlook the fact that in a system of competing Nazi agencies, representing a plurality of ideological tendencies, there could have been more than one possible outcome', as pointed out by Michael Burleigh: 'Nazi Europe: what if Nazi Germany had defeated the Soviet Union', in Niall Ferguson ed.: *Virtual History*, p. 326.

# Appendix 3

# Mahatma Gandhi's Letters to Hitler

(This essay was written in January 2004. A Dutch version was published in the conservative Catholic monthly *Nucleus*, Bruges, February and March 2006. Para 5 is a postscript written in August 2006. The entire paper was included in K. Elst: *Return of the Swastika*, Voice of India, Delhi, 2007, as ch. 2.)

Mahatma Gandhi's admirers are not in the habit of confronting embarrassing facts about their favourite saint. His critics, by contrast, gleefully keep on reminding us of a few facts concerning the Mahatma which seem to undermine his aura of wisdom and ethical superiority. One of the decisive proofs of Gandhi's silly lack of realism, cited by both his Leftist and his Hindutva detractors, is his attempted correspondence with Adolf Hitler, undertaken with a view to persuading Germany's dictator of the value of non-violence. I will now take upon myself the thankless task of arguing that in this attempt, Gandhi was (1) entirely Gandhian, and (2) essentially right.

## 1. GANDHI'S FIRST LETTER TO HITLER

Both of Gandhi's letters to Hitler are addressed to 'my friend'. In the case of anyone else than the Mahatma, this friendliness would be somewhat strange given the advice which Hitler had tendered to the British government concerning the suppression of India's freedom movement. During a meeting in 1937 with government envoy Lord Edward Halifax (who had, under the name Lord Irwin, been Viceroy in India in 1926–31 and with whom Gandhi had signed the Irwin pact in 1931), Hitler had pledged his support to the preservation of the British empire and offered his formula for dealing with the Indian National Congress: shoot Gandhi; if that isn't enough then kill the other leaders too; if that isn't enough then two hundred more activists, and so on until the Indian people will give up the hope of independence. Gandhi may of course have been unaware of Hitler's advice, but it would also be characteristically Gandhian to remain friendly towards his own would-be killer.

Some people will be shocked that Gandhi called the ultimate monster a 'friend'. But the correct view of sinners, view which I imbibed as the 'Christian' attitude but which I believe has universal validity, is that they are all but instances of the general human trait of sinfulness. Hitler's fanaticism, cruelty, coldness of heart and other reprehensible traits may have differed in intensity but not in essence with those very same traits in other human beings. As human beings gifted with reason and conscience, sinners are also not beyond redemption: your fiercest persecutor today may repent and seek your friendship tomorrow. If Gandhi could approach heartless fanatics like Mohammed Ali Jinnah in a spirit of friendship, there is no reason why he should have withheld his offer of friendship from Hitler.

In his first letter dd. 23 July 1939 (*Collected Works*, vol. 70, pp. 20–21), and which the Government did not permit to go, Gandhi does mention his hesitation in addressing Hitler. But the reason is modesty rather than abhorrence: 'Friends have been urging me to write to you for the sake of humanity. But I have resisted their request, because of the feeling that any letter from me would be impertinence.' But the sense of impending war, after the German occupation of Czech-inhabited Bohemia-Moravia (in violation of the 1938 Munich agreement and of the principle of the 'self-determination of nations' which had justified the annexation of German-inhabited Austria and Sudetenland) and rising hostility with Poland, prompted him to set aside his scruples: 'Something tells me that I must not calculate and that I must make my appeal for whatever it may be worth.' Even so, the end of his letter is again beset with scruples and modesty: 'Anyway I anticipate your forgiveness, if I have erred in writing to you. I remain, your sincere friend, Sd. M. MK Gandhi.'

The remainder and substance of this short letter reads: 'It is quite clear that you are today the one person in the world who can prevent a war which may reduce humanity to the savage state. Must you pay that price for an object however worthy it may appear to you to be? Will you listen to the appeal of one who has deliberately shunned the method of war not without considerable success?'

This approach is held in utter contempt by post-War generations. Thus, the Flemish Leftist novelist and literature Professor Kristien Hemmerechts has commented ('Milosevic, Saddam, Gandhi en Hitler', De Morgen, 16-4-1999): 'In other words, Gandhi was a naïve fool who tried in vain to sell his non-violence as a panacea to the Führer.'

This presupposes that Gandhi was giving carte blanche to Hitler for doing that which we know Hitler to have done, viz. the deportation of Jews and others, the mass killings, the ruthless oppression of the subject populations, the self-destructive military policies imposed on the Germans in the final stage of the war. But in reality, Gandhi's approach, if successful, would precisely have prevented that terrible outcome. Most of Hitler's atrocities were made possible by the war circumstances. In peacetime, the German public would not have tolerated the amount of repression which disfigured their society in 1941–45. Indeed, even in the early (and for German civilians, low-intensity) part of the war, protests from the public forced Hitler to stop the programme of euthanasia on the handicapped.

Moreover, it was the paranoia of the Nazi leadership about Jews as a 'fifth column', retained from their (subjective and admittedly distorted) World War I experience of Leftist agitators in the German cities stabbing the frontline soldiers in the back, which made them decide to remove the Jews from society in Germany and the occupied countries. This is clear from official Nazi statements such as Heinrich Himmler's Posen speech of October 1943. In a non-war scenario, at least an organized transfer of the Jews to a safe territory outside Europe could have been negotiated and implemented. Under a peace agreement, especially one backed up by sufficient armed force on the part of the other treaty powers, Hitler could have been kept in check. By escalating rather than containing the war, the Allied as much as the Axis governments foreclosed the more humane options.

When you start a war, you don't know beforehand just what terrible things will happen, but you do know in general that they will be terrible. That is the basic rationale of pacifism, and Gandhi was entirely correct to keep it in mind when most political leaders were getting caught up in war fever. Containing Hitler for a few more decades would have been a trying and testing exercise for Germany's neighbours, but Gandhi never claimed that non-violence was the way of the weak and the lazy. At any rate, would this effort in long-term vigilance not have been preferable to a war with fifty million dead, many more lives ruined, many countries overrun by Communism and fated to further massacres, and the unleashing of nuclear weapons on the world?

## 2. THE CHANCES FOR PEACE IN 1939

At that point in time, Hitler's 'worthy object' to which Gandhi refers, the topic of heated diplomatic exchanges and indeed the professed casus belli of the impending German invasion of Poland, was the rights of the German minority in Poland along with the issue of the 'corridor'. This was a planned over ground railway-cum-motorway which should either link German Pomerania with German East Prussia through Polish West Prussia (including the city of Danzig); or, in case a referendum in West Prussia favoured the region's return to Germany from which it had been taken in 1919, link land-locked Poland with a harbour set aside for the Poles on the Baltic coast through West Prussia. In 1945, all the regions concerned were ethnically cleansed of Germans and allotted to Poland, and Germany no longer claims any of them, but in 1939 many observers felt that the German demands were reasonable or at any rate not worth opposing by military means ('Who would want to die for Danzig?').

It was common knowledge that Poland was oppressing its German and Jewish minorities, so a case could be made that the advancement of the German minority (it goes without saying that Hitler cared less for the Polish Jews) was a just cause. It was also the type of cause which could be furthered through non-violent protests and mobilizing non-violent international support. It wouldn't formally humiliate Poland by making it give up territory or sovereignty, so perhaps the Polish government could be peacefully persuaded to change its ways regarding the minorities. On this point, Gandhi was undeniably right as well as true to himself by highlighting the non-violent option in striving for a worthy political object.

The question of the corridor was less manageable, as it did involve territory and hence unmistakable face-losing concessions by one of the parties. The apprehension which troubled the Poles and their well-wishers was that the demand of a corridor was merely the reasonable-sounding opening move for a total conquest of Poland. It is difficult to estimate Nazi Germany's exact plans for conquest, which was then already and has since remained the object of mythomanic war propaganda. Among the uninformed public, it is still widely believed that the Nazis aimed at 'conquering the world', no less; but this is nonsense. Hitler was ready to respect the British Empire, and his alleged plan for an invasion of America was shown to be a British forgery planted in order to gain American support. In repeated peace offers to France and Britain in autumn 1939 and throughout 1940, Hitler proposed to withdraw from all historically non-German territories (which would still leave him in control of Austria, Sudetenland, West Prussia and some smaller border regions of Poland and, from May–June 1940 on, also Luxemburg, Belgium's East Cantons and French Elzas-Lotharingen) and maintain a territorial status-quo thenceforth.

It is possible that he meant it when he agreed to limit his territorial ambitions to historically German regions, at least where the competition consisted of allied or somehow respected nations such as the Italians or the French. However, in the case of the despised Slavic countries, Poland and Ukraine, the fear of German conquest was more thoroughly justified.

In early 1918, the Treaty of Brest-Litovsk with the fledgling Soviet Union gave Germany control of Poland and western Ukraine. As a soldier, Hitler had applauded this gain of 'living space', which was to be settled with German farmers after moving the Slavs to Siberia. It was also this brief gain which made the subsequent defeat in World War I and the implied loss of territory so unbearable for Hitler and many Germans of his generation. There is no doubt that the Nazi leaders had an eye on these fertile territories for a future expansion of Germany. It was less certain that they wanted to conduct this annexation at once: would they abide by an agreement on a mere corridor if one were concluded, respecting Poland's sovereignty over the rest of its territory?

The safest course was not to take chances and contain Hitler's expansionism by military deterrence. As Poland itself could not provide this, it sought and received the assurance of help from Britain and France. This implied that a brief local war triggered by German aggression against Poland would turn into a protracted international war on the model of the Serb-Austrian crisis of 1914 triggering the Great War now known as World War I. It was at this point that Gandhi asked Hitler to desist from any plans of invading Poland. There can be no doubt that this was a correct demand for a pacifist to make. Was it perhaps a foolish demand, in the sense that no words should have been wasted on Hitler? We will consider this question later on, but note for now that in July 1939 everything was still possible, at least if we believe in human freedom.

### 3. GANDHI'S SECOND LETTER TO HITLER

On 24 December 1940, on the eve of Christmas, which to Christians is a day of peace when the weapons are silenced, Gandhi wrote a lengthy second letter to Hitler. The world situation at that time was as follows: Germany and Italy controlled most of Europe and seemed set to decide the war in their favour, the German-Soviet pact concluded in August 1939 was still in force, and under Winston Churchill, a lonely Great Britain was continuing the war it had declared on Germany immediately after Germany's invasion of Poland in September 1939.

On this occasion, Gandhi took the trouble of justifying his addressing Hitler as 'my friend' and closing his letter with 'your sincere friend', in a brief statement of what exactly he stood for: 'That I address you as a friend is no formality. I own no foes. My business in life has been for the past 33 years to enlist the friendship of the whole of humanity by befriending mankind, irrespective of race, colour or creed.' This very un-Hitlerian reason to befriend Hitler, what Gandhi goes on to call the 'doctrine of universal friendship', contrasts with the Hitler-like hatred of one's enemy which is commonly thought to be the only correct attitude to Hitler.

Gandhi certainly earns the ire of post-war public opinion

by stating: 'We have no doubt about your bravery or devotion to your fatherland, nor do we believe that you are the monster described by your opponents.' To be sure, this was written in a period of fairly limited warfare, well before the total war with the Soviet Union and the USA, and well before the mass killing and deportation of Jews. But the prevailing attitude today is one of judging Hitler and his contemporaries' dealings with him as if they all had the knowledge that we have acquired in and since 1945. By that standard, anyone doubting the British government's hostile depiction of Hitler, including Gandhi, was practically an accomplice to Hitler's crimes.

However, while not giving up on the chance of converting Hitler to more peaceful ways, Gandhi was not that mild in judging the crimes Hitler had already committed. In particular, he criticized the already well-publicized Nazi conviction that the strong have a right to subdue the weak: 'But your own writings and pronouncements and those of your friends and admirers leave no room for doubt that many of your acts are monstrous and unbecoming of human dignity, especially in the estimation of men like me who believe in human friendliness. Such are your humiliation of Czechoslovakia, the rape of Poland and the swallowing of Denmark. I am aware that your view of life regards such spoliations as virtuous acts. But we have been taught from childhood to regard them as acts degrading humanity.'

So, Gandhi felt forced to join the ranks of Hitler's opponents: 'Hence we cannot possibly wish success to your arms.' Yet this did not make him join the British war effort nor even some non-violent department of the British Empire's cause: 'But ours is a unique position. We resist British imperialism no less than Nazism.' To Gandhi, British imperialism is closely akin to Nazi imperialism: 'If there is a difference, it is in degree. One-fifth of the human race has been brought under the British heel by means that will not bear scrutiny.'

In outlining his position vis-à-vis British imperialism, Gandhi at once explained his attitude vis-à-vis Nazism: 'Our resistance to it does not mean harm to the British people. We seek to convert them, not to defeat them on the battle-field.' This was exactly what Gandhi was now trying out on Hitler: to convert him rather than defeat him, thus sparing him defeat if only he had listened.

Follows an explanation of the Gandhian method of making 'their rule impossible by non-violent non-co-operation', based on 'the knowledge that no spoliator can compass his end without a certain degree of co-operation, willing or unwilling, of the victim.' In a slogan: 'The rulers may have our land and bodies but not our souls.' To this, Hitler probably made a mental comment that prisoners, such as the many people whom he himself was locking away, were quite entitled to their souls, as long as they left their land as living space and their bodies as slave labour to the rulers.

Unlike many of his countrymen, Gandhi rejected the idea of achieving freedom from British rule with German help: 'We know what the British heel means for us and the non-European races of the world. But we would never wish to end the British rule with German aid.' Instead, Gandhi explained to Hitler, the non-violent method could defeat 'a combination of all the most violent forces in the world.'

In Gandhi's view, a violent winner is bound to be defeated by superior force in the end (a prediction proven true in Hitler's case), and even the memory of his victory will be tainted by its violent nature: 'If not the British, some other power will certainly improve upon your method and beat you with your own weapon. You are leaving no legacy to your people of which they would feel proud.' Here Gandhi probably projected his own disapproval of violent methods onto the masses of mankind, who are less inhibited by scruples about glorifying violent winners. Look at the lionization of Chengiz Khan in Mongolia, of Timur and Babar in Uzbekistan, of Alexander in Greece and Macedonia, even though their empires didn't last forever; and rest assured that most Germans would likewise have been proud of Hitler if he had been victorious.

## 4. GANDHI'S SACRED DUTY TO ADDRESS HITLER

Gandhi would not have been Gandhi if he hadn't attempted to prevent World War II. This was, to our knowledge, the single most lethal war in world history, with a death toll estimated as up to fifty million, not mentioning the even larger number of refugees, widows and orphans, people deported, people maimed, lives broken by the various horrors of war. It would be a strange pacifist who condoned this torrent of violence.

Nowadays it is common to lambast those who opposed the war. American campaigners against involvement in the war, such as aviator Charles Lindbergh, are routinely smeared as Nazis for no other reason than that they opposed war against the Nazis (or more precisely, war against the Germans, for only a minority of the seven million Germans killed during the war were Nazis). Leftist readers may get my point if they recall how those who opposed anti-Communist projects such as the Bay of Pigs invasion of Cuba or the Vietnam War were automatically denounced as being Communists themselves. Do they think this amalgamation of opposition to war and collusion (or actual identity) with the enemy is justified?

Gandhi's utterances regarding Nazism leave no doubt about his firm hostility to this militaristic and freedom-hating doctrine. Yet, he opposed war against Nazism. This was entirely logical, for he rejected the militaristic element in both Nazism and the crusade against it. He did support the fight against Nazism but envisioned it as a non-violent struggle aimed at convincing rather than destroying.

It is not certain that this would have worked, but then Gandhism is not synonymous with effectiveness. Gandhi's methods were successful in dissuading the British from holding on to India, not in dissuading the Muslim League from partitioning India. From that angle, it simply remains an open question, an untried experiment, whether the Gandhian approach could have succeeded in preventing World War II. By contrast, there simply cannot be two opinions on whether that approach of non-violent dissuasion would have been Gandhian. The Mahatma would not have been the Mahatma if he had preferred any other method. Our judgement of his letters to Hitler must be the same as our judgement of Gandhism itself: either both were erroneous and ridiculous, or both represented a lofty ethical alternative to the more common methods of power politics.

## 5. POSTSCRIPT

Some readers have wondered how I could possibly think that it made sense to reason with a monster like Adolf Hitler. They cannot get out of the amazingly strong consensus that World War II was a good and necessary war and that pacifism in those circumstances was nothing less than a crime. They ask rhetorically: how on earth could anyone countenance leaving in power the man who ordered the Holocaust?

I need not limit my answer to the matter of double standards, viz. the fact that none of these critics seems to have a problem with the world community's decision not to interfere with the regimes of Josef Stalin and Mao Zedong, who killed a lot more people than Hitler did. None of them says: 'Yes, it would have been worth the price if we had sacrificed a hundred million lives for the sake of regime change in the Soviet Union and the People's Republic of China. That was our ethical duty.' So, it turns out to be very easy to countenance leaving totalitarian mass-murderers in peace. Especially since the implosion of the Soviet system in 1989–91 has revealed that even such seemingly impregnable regimes can be dismantled from the inside. Left to itself, even the Nazi regime would have proven to be subject to the law of impermanence.

More compelling and more specific is the point that in the case of no war, there would have been no Holocaust. There is ample evidence that in case of British cooperation, Nazi Germany would have transferred the Jewish population under its control to some colonial territory (just as Stalin planned to transfer the Soviet Jews to Birobijan in Russia's Far East). With hindsight, the question in 1939–40 was: shall we defeat Hitler but let him eliminate his Jewish hostages while the war lasts, or shall we save the Jews and leave Hitler in power for another while? That would then have been a Hitler without the Holocaust, still not a nice man to know but not the incarnation of evil either.

And World War II was a lot more than the Holocaust. Were all those dozens of millions of victims, combatant and civilian, really worth it? Possibly, but I would like to hear the people who imply this speak it out more clearly: 'Yes, I am all in favour of getting fifty million people killed for the sake of regime change in Germany.'

War necessarily increases the evil and the will to harm in men; after the first exchanges of fire, after you've seen some of your comrades killed by the conscripts on the other side, the initial sportsmanlike will to victory gives way to a far more frenzied desire for vengeance. After the declarations of war, the Phoney War of 1939 led to the gentlemen's war between soldiers in the Battle of Britain of 1940 and the struggle in North Africa of 1941–42, then to far more gruesome war on the Eastern Front, the deportations and mass killings in the camps, the actions of the Resistance and the reprisals against them, the mass fire bombings of cities, the mass rapes and mass expulsions of civilians, and the use of the atom bombs. Around the sixtieth anniversary of the bombing of Dresden in February 1945, an Anglican clergyman made the decisive observation in the debate over the rights and wrongs of it all, viz. that after years of war, all those involved had gotten brutalized, their moral sensitivity numbed. And that escalation of grimness is what always happens in the course of a war. Every war is different, but in each case it is a safe prediction at the outset that you will get far more atrocities and damage than you bargained for.

Those who nonetheless maintain that World War II was worth it, should face the fact that this position makes it difficult for them to oppose any other war. If killing tens of millions in World War II was justified, why should the Iraq war not be justified, where the dead are only counted in tens of thousands? If denying the convention-sanctioned 'prisoner of war' status (with guarantees of decent treatment) to prisoners of war was justified when the Americans did it to hundreds of thousands of Germans in 1945, why should you protest against it when the Americans do it to hundreds of Muslims in Guantanamo Bay in 2005? If killing hundreds of thousands of Japanese with atomic bombs was justified, why hold protest demonstrations when Israeli bombing kills hardly a thousand Lebanese? If raping millions of German women and even thousands of liberated prisoners was part of the just and sacred victory over evil incarnate, why worry about mass rape in Bangladesh 1971 or in Darfur at the time of this writing? All that evil was unleashed the day it was decided to prefer the Holy War to what would allegedly have been a shameful peace.

Nowadays, wars are typically justified with references to the sacred duty of waging World War II. You want to bomb Serbia? 'Slobodan Milosevic is the new Hitler!' You want to invade Iraq? 'Saddam Hussein is the new Hitler!' You hear people opposing these wars? 'They have the Munich spirit, and we all know where that leads!'

This can have pretty perverse effects. US President Bill Clinton's Secretary of State Madeleine Albright, born in Munich-age Czechoslovakia, was obsessed with 'the Munich spirit' of appeasement so she always advocated the hard line. When UN data indicated that the American-imposed embargo on Iraq had led to the death of hundreds of thousands of Iraqi children, she bluntly asserted that the pressure on Saddam Hussein affected by the embargo 'was worth the price'. And what did she achieve, in Munich terms, with her aggression on Serbia over the Serbian province of Kosovo? In Munich 1938, the European powers accepted the secession of a part (Sudetenland) of a small Central-European country (Czechoslovakia) where a minority ethnic group with foreign ties (Germany) formed the majority. With the Kosovo war of 1999, the Americans imposed the de facto secession of a province (Kosovo) of a small Central-European country (Serbia) where a minority ethnic group with foreign ties (Albania) formed the majority. There are more Nazi parallels to the Kosovo war, though not the kind to which Madeleine Albright would like to draw attention, e.g. just as Hitler justified his invasion of Poland with false allegations of Polish aggression on German border posts, the USA justified its bombing of Serbia with totally confabulated allegations of a Serb 'genocide' on a quarter million Albanians.

The uncritical, indeed virtually religious extolling of World War II as a necessary and good war forms a permanently fertile soil for the justifications of all future wars. If anyone says that he is in favour of peace, the theory part of my litmus test would be whether he can bring himself to favouring or at least mentally exploring non-violent alternatives to World War II. For if he accepts the most lethal war in history as good, he loses all standing to denounce smaller wars as evil. There is a way out here for him, viz. to say that that war too was evil, but unfortunately a necessary evil. That claim is dependent on (the usually unexamined assumption of) the unavailability of less violent alternatives, which then becomes a matter of historical investigation of fact rather than of moral evaluation.

Another objection that has been made is that the British and other civilized nations simply were in no position to choose a non-violent alternative since war was forced upon them by the Nazis. This may now seem obvious and certainly has become an unquestioned assumption, but in 1939–41 the Communists made common cause with the Nazis (and jointly, they enjoyed a lot of goodwill among non-European populations, so theirs may have been the majority opinion worldwide) in denouncing the bourgeois democracies and particularly the colonial racist Winston Churchill as having inflicted the war on mankind. But then, the argument continues, his hand was forced by the prospect of seeing Germany break ever[y] new peace treat[y] and conquering one country after another, as had been done with Czechoslovakia and Poland. Indeed, this reasoning goes, even if the Nazis had been talked into peace in 1939–40, their intrinsic lust for war would only have erupted with greater force a few years later.

In that case, there was still a solution short of war. But at this point, the Gandhian strategy falters and a non-Gandhian alternative has to fill the little gap in the Mahatma's grand strategy for peace. In spite of the love of war for war's sake that you do find in some vaguely fascist authors, there was still some rationality left in Nazi Germany. Both Hitler and the Army High Command were reportedly downhearted when Britain and France followed up the invasion of Poland with a declaration of war on Germany. A bit of territorial expansion once in a while was welcome, but not at any price, especially not for men who had been German soldiers in the fateful Great War of 1914–18. So, the solution was to let them feel beforehand that more conquest would come at an intolerably high price. Had Britain and France built up their military force in the 1930s, presenting a real deterrent to German ambitions, it could have dissuaded the German leadership from further adventures.

This alternative was not tried, partly because the socialists and many others in Britain and France figured that fighting Nazi militarism should not be done by imitating it. To that extent, they had the Gandhian spirit: don't fight violence with violence, 'An eye for an eye makes the whole world blind.' This approach would have been alright if they had had the soul force that Gandhi always talked about, the kind of soul force that turns the tiger into a lamb. Send out those good vibrations and all evil people will turn good. Not that Gandhi had this soul force when he needed it (as when facing the Pakistan movement), but as an idea, as a pipe-dream, it was Gandhian par excellence.

In this case, however, the approach with a better chance of success would have been the one advocated by Gandhi's political opponent Vinayak Damodar Savarkar. In anticipation of the communal conflagration that brought forth Pakistan, he advised that Hindus build up their fighting strength so that the Muslims wouldn't dare to take them on and impose their separatist plans on them. The aggressor would have abstained from violence out of fear for the consequences, and justice would have prevailed without a shot being fired. This strategy was not tried in India, with the bloody results we all know, but elsewhere it has proved its worth. In the Cold War, smaller battles were fought between the American-led and the Soviet-led camps, but the big confrontation was averted because Soviet ambitions were deterred by NATO vigilance. The miracle formula for coexisting with an aggressor without having to suffer his aggression did exist, but it was more Savarkarite than Gandhian: 'peace through strength.'

As a teenage leftist, I joined anti-NATO, anti-armament and 'anti-war' demonstrations. We shouted slogans like: 'Belgium out of NATO, NATO out of Belgium!' With the wilful deafness of an ideological fanatic, I remained unmoved by the apt rightist reply to all our sloganeering: 'Peace? Gladly, NATO provides it.' And I pitied our Latin teacher, that stone-age obscurantist, who reminded us: '*Si vis pacem, para bellum*' ('If you want peace, be prepared for war'). Maybe the Romans had that one from Savarkar, or maybe the other way around, but it was perfect common sense.

Gandhi was gravely mistaken in thinking that you can make the enemy disarm by first disarming yourself. Yet, he was right in setting his sights on peace. Being prepared for war was the right tactic, but its target should have been a bloodless crisis management, not war. Strength should be mustered not to make but to avoid war, the source of many evils.

## BIBLIOGRAPHY

*The Collected Works of Mahatma Gandhi*, Volume 76 (31 May 1939 to 15 October 1939), Publications Division, Ministry of Information and Broadcasting, Government of India 1979, 1st Reprint 1994, 2nd Revised Edition 2000, pp. 156–157, Letter No. 200, dated July 23, 1939.

*The Collected Works of Mahatma Gandhi*, Volume 79 (16 July 1940 to 27 December 1940), Publications Division, Ministry of Information and Broadcasting, Government of India 1980, 1st Reprint 1994, 2nd Revised Edition 2001, pp. 453–456, Letter No. 520, dated December 24, 1940 (This letter was suppressed by the Government of India, ibid., p. 453).

# Appendix 4

# Learning from Mahatma Gandhi's Mistakes

(This article was written in January 2004, originally as the text for some lectures to the general public in the Western world.)

Mahatma Gandhi is often praised as the man who defeated British imperialism with non-violent agitation. It is still a delicate and unfashionable thing to discuss his mistakes and failures, a criticism hitherto mostly confined to Communist and Hindutva publications. But at this distance in time, we shouldn't be inhibited by a taboo on criticizing India's official patron saint.

## 1. GANDHIJI'S MISTAKES

Without attempting to approach completeness, we may sum up as Gandhi's biggest political failures the following events:

(a) Recruiting Indian soldiers for the British war effort in 1914–18 without setting any conditions, in the vain hope that this unilateral gift to Britain would bring about sufficient goodwill in London for conceding to India the status of a self-ruling dominion within the British Empire, on a par with Canada or Australia. While it was already off line for a pacifist to cooperate in such a wasteful war (as contrasted with World War II, to both sides a kind of holy war where fundamental principles were at stake), Gandhiji's stance was also a glaring failure of political skill, since he neglected to extract any tangible gains for India in return for the thousands of Indian lives which he sacrificed to British imperial interests.

(b) Committing the mobilization potential of the freedom movement to the Khilafat agitation in 1920–22, again a non-negotiated unilateral gift. The Khilafat Movement was a tragicomical mistake, aiming at the restoration of the Ottoman Caliphate against which the Arabs had risen in revolt and which the Turks were dissolving, a process completed with the final abolition of the institution of the Caliphate in 1924. It was a purely retrograde and reactionary movement, and more importantly for Indian nationalism, it was an intrinsically anti-nationalist movement pitting, specifically, Islamic interests against secular and non-Muslim interests. Gandhi made the mistake of hubris by thinking he could reconcile Khilafatism and Indian nationalism, and he also offended his Muslim allies (who didn't share his commitment to non-violence) by calling off the agitation when it turned violent. The result was even more violence, with massive Hindu-Muslim riots replacing the limited instances of anti-British attacks, just as many level-headed freedom fighters had predicted. Gandhiji failed to take the Khilafat Movement seriously whether at the level of principle or of practical politics, and substituted his own imagined and idealized reading of the Khilafat doctrine for reality.

(c) His autocratic decision to call off the mass agitation for complete independence in 1931, imposed upon his mass following and his close lieutenants against their wishes and better judgement, in exchange for a few puny British concessions falling far short of the movement's demands. His reputation abroad didn't suffer, but to informed observers, he had thrown away his aura as an idealist leader standing above petty politics; the pact between Gandhi and Viceroy Lord Irwin amounted to the sacrifice of a high national goal in favour of a petty rise in status for the Congress. Also, every delay in the declaration of Independence gave the emerging separatist forces the time to organize and to strengthen their position.

(d) Taking a confused and wavering position vis-à-vis India's involvement in World War II. His initial refusal to commit India to the war effort could have been justified on grounds of pacifist principle as well as national pride (the Viceroy had committed India without consulting the native leadership), but it was a failure because his followers weren't following. Indian recruits and business suppliers of the Army eagerly joined hands with the British rulers, thus sidelining Gandhi into political irrelevance. By contrast, the Muslim League greatly improved its bargaining positions by joining the war effort, an effect not counterbalanced by the small Hindu Mahasabha's similar strategy. The pro-Partition case which the Muslim League advocated was bolstered while Gandhi's opposition to the imminent Partition was badly weakened. Gandhi was humiliated by his impotence before the degeneration of his 'Quit India' agitation into violence and by ultimately having to come around to a collaborationist position himself.

(e) Taking a confused and wavering position vis-à-vis the Partition plan, including false promises to the Hindus of the designated Pakistani areas to prevent Partition or at least to prevent their violent expulsion. He chose not to use his weapon of a fast unto death to force Mohammed Ali Jinnah into backing down from Partition, a move which cast doubt on the much-touted bravery of all his other fasts unto death performed to pressurize more malleable opponents. If acquiescing in the Partition could still be justified as a matter of inevitability, there was no excuse for his insistence on half measures, viz. his rejecting plans for an organized exchange of population, certainly a lesser evil when compared to the bloody religious cleansing that actually took place. Gentle surgeons make stinking wounds.

(f) Refusing to acknowledge that Pakistan had become an enemy state after its invasion of Kashmir, by undertaking a fast unto death in order to force the Indian government to pay Pakistan fifty-five crore rupees from the British-Indian treasury. Pakistan was entitled to this money, but given its aggression, it would have been normal to set the termination of its aggression, including the withdrawal of its invading troops, as a condition for the payment. Indeed, that would have been a sterling contribution to the cause of enduring peace, saving the lives of the many thousands who fell in subsequent decades because of the festering wound which Kashmir has remained under partial Pakistani occupation. Coming on top of Gandhi's abandonment of the Hindus trapped in Pakistan in August 1947, it was this pro-Pakistani demand, as well as his use of his choice moral weapon (left unused to save India's unity or the persecuted Hindus in Pakistan) in the service of an enemy state's treasury, that angered a few Hindu activists to the point of plotting his murder.

## 2. PROBLEMS WITH PACIFISM

The common denominator in all these costly mistakes was a lack of realism. Gandhi refused to see the realities of human nature; of Islamic doctrine with its ambition of domination; of the modern mentality with its resentment of autocratic impositions; of people's daily needs making them willing to collaborate with the rulers in exchange for career and business opportunities; of the nationalism of the Hindus who would oppose the partition of their Motherland tooth and nail; of the nature of the Pakistani state as intrinsically anti-India and anti-Hindu.

In most of these cases, Gandhi's mistake was not his pacifism per se. In the case of his recruiting efforts for World War I, there wasn't even any pacifism involved, but loyalty to the Empire whether in peace or in war. The Khilafat pogroms revealed one of the real problems with his pacifism: all while riding a high horse and imposing strict conformity with the pacifist principle, he indirectly provoked far more violence than was in his power to control. Other leaders of the freedom movement, such as Annie Besant and Lala Lajpat Rai, had warned him that he was playing with fire, but he preferred to obey his suprarational 'inner voice'.

The fundamental problem with Gandhi's pacifism, not in the initial stages but when he had become the world-famous leader of India's freedom movement (1920–47), was his increasing extremism. All sense of proportion had vanished when he advocated non-violence not as a technique of moral pressure by a weaker on a stronger party, but as a form of masochistic surrender. Elsewhere (above, *Gandhi and His Assassin*, p. 94) I have cited four instances of his advice to the victims of communal violence which is simply breathtaking for its callousness in the face of human suffering. Two more instances follow.

During his prayer meeting on 1 May 1947, he prepared the Hindus and Sikhs for the anticipated massacres of their kind in the upcoming state of Pakistan with these words: 'I would tell the Hindus to face death cheerfully if the Muslims are out to kill them. I would be a real sinner if after being stabbed I wished in my last moment that my son should seek revenge. I must die without rancour. (…) You may turn round and ask whether all Hindus and all Sikhs should die. Yes, I would say. Such martyrdom will not be in vain.' (*The Collected Works of Mahatma Gandhi*, vol. LXXXVII, p. 394–5) It is left unexplained what purpose would be served by this senseless and avoidable surrender to murder.

Even when the killing had started, Gandhi refused to take pity on the Hindu victims, much less to point fingers at the Pakistani aggressors. More importantly for the principle of non-violence, he failed to offer them a non-violent technique of countering and dissuading the murderers. Instead, he told the Hindu refugees from Pakistan to go back and die. On 6 August 1947, Gandhiji commented to Congress workers on the incipient communal conflagration in Lahore thus: 'I am grieved to learn that people are running away from the West Punjab and I am told that Lahore is being evacuated by the non-Muslims. I must say that this is what it should not be. If you think Lahore is dead or is dying, do not run away from it, but die with what you think is the dying Lahore. (...) When you suffer from fear you die before death comes to you. That is not glorious. I will not feel sorry if I hear that people in the Punjab have died not as cowards but as brave men. (...) I cannot be forced to salute any flag. If in that act I am murdered I would bear no ill will against anyone and would rather pray for better sense for the person or persons who murder me.' (*Hindustan Times*, 8-8-1947, CWoMG, vol. LXXXIX, p. 11)

So, he was dismissing as cowards those who saved their lives fleeing the massacre by a vastly stronger enemy, viz. the Pakistani population and security forces. But is it cowardice to flee a no-win situation, so as to live and perhaps to fight another day? There can be a come-back from exile, not from death. Is it not better to continue life as a non-Lahorite than to cling to one's location in Lahore even if it has to be as a corpse? Why should staying in a mere location be so superior to staying alive? To be sure, it would have been even better if Hindus could have continued to live with honour in Lahore, but Gandhi himself had refused to use his power in that cause, viz. averting Partition. He probably would have found that, like the butchered or fleeing Hindus, he was no match for the determination of the Muslim League, but at least he could have tried. In the advice he now gave, the whole idea of non-violent struggle got perverted.

Originally, in Gandhi's struggle for the Indians' rights in South Africa, non-violent agitation was tried out as a weapon of the weak who wouldn't stand a chance in an armed confrontation. It was a method to achieve a political goal, and a method which could boast of some successes. In the hands of a capable agitator, it could be victorious. It was designed to snatch victory from the jaws of powerlessness and surrender. By contrast, the 'non-violent' surrender to the enemy and to butchery which Gandhi advocated in 1947 had nothing victorious or successful about it.

During the anti-colonial struggle, Gandhi had often said that oppression was only possible with a certain cooperation or complicity from the oppressed people. The genius of the non-violent technique, not applicable in all situations but proven successful in some, was to create a third way in the violent confrontation between the oppressed and the oppressor, fatally ending in the defeat of the weak, and the passive resignation of the oppressed in their state of oppression. Rather than surrendering to the superior power of the oppressor, the oppressed were given a method to exercise slow pressure on their oppressor, to wrest concessions from him and to work on his conscience. No such third way was left to the minorities in Pakistan: Gandhi's only advice to them was to surrender, to become accomplices in their extermination by meekly offering their necks to the executioner's sword.

My point is not that Gandhi could and should have given them a third way, a non-violent technique that would defeat the perpetrators of Partition and religious cleansing. More realistically, he should have accepted that this was the kind of situation where no such third option was available. Once the sacrifice of a large part of India's territory to a Muslim state had been conceded, and given previous experiences with Muslim violence against non-Muslims during the time of Gandhi's own leadership, he should have realized that an exchange of population was the only remaining bloodless solution. The Partition crisis was simply beyond the capacity of Gandhian non-violence to control. If he had had the modesty to face his powerlessness and accept that alternatives to his own preferred solution would have to be tried, many lives could have been saved.

## 3. ROBUST PACIFISM

It cannot be denied that Gandhian non-violence has a few successes to its credit. But these were achieved under particularly favourable circumstances—the stakes weren't very high and the opponents weren't too foreign to Gandhi's ethical standards. In South Africa, he had to deal with liberal British authorities who weren't affected too seriously in their power and authority by conceding Gandhi's demands. Upgrading the status of the small Indian minority from equality with the Blacks to an in-between status approaching that of the Whites made no real difference to the ruling class, so Gandhi's agitation was rewarded with some concessions. Even in India, the stakes were never really high. Gandhi's Salt March made the British rescind the Salt Tax, a limited financial price to pay for restoring native acquiescence in British paramountcy, but he never made them concede Independence or even Home Rule with a non-violent agitation. The one time he had started such an agitation, viz. in 1930–31, he himself stopped it in exchange for a few small concessions.

It is simply not true that India's Independence was the fruit of Gandhian non-violent agitation. He was close to the British in terms of culture and shared ethical values, which is why sometimes he could successfully bargain with them, but even they stood firm against his pressure when their vital interests were at stake. It is only Britain's bankruptcy due to World War II and the emergence of the anti-colonial United States and Soviet Union as the dominant world powers that forced Clement Attlee's government into decolonizing India. Even then, the trigger events in 1945–47 that demonstrated how the Indian people would not tolerate British rule for much longer, had to do with armed struggle rather than with non-violence: the naval mutiny of Indian troops and the ostentatious nationwide support for the officers of Subhas Bose's Axis-collaborationist Indian National Army when they stood trial for treason in the Red Fort.

So, non-violence need not be written off as a Quixotic experiment, for it can be an appropriate and successful technique in particular circumstances; but it has its limitations. In many serious confrontations, it is simply better, and on balance more just as well as more bloodless, to observe an 'economy of violence': using a small amount of armed force, or even only the threat of armed force, in order to avoid a larger and bloodier armed confrontation. This is the principle of 'peace through strength' followed by most modern governments with standing armies. It was applied, for example, in the containment of Communism; though relatively minor wars between Communist and anti-Communist forces were fought in several Third World countries, both the feared Communist world conquest and the equally feared World War III with its anticipated nuclear holocaust were averted.

The ethical framework limiting the use of force to a minimum is known as 'just war theory', developed by European thinkers such as Thomas Aquinas and Hugo Grotius between the thirteenth and eighteenth century, but in essence already present in the Mahabharata as well. Thus, waging war can be a just enterprise when it is done in self-defence, when all non-violent means of achieving the just objective have been tried, when non-combatants are respected as such, when the means used are in proportion to the objective aimed for, etc.

One of the less well-known criteria for just warfare which deserves to be mentioned here in the light of Gandhi's advice to the Hindus in Pakistan is that there should be a reasonable chance of success. No matter how just your cause, it is wrong to commit your community to a course of action that only promises to be suicidal. Of course, once a group of soldiers is trapped in a situation from which the only exit is an honourable death, fighting on may be the best course remaining, but whenever possible, such suicide should be avoided. This criterion is just as valid in non-armed as in armed struggle; it was wrong to make the Hindus stay among their Pakistani persecutors when this course of action had no chance of saving lives nor even of achieving certain political objectives.

As the Buddha, Aristotle, Confucius and other ethical guides already taught, virtue is a middle term between two extremes. In this case, we have to sail between the two extremes of blindness to human fellow-feeling and blindness to strategic ground realities. It is wrong to say that might makes right and that anything goes when it comes to achieving victory, no matter what amount of suffering is inflicted on the enemy, on bystanders or even on one's own camp. It is equally wrong to strike a high moral posture which haughtily disregards, and hence refuses to contain or subdue, the potential for violence in human confrontations and the real pain it causes. In between these two extremes, the mature and virtuous attitude is one which desires and maintains peace but is able and prepared to fight the aggressor.

Limiting the use of force to a minimum is generally agreed to be the correct position. In this case, disagreeing with Gandhi is not an instance of Communist or Hindu-chauvinist extremism, but of the accumulated wisdom of civilized humanity. Excluding the use of force entirely, by contrast, may simply whet the aggressor's appetite and provoke far more violence than the achievable minimum. This is a mistake which an overenthusiastic and inexperienced beginner can forgivably make, but in an experienced leader like Mahatma Gandhi during his time at the head of the freedom movement, it was a serious failure of judgement. The silver lining in the massacres which his mistakes provoked, is that they have reminded us of the eternal wisdom of 'the golden mean', the need for a balanced policy vis-à-vis the ever-present challenge of violence and aggression. It has been known all along and it is crystal-clear once more that we should avoid both extremes, Jinnah's self-righteousness and Gandhi's sentimentalism.

# Appendix 5

# Questioning the Mahatma

(Book review published in *The Sunday Pioneer*, Delhi, 15 May 2011)

Mahatma Gandhi was a heartless and manipulative tyrant without the redeeming feature of political merit. On the contrary, his vision for India was confused, he twisted the meaning of straightforward terms like Swarajya (independence) to suit his own eccentric fancies, he never overcame his basic loyalty to the British Empire, and he didn't have the courage of his conviction when it was needed to avert the Partition of India. While playing the part of a Hindu sage in sufficient measure to keep the Hindu masses with him, he never championed and frequently harmed Hindu interests. Finally, his sexual experiments with young women were not a private matter but had an impact on his politics. Thus says a new study of Gandhi's political record by Hindu scholar Mrs Radha Rajan.

The latest American book on Mohandas Karamchand Gandhi, Joseph Lelyveld's *Great Soul*, has drawn a lot of attention. This was mainly because of its allegations about yet more eccentric sexual aspects of his Mahatmahood on top of those already known. In particular, Lelyveld overinterprets Gandhi's correspondence with German-Jewish architect Hermann Kallenbach as evidence of a homosexual relationship. Bapu's fans intoned the same mantra as the burners of Salman Rushdie's book *The Satanic Verses*: 'Freedom of expression doesn't mean the right to insult revered figures.' Well, if it doesn't mean that, it doesn't mean much.

In particular, Lelyveld has all the more right to disclose what he found in the Mahatma's bedroom because the latter was quite an exhibitionist himself, detailing every straying thought and nocturnal emission in his sermons and editorials. But do these tickling insinuations carry any weight? Other, more troubling aspects of Gandhi's résumé are far more deserving of closer scrutiny. Some unpleasant instances of his impact on India and Hinduism have been discussed thoroughly in a new book, *Eclipse of the Hindu Nation: Gandhi and His Freedom Struggle* (New Age Publ., Kolkata), by Mrs Radha Rajan, editor of the Chennai-based nationalist website, www.vigilonline.com.

Radha Rajan was already the author, with Krishen Kak, of *NGOs, Activists and Foreign Funds: Anti-Nation Industry* (2006), a scholarly X-ray of the NGO scene, exposing this holier-than-thou cover for both corruption and anti-India machinations. The present book likewise takes a very close look at a subject mostly presented only in the broad strokes of hagiography. In particular, she dissects the Hindu and anti-Hindu content of Gandhi's policies. Both were present, the author acknowledges his complexity, but there was a lot less Hindu in him than mostly assumed.

Rama had Vasishtha, Chandragupta had Chanakya, Shivaji had Ramdas as spiritual advisers, but Gandhi never solicited the guidance of any Hindu rajguru. By contrast, every step of the way in his long formative years, he read Christian authors and welcomed the advice of Christian clergymen. This way, he imbibed many monotheistic prejudices against heathen Hinduism, to the point that in 1946 he insisted for the new temple on the BHU campus not to contain an 'idol'. (p.466)

Gandhi took his Hindu constituents for granted but never

showed any concern for specific Hindu interests. The story that he staked his life to quell the massacres of Hindus in Noakhali in 1947, turns out to be untrue; his trip to East Bengal took place under security cover and well after the worst violence had subsided. There and wherever Hindus were getting butchered en masse in 1947–48, he advised them to get killed willingly rather than fight back or flee. It is breathtaking how often his writings and speeches contain expressions like: 'I don't care if many die.' And it was the first time in Hindu history that anyone qualified going down without a fight against a murderous aggressor as 'brave'.

All his fasts unto death proved to be empty play when he refused to use this weapon to avert the Partition, in spite of promises given. It was the only time when he ran a real risk of being faced with an opponent willing to let him die rather than give in. Radha Rajan documents how unpopular he had become by then, not only among fellow politicians who were exasperated at his irrationality, but also among the masses suffering the effects of his confused policies. Had Gandhi not been murdered, his star would have continued to fall and he would have been consigned to the dustbin of history.

Gandhi made a caricature of Hinduism by presenting his own whimsical and eccentric conduct as quintessentially Hindu, such as the rejection of technological progress, maintaining sexual abstinence even within marriage, and most consequentially, extreme non-violence under all circumstances. This concept owed more to Jesus' 'turning the other cheek' than to Hindu-Buddhist ahimsa. He managed to read his own version of non-violence into the Bhagavad Gita, which in fact centres on Krishna's rebuking Arjuna's plea for Gandhian passivity. He never invoked any of India's warrior heroes and denounced the freedom fighters who opted for armed struggle, under the quiet applause of the British rulers whose lives became a lot more comfortable with such a toothless opponent.

The author acknowledges Gandhiji's sterling contribution to the weakening of caste prejudice among the upper castes. His patronizing attitude towards the Harijans will remain controversial, but the change of heart he effected among the rest of Hindu society vis-à-vis the Scheduled Castes was revolutionary. However, once educated Scheduled Caste people started coming up and speaking for themselves, his response was heartless and insulting. Thus, a letter is reproduced in which the Mahatma, with chilling pedantry, belittles an admiring Constituent Assembly candidate from the scavengers' caste for his 'bookish English' and because: 'The writer is a discontented graduate. (…) I fear he does no scavenging himself' and thus 'he sets a bad example' to other scavengers. (p.480) Few readers will have expected the sheer nastiness of this saint's temper tantrums.

Likewise, his supposed saintliness is incompatible with his well-documented mistreatment of his sons (to whom he refused a proper education) and especially of his faithful wife, whom he repeatedly subjected to public humiliation. Here too, Gandhi's sexual antics receive some attention. The whole idea of an old man seeking to strengthen his brahmacharya (chastity) by sleeping with naked young women is bad enough. Perhaps we had to wait for a lady author to give these victims a proper hearing. Radha Rajan documents the fear with which these women received Gandhi's call to keep him company, as well as their attempts to avoid or escape this special treatment and the misgivings of their families. She praises the self-control of Gandhi's confidants who, though horrified, kept the lid on this information out of concern for its likely demoralizing effect on the Congress movement. The Mahatma himself wasn't equally discreet, he revealed the names of the women he had used in his chastity experiments, unmindful of what it would do to their social standing.

When Sardar Patel expressed his stern disapproval of these experiments, Gandhi reacted with a list of cheap allegations, which Patel promptly and convincingly refuted. Lowly insinuations turn out to be a frequent presence in the Mahatma's correspondence.

As the author observes: 'Reputed historians and other eminent academicians have not undertaken so far any honest study of Gandhi's character. Just as little is known of his perverse experiments with women, as little is known of his vicious anger and lacerating speech that he routinely spewed at people who opposed him or rejected him.' While careful not to offend the powerful among his occasional critics, like his sponsor G.D. Birla, 'he treated those whom he considered inferior to him in status with contempt and in wounding language.' (p.389)

Unlike in Lelyveld's account, the references to Gandhi's sexual gimmicks here have political relevance. Gandhi's discomfort with Patel's disapproval was a major reason for his overruling the Congress workers' preference for Patel and foisting his flatterer Jawaharlal Nehru as Prime Minister on India instead. Thus, argues Radha Rajan, he handed India's destiny over to an emergent coalition of anti-Hindu forces. To replace Nehru as party leader, he had his yes-man J.B. Kripalani selected, not coincidentally the one among those in the know who had explicitly okayed the chastity experiments. The Mahatma's private vices spilled over into his public choices with grave political consequences.

# Appendix 6

# Gandhi and Mandela

(Article published in *Outlook*, Delhi, on 18 July 2013, Nelson Mandela's last birthday)

Now that Nelson Mandela is leaving the stage, we can take stock of his role in history. His name will remain associated with two major turnarounds: the conversion of the nonviolent African National Congress (ANC) to the armed struggle in 1961, and the non-violent transition of South Africa from a white minority regime to non-racial majority rule in 1994. The latter leads to the frequent comparison of Mandela with Mahatma Gandhi, but the former was a conscious break with a policy that was inspired by the same Gandhi.

When the ANC was founded in 1912 (then as Native National Congress), Gandhi lived in South Africa and led the non-violent struggle of the Indian community for more equal rights with Europeans, with some success. Note that Gandhi did not work for the coloureds or blacks, and found it a great injustice that the diligent Indians were treated on a par with the 'indolent' and 'naked' blacks. He did not question the disparity between black and white, only the ranking of the Indians as black rather than white. Nevertheless, the budding ANC took over the non-violent strategy typical of Gandhi's movement.

Later in India, he would lead the fight for a very ambitious goal, namely home-rule and finally the full independence of England's largest colony. That was more than the English would grant him, and in spite of the usual myths, Gandhi's mass movement (by 1947 a fading memory) contributed but little to the eventual decolonization. As Clement Attlee, Prime Minister at the time of India's independence, testified later, Gandhi's importance in the decision to let go of India was 'minimal'. In South Africa, however, the stakes were not that high. The struggle was over the status of the small Indian minority, without much effect on the British administration. For example, the overzealous decision to only recognize Christian marriages was a great source of annoyance to the Indians, but without much importance to the maintenance of colonial rule; it could easily be reversed on Gandhi's insistence.

The fight for the rights of the Indians was conducted non-violently. The Mahatma did not tarnish the fight for a noble cause with the use of evil means. However, he was not entirely averse to violence; he took part in the Boer War (1899–1902) and Second Zulu War (1906) as a voluntary stretcher-bearer and recruited among Indians to participate in the First World War. His somewhat naive calculation was that for his sincere cooperation in the war, the British rulers would grant him political concessions in return.

In Mandela, we see that combination of armed struggle and non-violent political achievements. In 1961, the ANC noted that the peaceful struggle had only yielded failure and decline; the blacks were even worse off in the self-governing South Africa than under British colonial rule. A Gandhian analysis would be that the ANC had mastered the method of non-violent protest insufficiently, but it is understandable that the ANC saw as this as a failing method.

Spurred on by younger leaders like Nelson Mandela, the organization founded an armed wing, the Umkhonto we Sizwe, 'Spear of the Nation'. It is no exaggeration to label the policy of the ANC and Mandela in the following years as 'terrorist'. When

Mandela was put in prison, he was in possession of a large quantity of weapons and explosives. Very recently, my compatriot Hélène Passtoors admitted that she was complicit in a 1983 ANC bomb attack with nineteen fatalities and two-hundred injuries.

As the memory of this face of the ANC dies, we pay more attention to the Mandela of 1994 and subsequent years. While the armed struggle was bloody but militarily fruitless, the ANC gained much more on another front—the mobilization of international public opinion against the Apartheid Government. This forced the white rulers to negotiate with the released Mandela, who now showed a lot of conciliatory goodwill. It was due to him that the transfer of power was peaceful. Later there would nonetheless be a wave of violence against the whites, with the frequent *plaasmoorde* (farm murders), but by then Mandela had already retired from politics.

Like Gandhi, he deserves a nuanced assessment. Both remain associated in our memory with a non-violent transfer of power, but have had their share of armed conflict too.

# Appendix 7

# Gandhi the Englishman

(*The Pioneer*, Delhi, 1 January 2014)

Shortly before Independence, Mahatma Gandhi asked Sardar Vallabhbhai Patel to step down as candidate for the Congress leadership and hence for the upcoming job of Prime Minister. It was the only way to foist Jawaharlal Nehru on India, as Sardar Patel would easily have gotten a majority behind him. Yet, Nehru was overtly Westernized and known to be in favour of industrialization and modernization, while Gandhi was reputedly opposed to this approach.

Was Patel's outlook not more capable, more popular and more Gandhian? With the benefit of hindsight, we can moreover say that the choice for Nehru ultimately led to the festering Kashmir problem, to proverbial socialist poverty, and to the communalization of the polity. Yet, when Gandhi made his fateful pro-Nehru move, he tried to minimize its importance and laughed it off: 'Jawaharlal is the only Englishman in my camp.' This was a most curious reason, as Gandhism was popularly taken to imply a choice for native culture and against Westernization. But then, Gandhi himself was not really a votary of Gandhism.

## 1. BACKWARDNESS

Superficially, of course, with his spinning-wheel, he seemed to be the colourful paragon of Indian *swadeshi* (native produce) ideals. But there already, the problem starts. Indian culture had never opted for willful backwardness. In its time, the Harappan culture played a vanguard role in industry and trade. When you compare the Ramayana and the Mahabharata, you find decisive technological progress—Arjuna has abandoned Rama's bow and arrow (not to speak of Hanuman's mace, the primitive weapon par excellence) for a sword and a chariot. Jokes about Hindus highlight their uptight and greedy nature, but none would question their entrepreneurial skills. Indeed, Indian emigrants to more libertarian countries, and now also the native Indians relatively freed from socialist controls, have surprised everyone with their economic success.

It is the British who de-industrialized India, thus dooming it to backwardness and poverty. In order to give some justification to their policy, they fostered the idea of a 'spiritual' India, uninterested in material progress. Gandhi proved to be a faithful propagator of this British notion. He also tapped into an anti-modern fashion in the West, where some intellectuals got tired of industrialization and set up autarchic communes.

Although Gandhi led the Freedom Movement, he was also a British loyalist. He volunteered for military service in the Boer War and in the suppression of the Zulu rebellion, and recruited for the British war effort in the First World War. From 1920 onwards, as the formal leader of the Indian National Congress, he got crowds marching but didn't achieve much in reality. He let his enthusiastic foot-soldiers down. Initially, it was still possible to be both pro-British and pro-Indian, e.g. Annie Besant's Home Rule League aimed for autonomy (*swaraj*) within the British Empire, on a par with 'grown-up' states like Canada and Australia. In 1929, however, Congress redefined its goal as 'complete independence' (*purna swaraj*). Mass agitation highlighted and popularized this goal, but Gandhi's subsequent conclusion of a far less ambitious pact with Viceroy Lord Irwin betrayed his own pro-British feelings, not shared by his disappointed younger followers. In 1927, he had indeed blocked a similar resolution for full independence, pleading for dominion status instead. From 1942 onwards, as India's independence was being prepared, he was relegated to the sidelines. When Prime Minister Clement Attlee finally announced the transfer of power, the memory of Gandhi's mediagenic mass campaigns was only a 'minimal' factor, as he confided later in an interview.

Being a loyalist of a world-spanning empire, Gandhi was at least immune to a rival Western fashion: nationalism. His opponent Vinayak Damodar Savarkar took inspiration from small nations seeking their nationhood, like the Czechs and Irish wanting independence, or Germany and Italy forging their unity, as exemplified by Savarkar's translation of Giuseppe Mazzini's book championing Italian nationalism. His 'Hindu nation' was numerous enough, but centuries of oppression had given it the psychology of a defensive nation. Gandhi, by contrast, had the outlook of the multinational empire. That helps explain why in 1920 he could become enamoured of the Caliphate movement, defending the Muslim empire from which the Arabs had just freed themselves. It certainly explains his incomprehension for the founding of Hindu nationalist organizations (Hindu Mahasabha 1922, RSS 1925) in reaction against his tragicomical Caliphate agitation.

## 2. UNIVERSALISM

In his youth, Gandhi had been influenced by Jain and Vaishnava saints, but as an adult, he mainly took inspiration from Christian writers like Leo Tolstoy and befriended Westerners like architect Hermann Kallenbach. His name was elevated into an international synonym of non-violent agitation by American journalists. It is logical to suspect a direct transmission from the West for his voguish doctrines, like this political non-violence or his slogan of *sarva-dharma-samabhava*, 'equal respect for all religions'.

The marriage of non-violence and political agitation seems an innovative interpretation of Hinduism's old virtue of *Ahimsa*. But Hinduism had tended to keep ascetic virtues separate from *Raja Dharma*, a politician's duties. When the Jain *Oswal* community decided to opt for uncomproming *Ahimsa*, it gave up its *Kshatriya* (warrior) status and adopted *Vaishya Dharma*, the bloodless duties of the entrepreneur. The personal practice of virtues was always deemed different from the hard action that politics sometimes necessitates. From the start, Gandhi's philosophy of non-violence was tinged with the Christian ideal of self-sacrifice, of being killed rather than killing. Not that many Christian rulers had ever applied this principle, but at least it existed in certain Gospel passages such as the Sermon on the Mount. When, during the Partition massacres, Gandhi told Hindu refugees to go back to Pakistan and willingly get killed, he did not rely on any principle taught in the wide variety of Hindu scriptures. But in certain exalted Christian circles, it would be applauded.

This is even clearer in Gandhi's religious version of what Indians call 'secularism', i.e. religious pluralism. This was a growing value in the modern anglosphere. Within Christianity, Unitarianism had set out to eliminate all doctrinal points deemed divisive between Christians, even the fundamental dogma of the Trinity. On the fringes, the Theosophists and Perennialists sought common ground between 'authentic' Christianity, Vedicism and 'esoteric' Buddhism as expressions of the global 'perennial' truth. Gandhi's contemporary Aldous Huxley juxtaposed the goody-goody points of all religions in a book aptly titled *The Perennial Philosophy*. Outside the West, this trend was imitated by progressive circles, such as the *Baha'i* reform movement in Iran, harbinger of modern values like egalitarianism and internationalism (e.g. promotor of Esperanto, the linguistic embodiment of the globalist ideal). In India, the British-influenced *Brahmo Samaj* and *Ramakrishna Mission* had promoted the idea of a universal religion transcending the existing denominations. Hinduism had always practised pluralism as a pragmatic way to live and let live, but these movements turned it into an ideological dogma.

## 3. SYRUPY

So, Gandhi's religious pluralism, today his main claim to fame, was essentially the transposition of a Western ideological fashion. Of Vivekananda, it is routinely claimed that he was besieged by alternative religionists as soon as he set foot in the USA, and that this influence coloured his view and presentation of Hinduism. Gandhi's worldview, too, was determined by Western contacts, starting in his student days in England, when he frequented vegetarian eateries, the meeting-place par excellence of various utopians and Theosophists. It must be emphasized that he borrowed from one current in Western culture while ignoring another, viz. the critical questioning of religion. Historical Bible studies had reduced Jesus to a mere accident in human history, neither the Divine incarnation worshipped by Christians nor the spiritual teacher venerated by many Hindus. In the pious Mahatma, this very promising rational approach to religion was wholly absent.

Hindus themselves are partly to blame, having long abandoned their own tradition of philosophical debate, embracing sentimental devotion instead. This has led to a great flowering of the arts but to a decline in their power of discrimination. Great debaters like Yajñavalkya or Shankara would not be proud to see modern Hindus fall for anti-intellectual sound bites like 'equal respect for all religions'. Very Gandhian, but logically completely untenable. For example, Christianity believes that Jesus was God's Son while Islam teaches that he was merely God's spokesman: if one is right, the other is wrong, and nobody has equal respect for a true and a false statement (least of all Christians and Muslims themselves). Add to this their common scapegoat Paganism, in India represented by 'idolatrous' Hinduism, and the common truth of all three becomes unthinkable. It takes a permanent suspension of the power of discrimination to believe in the syrupy Gandhian syncretism which still prevails in India.

The Mahatma's outlook was neither realistic nor Indian. Not even the Jain doctrine of *Anekantavada*, 'pluralism', had been as mushy and anti-intellectual as the suspension of logic that is propagated in India in Gandhi's name. It could only come about among post-Christian Westerners tired of doctrinal debates, and from their circles, Gandhi transplanted it to India.

# Bibliography

Akbar, M.J., *Nehru, the Making of India*, Penguin, Delhi, 1991.

Ambedkar, B.R., *What Congress and Gandhi Have Done to the Untouchables*, Thacker, Bombay, 1946.

Ambedkar, B.R., *Pakistan, 1940*, Vol. 8 of his Writings and Speeches, Education Dpt., Gvt. of Maharashtra, 1990.

Attwood, D.W. et al, eds., *City, Countryside and Society in Maharashtra*, Univ. of Toronto Press, Toronto, 1988.

Baxter, Craig, *The Jana Sangh*, OUP, Bombay, 1972.

Bharti, Brahma Datt, *Gandhi and Gandhism Unmasked: Was Gandhi a Traitor?* Era Books, Delhi, 1992.

Bhave, Vinoba, *The Essence of the Quran*, Akhil Bharat Sarva Seva Sangh, Varanasi, 1985 (1962).

Chakravarthy, Gargi: *Gandhi, a Challenge to Communalism: A Study of Gandhi and the Hindu-Muslim Problem, 1919–1929*, EBC, Delhi, 1992 (1987).

Collins, Larry, and Lapierre, Dominique: *Freedom at Midnight*, Vikas, Delhi, 1988 (1975).

Dalton, Dennis, *Mahatma Gandhi, Nonviolent Power in Action*, OUP, Delhi, 2001 (2000).

Daniélou, Alain, *Histoire de l'Inde*, Fayard, Paris, 1983 (1971).

Daniélou, Alain, *Le Chemin du Labyrinthe*, Laffont, Paris, 1981.

Durga Das, *India from Curzon to Nehru and After*, Rupa, Delhi, 1977 (1975).

Edwards, Michael, *The Myth of the Mahatma*, Constable, London, 1986.

Elst, Koenraad, *Return of the Swastika*, Voice of India, Delhi, 2007.

Fischer, Louis, *The Life of Mahatma Gandhi*, Bharatiya Vidya Bhavan, Bombay, 1965.

Gandhi, M.K., *The Hindu-Muslim Unity*, Bharatiya Vidya Bhavan, Bombay, 1965.

Gandhi, M.K., *Trusteeship*, Navajivan, Ahmedabad, 1966.

Gandhi, M.K., *Satyagraha in South Africa*, Navajivan, Ahmedabad, 1966.

Gandhi, M.K., *Hind Swaraj*, Navajivan, Ahmedabad, 1982 (1909).

Gandhi, M.K., *Collected Works*, vols. 24, 75, 79, 80, Pub. Div., Delhi, 1993.

Ghosh, Tapan, *The Gandhi Murder Trial*, Asia, Bombay, 1973.

Godse, Gopal, *Gandhiji's Murder and After*, Surya Prakashan, Delhi, 1989.

Godse, Nathuram, *Why I Assassinated Gandhi*, Surya Bharti Prakashan, Delhi, 1993.

Goel, Sita Ram, *Perversion of India's Political Parlance*, Voice of India, Delhi, 1995.

Goel, Sita Ram, ed., *Freedom of Expression*, 'Secular Theocracy vs. Liberal Democracy', Voice of India, Delhi, 1998.

Goel, Sita Ram, *History of Hindu-Christian Encounters*, 2nd ed., Voice of India, Delhi, 1996.

Goyal, Des Raj, *Rashtriya Swayam Sevak Sangh*, Radha Krishna, Delhi, 1979.

Huq, Fazlul, *Gandhi Saint or Sinner?*, Dalit Sahitya Akademi, Bangalore, 1992.

Inamdar, P.L., *The Story of the Red Fort Trial 1948–49*, Popular Prakashan, Bombay, 1979.

Johnson, Paul, *Modern Times*, Orion, London, 1992.

Jordens, J.T.F., *Swami Shraddhananda. His Life and Causes*, OUP, Delhi, 1981.

Karanjia, R.K., *The Mind of Mr. Nehru*, London, 1960.

Khosla, G.D., *The Murder of the Mahatma and Other Cases from a Judge's Note Book*, Jaico, Delhi, 1977.

Khosla, G.D., *Stern Reckoning: A Survey of the Events Leading up to and Following the Partition of India*, OUP, Delhi, 1989.

Kothari, M.M., *Critique of Gandhi*, Critique Publ., Jodhpur, 1996.

Madhok, Balraj, *Rationale of Hindu State*, Indian Book Gallery, Delhi, 1982.

Majumdar, R.C., *British Paramountcy and Indian Renaissance*, Bharatiya Vidya Bhavan, Bombay, 1963.

Majumdar, R.C., *The Struggle for Freedom*, Bharatiya Vidya Bhavan, Bombay, 1969.

Malgonkar, Manohar, *The Men Who Killed Gandhi*, Vision Books, Delhi, 1981.

Malkani, K.R., *The Politics of Ayodhya and Hindu-Muslim Relations*, Har Anand, Delhi, 1994.

Mehta, Ved, *Mahatma Gandhi and His Apostles*, India Book Co., Lucknow, 1978.

Nanda, B.R., *Gandhi and His Critics*, OUP, Delhi, 1985.

Nandy, Ashis, *At the Edge of Psychology*, OUP, Delhi, 1980.

Orwell, George, *Collected Essays*, vol. 4, London, 1968.

Pande, B.N., *Islam and Indian Culture*, Khuda Bakhsh Oriental Public Library, Patna, 1985.

Rajshekar (Shetty), V.T.: *Why Godse Killed Gandhi*, Dalit Sahitya Akademi, Bangalore, 1983.

Ram Gopal, *Hindu Culture during and after Muslim Rule: Survival and Subsequent Challenges*, MD Pub., Delhi, 1994.

Seervai, H.M., *Partition of India: Legend and Reality*, Emmenem Pub., Bombay, 1989.

Shaikh, Anwar, *The Tale of Two Gujarati Saints*, A. Ghosh, Houston, 1997.

Shourie, Arun: *Individuals, Institutions, Processes: How One may Strengthen the Other in India Today*, Viking, Delhi, 1990.

Shourie, Arun, *Worshipping False Gods; Ambedkar, and the Facts which have been Erased*, ASA, Delhi, 1997.

Sri Aurobindo, *India's Rebirth*, Mysore, 1993.

Talageri, Shrikant, *Aryan Invasion Theory and Indian Nationalism*, Voice of India, Delhi, 1993.

Tendulkar, D.G., *Mahatma Gandhi*, Vol. 1, Bombay, 1961.

Waterstone, Richard, *De Wijsheid van India*, Librero, Kerkdriel, 2001.

Wolpert, Stanley A., *Jinnah of Pakistan*, OUP, Delhi, 1984.

Wolpert, Stanley A., *Tilak and Gokhale*, Surjeet Pub., Delhi, 1989.

Zelliot, Eleanor, and Berntsen, Maxine, eds., *The Experience of Hinduism*, Sri Satguru, Delhi, 1995.

# Index